CONFESSIONS OF A
CARTEL
HITMAN

MARTIN CORONA
WITH TONY RAFAEL

EBURY
PRESS

Although this book is based on real people and real events,
some names, places and identifying features have been
changed in order to preserve their privacy.

3 5 7 9 10 8 6 4 2

Ebury Press, an imprint of Ebury Publishing
20 Vauxhall Bridge Road
London SW1V 2SA

Ebury Press is part of the Penguin Random House group of companies
whose addresses can be found at global.penguinrandomhouse.com

 Penguin
Random House
UK

First published by Dutton, an imprint of Penguin Random
House LLC, in 2017
This edition published by Ebury Press in 2017

www.penguin.co.uk

A CIP catalogue record for this book is available from the British Library

ISBN 9781785037344

Printed and bound in Great Britain by Clays Ltd, St Ives PLC

Penguin Random House is committed to a
sustainable future for our business, our readers
and our planet. This book is made from Forest
Stewardship Council® certified paper.

Contents

Foreword   vii

PART ONE: SORROW

1. The Letter   3
2. Posole   9
3. The Beach   21
4. Gladiator School   27
5. The Ones That Got Away   39
6. Power Boosting   47
7. Surenos Don't Stoop   55
8. A Chance in Hawaii   69
9. Baby   83

PART TWO: EDUCATION

10. Big D's Tickets   95
11. Circus Circus   107
12. Small Fish, Big Ocean   115
13. The First Order of Business   129

CONTENTS

14. Mainline   139
15. I Want to Kill Him   149
16. The Hole   159
17. Plastic Knives   169
18. Real Great Dudes   177

PART THREE: PROFESSION

19. A Big Enterprise   189
20. Bullet Hoses   199
21. The Fat Guy   213
22. Getting It Done Right   225
23. Respect   235
24. Wasn't for Her   249
25. Bad Karma   261
26. Neglected Business   275
27. "Are You Against Us?"   281
28. Out of My Life   291

CONFESSIONS OF A
CARTEL
HITMAN

Foreword

Steve Duncan, Special Agent, California Department of Justice

We got a multiple murderer, a brutal hit man who participated in many killings and murdered at least eight people himself. He had often left victims near death. He had destroyed families in the United States and Mexico. We got him. Martin Corona, an accomplished hit man for the extremely violent Tijuana Cartel, also known as the Arellano Félix Organization, signed a plea agreement created by the prosecutor and me. Corona then stood before a federal judge and pled guilty to cocaine distribution. He was sentenced to roughly twenty-five years.

Wait! He pled to cocaine distribution when he was a multiple murderer and you're good with this? Hold on now, there's more.

Corona was thirty-seven years of age. In the federal system, you do eighty-five percent of your sentence. In his case, 20.6 years. Corona would be released when he was fifty-eight years old. Corona was sentenced in October 2001 and would not be released until 2022.

During intensive debriefings with Corona in 2001, he confided to our team that he had hepatitis C, a virus that is chronic and can lead to an early death. We feigned sympathy, but after we locked Corona back into his cell, we smiled. We truly believed he would die in prison. "Divine intervention," I thought.

Let me get to the facts.

It was September 1999 and my cell phone rang. As I answered, Bill Ziegler, a parole agent, cut me off and said, "Get your ass down here right now." He explained that Martin Corona was in a vulnerable situation and it might be the time to break him. Ziegler's office was in Oceanside, about a forty-five-minute drive from San Diego. I put down everything, grabbed my partner, California Department of Justice special agent Javier Salaiz, and we headed north.

From 1992 to 1996, I was a member of the Violent Crimes Task Force—Gang Group comprised of the Drug Enforcement Administration, Federal Bureau of Investigation, San Diego Police Department, San Diego County Sheriff's Department, US Marshals Service, San Diego County Probation Department, US Attorney's Office, the District Attorney's Office, the Immigration and Naturalization Service, and the California Department of Justice. I was deputized by the Drug Enforcement Administration to enforce the federal drug laws, or Title 21 of the United States Code. At the time, I was investigating members of the Logan Heights street gang and other Hispanic gangs working as assassins for the Tijuana Cartel.

On May 24, 1993, at the Guadalajara International Airport in Jalisco, Mexico, Cardinal Juan Jesus Posadas Ocampo was shot and killed by enforcers for the Tijuana Cartel. It was a case of mistaken identity, as the enforcers believed that their drug rival, Joaquin "Chapo" Guzman Loera, was in the white Grand Marquis that the cardinal was being escorted in. About a dozen of the enforcers present were Logan Heights gang members. The Arellano Félix brothers, who headed the cartel, instantly became some of the world's most wanted criminals, and Mexico wanted justice. Many of the enforcers were rounded up in the US and Mexico and sent to Mexican prisons to face charges related to the cardinal's murder. In those days in Mexico, their system was described as Napoleonic and suspects were "guilty until proven innocent."

In 1995, the Arellano Félix Organization Task Force was created to target and dismantle the Tijuana Cartel. DEA agent Jack Robertson was the case agent of the Tijuana Cartel and he led the charge at the AFO Task Force. Jack had recruited me to assist in his investigation in 1993.

The government of Mexico eventually dropped the charges on many of the gang members involved in the murder of the cardinal. So much for Napoleon. As the enforcers were released, many returned to San Diego and other parts of the US. An angry US Attorney, Alan Bersin, tasked one of his federal prosecutors to lead the prosecution against the enforcers in the Southern District of California. I was assigned as the case agent. We developed a federal Drug Kingpin case against David Barron Corona and ten enforcers and secretly indicted them in June 1997.

Barron, a Logan Heights gang member and Mexican Mafia prison gang member, had become a top enforcer for the Tijuana Cartel after his heroics at Christine's disco in Puerto Vallarta in November 1992. As an escort for the cartel's top brass, he got them safely out of the disco as Chapo's troops attempted to ambush and kill them. After the dust settled, Benjamin Arellano Félix, the cartel's leader, personally assigned him to head the cartel's enforcement arm, and Barron began to recruit his fellow gang members from San Diego. Barron was a "one percenter," a term we use in law enforcement for the gang leaders. Barron, like other one percenters, was charismatic, aggressive, and ambitious.

In November 1997, Barron was killed while he ambushed and shot a Tijuana newspaper editor. We unsealed the indictment and arrested several of the enforcers who were in the US. With the long sentences each was exposed to, we received their cooperation, and the prosecutor and agents were soon able to debrief several defendants who pled guilty for their parts in the murder of the cardinal. Every defendant mentioned Corona as a member of the "Death Squad," a special group of cartel enforcers with tactical ability. They had all witnessed Corona being paid $15,000 to $25,000 for murders. Corona was put at the top of the list for the second round of indictments.

So a year or so later, Javier and I went into an interview room, where I met Corona for the first time. I was direct. I told him that I was preparing to indict him and that I knew he was a high-level enforcer for the Tijuana Cartel. Corona did not mention any violence but did admit guarding stash houses for the cartel. We also spoke about family, fishing, and the beauty of the Sierra Nevada mountains, for which we shared a fondness. After a couple hours of conversation, I told him he had a decision to make: "Cooperate with the government or go to jail for the rest of your life." He responded that the statute of limitations was up for his drug activity and he no longer worked for the cartel. I told him there was no statute of limitations for murder.

Months later, Corona's attorney contacted me and said that Corona wanted to cooperate.

As I entered the interview room at the US Attorney's Office, a handcuffed and leg-chained Corona was seated across the table with his attorney. Corona began to talk about his recruitment and violence with the Tijuana Cartel. However, his attorney stopped him and said he wanted to know what the charges would be. The prosecutor called for a break, and we went into her office to discuss the evidence we had on Corona. I explained that I still had witnesses who spoke of several murders for which he was paid and that he could still be facing indictments based on the cardinal murder federal conspiracy case—but that was not a sure thing.

The prosecutor and I constructed a plea agreement with minimal and vague information charging Corona with 21 USC 841(a)(1), Distribution of Cocaine, and submitted the plea to Corona and his attorney at the next interview. After reviewing the document, Corona's attorney saw how vague it was and wanted to know what we had on his client. Our response was, "You came to us and we are not putting our cards on the table." I now believe Corona wanted to cooperate no matter what evidence we had. He was tired of the life and wanted to clear his conscience. But my ego still likes to think we bluffed him.

I have sat through many debriefings and heard many stories of murder from cartel leaders and gang members. The suspect typically minimizes and qualifies the killings and often blames someone else. Martin Corona didn't do that. For the next year of weekly debriefings of Corona, I heard the actual killer and planner of several murders in the US and Mexico describe, in detail, how he and others savagely murdered people they deemed the enemy. We were able to find all but one of the bodies.

Corona testified to each murder in federal grand jury, oftentimes crying as he recounted the details to the jurors. He identified several other enforcers involved in those murders who were still walking the streets. His testimony assisted greatly in the indictment and subsequent prosecution and sentencing of many upper-echelon Tijuana Cartel members.

For years I continued to follow up on Corona's murders. I kept in touch with Corona too. He sent letters of apology to his victims and their families and has shown unflagging remorse. I respect Corona, but he can never know the depth of the damage he did to these victims and their families. It is heartbreaking to see the damage to each extended family unit and the way the misfortune continued after they were touched by Corona and the Tijuana Cartel.

Over a period of sixteen months during Corona's cartel hit man career, in three separate incidents, one family lost a son and a son-in-law and nearly lost two daughters who were both shot in the head. A nine-year-old girl witnessed her mother get shot in the head, and her aunt three times in the head, by Corona in San Diego. A month later, while visiting her father and grandmother in Tijuana, she witnessed Corona break into her father's home, tie up her and her grandmother, and take her father upstairs and beat him to death with a sledgehammer.

In 2001, I contacted the two daughters. One victim was cooperative, but had lost all recall of the incident due to the severe brain damage caused by three .45-caliber bullets to the head. At the time of the shooting, she had just returned from Paris, France, where she spent a year modeling for *Mademoiselle* magazine. Her sister, like most victims in this case, was reluctant to cooperate and had started a new life elsewhere and did not tell her new husband about her misfortune. The little girl was then sixteen years old and her mother refused to let me interview her. She is thirty years old today and still gets upset when I try talking to her. In 2015, when I contacted her to let her know Corona was released from prison, she asked me never to speak to her again. The majority of victims in our experience refuse to confront their offenders and try to forget about their past.

In 1995, Corona and others entered a home in Tijuana, tied up the extended family and groundskeepers, and took a married couple upstairs and stabbed them dozens of times and left them dead in separate bedrooms. In 2001, I found several family members who were present during the murders. None of them would cooperate because they were afraid of retaliation by the cartel. One brother did explain that arrests were made, and one of the groundskeepers was still in jail for the murders. I explained that we had the subjects involved identified and there was very little chance of retaliation by the cartel. After months of trying to convince them to cooperate, they left my telephone calls and home and work visits unanswered. The groundskeeper is probably still in jail for something he had nothing to do with.

In January 2003, one of the uncooperative brothers was kidnapped in Tijuana. In February 2003, I began receiving calls from his wife, who had also been uncooperative. Nevertheless, I helped her all I could.

In April 2003, I received credible information that the kidnap victim had been killed by members of the Tijuana Cartel. Once the information was corroborated, I broke the bad news to his wife. She refused to believe me and stated that her husband had run off with his "sancha," or mistress, after receiving a large inheritance. She continued to call me, telling me that she was being followed. Many times, I would respond to her house in San Diego to appease her, but I knew she was becoming delusional. After several months of trying to help her, I let her calls roll over to voice mail.

On August 10, 2005, I saw an article in *The San Diego Union-Tribune* detailing the murder-suicide of the wife and her two young sons—who had witnessed their father's kidnapping. San Diego Sheriff's officials found the bodies the day before.

There are other stories of continued misfortune in the lives touched by Corona and the Tijuana Cartel.

In the spring of 2014, Corona was released from federal prison.

He had told me he wanted to talk to law enforcement and the public to educate them on gangs, organized crime, and violence. So we put him to work, and he was a big hit telling his story to police officers all over the country. They saw the sincere, respectful former assassin humbly spill his guts and they appreciated his effort.

Corona, now free, has spent the majority of his life in prison. Most guys like him do not make it in society. I wish him the best and hope that he can make it through the internal struggle he has to deal with. This book, this testimony, is a step in that struggle. It is now your turn to be the judge.

CONFESSIONS
OF A
CARTEL HIT MAN

PART ONE

SORROW

1

The Letter

I was in Sandstone Federal Correctional Institution in Minnesota. It's a low-security facility that houses mostly nonviolent offenders—white-collar criminals who commit their robberies with gold-plated pens and computer spreadsheets and snake their way through the SEC systems with the hope of getting away clean.

In addition to the financial hustlers, crooked politicians, and their bagmen, there were also people like me at Sandstone—confidential witnesses who testified in court against their former criminal associates. We weren't white-collar guys.

Some people call Sandstone and places like it White-Collar Country Clubs. And in some ways, that's accurate, at least compared to the supermax facilities. At least in Sandstone. You don't have the hard-core gangsters, the unrepentant racists, the cold-blooded killers, and the various sociopaths that could go off without warning like a stick of dynamite. You don't have to fight for your life.

In my case, I'd like to say it was doing easy time. But it wasn't. The real prison I inhabited wasn't Sandstone. It was my own conscience. It was the guilt. Although I'm now technically free, I still carry my prison with me. There's no escape from this one. There's no crashing through the wall or even receiving a pardon. In every legal way, I've paid my debt, done my time, and fulfilled all the obligations of testifying against the people who sent me out to kill. But the freedom that most people take for granted, the freedom of an easy conscience, is something that I'll never again experience.

My handler at the time, Steve Duncan, was one of the first people in law enforcement who I could talk to and not feel like he was just trying to get some more information out of me for his case. By 2008, I'd spent a lot of time with him. He spent time with my parents and helped to get them someplace safe out of the reach of the Arellano Félix assassins.

One day I asked him if it would be okay for me to try to write a letter to the survivors of the people I killed and the ones who survived my attempt to murder them. He thought about it for a while and then said he thought it was a good idea. Not that it would reduce my sentence or get me any better deal with the US Attorney. That was all behind me at that point. My deal had been made. I knew I would be getting out of prison by a certain date and there was nothing I would get out of this except, hopefully, to communicate my sense of remorse to the people I wronged.

There's no manual on how to do this. I started and stopped a number of times. And I tore up the first few tries because it literally made me sick to think of the harm I'd done. But those people deserved . . . something.

This letter is addressed to all those whose lives I've affected personally as well as all humanity. I apologize for not addressing you by name, but I don't feel worthy of that intimacy. Please don't mistake my humility for lack of respect.

My name is Martin Corona and I am a murderer. It's . . . something I live with daily in shame and disgust.

I once worked for the Arellano Félix Drug Cartel. I served as one of their many puppets who were dispatched at the whim of the Arellano brothers to take the lives of those who posed a threat to their business . . .

I can begin by saying I'm sorry. But I can't help wonder what would that mean to me if someone took one of my loved ones away.

I don't seek forgiveness or empathy. Only an opportunity to tell you that I despise the man that I was and whom I must face each morning when I look in the mirror. I may have had a change of heart in my life, but it's still the same evil some of your loved ones had to look upon as they drew their last breath.

There is nothing I can do to repay the sins I've committed. I can literally offer you my life and it's one thing I would freely lay down if it would reverse the past. I've tried to take it by my own hands on more than one occasion but for some reason, I've been spared.

My other alternative is to continue the mission that I've set for myself. That is, to speak out against the people and the beliefs that I once claimed loyalty to. I never had any personal intention to harm you or

*anyone. I never woke up one day and decided to go on
a killing spree . . .*

"I'm sorry," is all I have to say . . .

Respectfully,

Martin Corona

Duncan forwarded the letter to some of the people I indicated. Most of them did not respond. One of them, a young female, contacted Duncan and told him she would like to meet me one day. But not just yet. Not enough time had passed and she wasn't ready to relive the nightmare I'd put her through. But the one thing that she wanted me to know was that she forgave me. She didn't blame me.

I'll tell you, it was the first time in decades that I was truly humbled and felt like a member of the human race again. To know that at least in her eyes I wasn't this subhuman monster seemed to lift at least a little of my guilt.

It wasn't long after her response that I began thinking about writing about my life. If I could make her understand, it was possible to make other people see that evil isn't always forever.

I don't believe anyone is born into the world to be evil. Something significant had to come along to be a turning point. Sometimes it's a circumstance like poverty, drug-abusive parents, sexual abuse, physical abuse, or maybe the overwhelming feeling that you just don't matter to anyone. And if you are finally convinced that you don't matter, it can cause you to do extraordinary things that finally get you noticed. What makes a kid want to commit suicide at the age of twelve? Or bring a gun to school? Or rebel so bad that their parents "don't even know who you are."

I've heard that one. Who knew who I was back in the nineties when I leaned down low, focused, armed, looking for the right moment to act? I mean, is anyone going to tell me that I was born to be sitting in a car, living my own version of a Mack Bolan novel? Watching three dealers serve dope fiends in the middle of the street in Los Angeles, in broad daylight, and I'm doing my best to figure out how to kill them without getting caught? And at the same time make sure that everyone connected to those three knows that my bosses, the Arellano Félix brothers, don't take no shit from their enemies?

Two days after that initial recon, two of those dealers will have clocked out permanently and the other would die six months later from mercury poisoning from the mercury-tipped slugs that I had fired into him. The fact of the matter is that my crew was crazier than anything Mack Bolan could have done and we were not fictional characters. We were for real and we didn't play at being assassins. I was one of the Arellanos' top hit men and that day I was making good on the contract the Arellanos had put out on Chapo Guzman and anyone connected to him. What brought me to that particular street with my machine gun loaded with mercury-tipped bullets? I wasn't born evil, but my life is what I made of it.

2

Posole

The family situation I was born into looks unremarkable from the outside. My father, Fred, was a career US Marine master gunnery sergeant who wore the uniform for thirty-three years. The anchor and globe they gave him when he finished boot camp was just acknowledging the code that he'd operated under for his entire life. In my mind, he had sprung full-blown as a Marine. I was insanely proud of my father. It didn't go the other way.

My family on my mother's side arrived in Oceanside, California, in 1917. They drove from Texas in a car and an old truck. In 1916, Pancho Villa stopped a train in Mexico and killed eighteen American citizens in cold blood to register his displeasure that President Woodrow Wilson was not backing Villa's faction in the revolution. That same year, Villa invaded the town of Columbus, New Mexico, burned it to the ground, and left another nineteen US citizens dead in the streets. When I think about that, I wonder if the violence I would eventually inflict in Mexico and the US drove some of the hundreds of thousands of illegal border crossers into California and the Southwest.

My grandmother's family found whatever jobs they could in an area that was still heavily agricultural and predominantly Mexican. My father's family had migrated from Mexico and settled in Texas. As soon as he could enlist, he did. He was assigned to Camp Pendleton, just north of San Diego, California. Oceanside is basically a bedroom suburb of Camp Pendleton. They used to say, "You can't swing a dead cat in Oceanside without hitting a Marine."

When my grandmother was young and living in Oceanside, she did field work. She picked oranges, lettuce, and strawberries. To make a few extra dollars, my great-grandmother and great-grandfather began cooking in the evenings for the unmarried workers who didn't have families. After a day stooped over cutting lettuce, they and my grandmother would go home and cook massive amounts of posole.

The British have their steak and kidney pie and boiled beef. The Italians have pasta, and the Germans have their sausages and sauerkraut. Mexicans have posole. It's a corn-based stew that originated in pre-Columbian Central America. It's as much a sacrament in Mexican life as Communion and baptism. You eat posole when you're sick to make you feel better. You eat it when you're well to stay healthy. And you eat it in honor of a culture that seems to have dissipated and dissolved under the hooves and flintlocks of Western European immigration. The woman who produces posole isn't exactly worshipped, but pretty damned close.

My grandmother became the "Posole Lady" in Oceanside. She sold the stew out of her kitchen and often delivered it. She became so connected to her cooking that the area in Oceanside she lived in eventually came to be known simply as Posole. For most of the twentieth century, Posole was just the name the locals called the area. By the 1960s, when neighborhoods began giving birth to street gangs, Posole became the name of our gang as well. Posole was my home gang. It was under the Posole umbrella that I began my criminal career. In a strange way, I felt like I owned the neighborhood because my family had been there longer than anyone else. My grandmother's cooking gave the entire neighborhood its name.

By the time a teenager is ready to be jumped into a gang, he is literally prepared to kill and die for his neighborhood. To an outsider, this level of commitment to the gang and the neighborhood seems insane. Maybe you need to have been raised in the varrio to understand how young men can turn their backs on their families and, frankly, the entire noncriminal world and volunteer for a suicide pact with their homeboys. I was probably a lot more committed to the gang than most of my homies. I lived the gang life right up to the point that it was going to kill me. I bought the ticket to the horror show and stayed for the entire nightmare performance. And I was one of the leading players.

Blood connections to the barrio weren't limited to young males. The girls had their own little cliques and groups. When my mother was growing up, she belonged to the Tangerines. It wasn't a gang in the strict sense of the word. It was more a social club or what would pass for a sorority in college. They had their own Tangerines jackets and they wore the same kind of hairstyle and makeup. The friendships they made as teenagers would last a lifetime. They would marry their girlfriends' brothers or cousins. And a lot of them would get pregnant with guys they never married but never really stopped socializing with in the neighborhood. Decades later, the whole neighborhood would basically become a huge extended family where everyone knew everyone else's history and we were all connected one way or another. I guess this social system played out in every Hispanic neighborhood in California.

When I was eight, my father was ordered to Camp Lejeune, North Carolina. Prior to this, the only place I'd been outside of California was to Mexico for holiday trips. In those days, Mexico wasn't the free-fire cartel killing ground that it became. There was always drug dealing and smuggling, but nothing on the scale that I would witness in the nineties.

Once, smuggling was almost considered an honorable profession on the Mexican border. Old-school paisas (Mexican villagers) hauled turquoise, mescal, gold, and silver into the US on donkeys. During Prohibition, they smuggled liquor imported from Europe and Mexican-brewed tequila. These farmers and traders had no ambition of becoming internationally celebrated criminals. They were subsistence smugglers who knew their way across the desert and could pick out their route over the mountains and across the desert by moonlight or a Zippo lighter. Those routes used by the mescal haulers are still in use today, but the subsistence smugglers were replaced by cartels like the Arellano Félix brothers, who became rich enough to buy the Mexican government.

I remember sitting in the rear bench seat of the Ford Torino station wagon we had and watching the Baja California landscape roll by the tinted windows. That was the brief time in my life when I was still a goofy kid who liked reading and writing, was good at math, and could not resist taking mechanical things apart. Years later, as a freshly released convict from the California Department of Corrections, I was driven down the same Highway 1D, the Tijuana to Ensenada road, in a blacked-out Chevy

SUV armed with a full-auto AK-47. We had hand grenades and pistols too.

My parents and I made the trip to Camp Lejeune in that Torino. To save money, we slept in the car. In North Carolina, we lived off base in military housing. There was a clear, fast-running creek behind the house that held fish and frogs. Beyond the creek, there were dense woods that went on for miles.

In addition to teaching me how to fish, my father would take me into the woods and teach me bushcraft. He taught me a half-dozen ways of making a fire using nothing but what was available on the ground. Catching, skinning, gutting, and eating squirrels was as natural as picking up a pork chop under plastic in the supermarket. And then there was the endurance program. We hiked and hiked for miles, soaked through with sweat or rain. Mud-caked boots. Eating and drinking whatever we could find in the woods.

I was by nature left-handed. But my father saw that as some sort of moral shortcoming.

Fathers deal with their sons. They toughen them up. They train them. Drill them. Dads make sure the beds are made, the yard is cleaned up, the garbage taken out, the clothes all folded and stacked in a footlocker. Dads conduct surprise white-glove inspections at night, and failure to execute correctly results in being hit with belts, broomsticks, and closed fists. I didn't know any different. I tried to become right-handed.

As in Oceanside, all our neighbors in North Carolina were in the Marine Corps. The Barkers lived two houses down from us. They were officer class. He was a captain. His wife, Margie, was an energetic Georgia girl who had a passion for growing vegetables and flowers. They had two blond daughters who were five years older than me. Margie and my mom became great friends and the two of them created a community garden. In the summertime, Margie would borrow me and we'd spend entire days together weeding, pruning, watering, and raising massive heads of lettuce. When we weren't in the garden, she took me to her house and taught me how to pickle and can just about anything the garden produced.

I played Little League baseball. I joined the Scouts and earned all sixteen merit badges. I played football.

Margie and her family were what I considered the rock-solid template of what a military family was supposed to be. Captain Barker was all business, but he wasn't mean or violent. I noticed the way he handled the two girls and his wife, Margie. There was love in that family. There was no yelling or broomsticks broken. There were no surprise 3:00 A.M. inspections and no double-time hikes in the woods. Margie and my mom remained friends for thirty years. When we were reassigned back to Camp Pendleton, the Barkers were already there. The two Barker girls would become babysitters for my little brother and sister.

After a year in North Carolina, my brother Fred was born. My grandmother came from Oceanside to live with us to help my mom. It was after Fred was born that the situation with my father got really bad.

My father and I would be in the car, with me riding shotgun. Suddenly, he'd scream as loud as he could and squeeze my thigh as hard as he could. According to him, he was teaching me how not to flinch in an emergency situation. Sometimes, without screaming, he'd swing a fist at me, just missing my face. If I flinched, I got punched.

We transferred back to Oceanside. While we were in North Carolina, my dad had rented out our house in Oceanside. The tenants had trashed the house so badly we had to move in temporarily with my grandmother until our house was fixed.

I could not sit still in class. I occasionally flew into rages and pounded on classmates with my fists.

When I was seven, my mother took me to the hospital on base and had me examined by a psychiatrist. The doctors prescribed phenobarbital. During the school year, I'd go to the nurse's office at noon every day and she'd give me my drugs. More often than not, I'd be asleep in an hour with my head on my desk, thanks to the pills.

One of my teachers, Mrs. Marsky, became concerned enough with my daily ritual of falling asleep that she contacted my mother. The teacher was told it was doctor's orders and she had no say in the matter. So by the time my cousin Tommy Garcia and I started getting high on street drugs at age twelve or thirteen, I'd already been a pill popper for half a decade.

I got out of the house and hung with Tommy, my cousin Roy Rivas, and some of the homeboys in the neighborhood. Tommy's home life was only a little better than mine, so we would go home just to sleep. We weren't quite throwaway or runaway kids because we had a home to go to. We just chose to avoid contact with our families.

Neither of us felt we really belonged anywhere except on the street. That's where our real friends were. I was twelve and already had one foot out the door. That was when my grandmother took me into her room and took a photo album out of the closet. She showed me a picture of my mother standing next to a Marine. This Marine was not Fred Corona, the man I knew as my father.

"That," she said, "is your real father. He got your mother

pregnant just before he left the Marines. He wanted to take her back to Michigan where he came from, but your mother wanted to stay here."

After that, Tommy and I did everything we could to stay on the streets and make a few dollars. We started a lawn mowing business. Our clients were all Marines, enlisted men as well as officers. Tommy and I were incredibly conscientious with the lawn mowing. When we finished a job, it was done to military precision. It would have gotten nothing but a grudging okay from my father, but the people we worked for were extremely happy with the work. On a good week, we could each make $150. In 1976, that was very decent money for a couple of twelve-year-olds.

Then one day we were cutting the lawn for an enlisted man who was having a party at his house. We could see that this party was offering more than beer and liquor to the guests. Tommy had already once tried marijuana and recognized it when he saw the Marines at the party passing joints. Tommy asked the Marine if he could give us some dope instead of cash for the lawn. He was happy to do it and he gave us a couple of joints.

After we were done mowing lawns for the day, Tommy and I went to a canyon where a lot of kids hung out to drink, ditch school, get laid, or get high. It was a party canyon. This was the first time I'd actually smoked cannabis, and at the time, it appeared like a salvation. Unlike the phenobarbital that made me groggy and then put me to sleep, cannabis was my happy drug. I could continue to function but still be high enough to put the brakes on my anxiety. It was a mental and emotional vacation. This was the drug I needed.

My mom had had a few surgeries and they gave her painkillers. I don't actually remember if my intention was to sell them or to give them away or take them, but I stole them from the bathroom cabinet where she kept them and took them to school. They rattled in my pocket all day and then I decided to take them. I had no fear of death, but I did think, if I'm going to die, I might as well do it in school with my friends around me. I swallowed the entire bottle of painkillers in the school bathroom.

I went back to class. A half hour later, it looked like the blackboard was melting. The voices around me started sounding very far away and I couldn't feel my arms or legs. The last clear memory I have is Barbara Soto's voice asking me, "Are you okay?" She was one of the homegirls that hung out with us Posoles. Then I remember her screaming and apparently I hit the floor like a deadweight.

I sort of came out of it a little bit. I remember being on the floor of the nurse's office, the same nurse that fed me the phenobarbital, and two paramedics were working on me. I had no fear, no anxiety. It was the most peaceful feeling I'd ever had in my life. I actually felt myself floating to the ceiling and I remember looking down at myself and the paramedics and just feeling serene. Years later, I found out they call this a near-death experience. I never saw the white light you're supposed to see, but I clearly remember looking down at myself and feeling nothing but peace. I was ready to go to wherever was the next place you go. Heaven, maybe, if I was lucky. I was still Catholic enough to believe in that.

I later found out that in the ambulance my heart stopped twice.

I remembered watching *The Bride of Frankenstein* as a young kid. There's a scene at the end where the monster tries to touch the woman that Dr. Frankenstein just made for him. His bride. She pulls away, scared out of her mind at the way he looks. You could see in the monster's face that he realizes there's something unnatural about him, the woman, and the doctors that made him. The monster lets Dr. Frankenstein and his wife leave. Then he turns to the bride and the other doctor and says, "We belong dead." He pulls the lever and the whole castle blows up. That phrase echoed in my head for years.

Four days later they finally got all the dope out of me.

They transferred me from the hospital ICU to the San Luis Rey mental hospital in Encinitas. As it happened, one of the Posole homegirls was there as well. She was there for drugs, running around with older guys, and basically screwing up her life. Like me.

As soon as they let me walk around the ward, I wandered around, looking for a way to get out. They had a balcony on the floor, with wooden slats and beams that would let the sun in but were close enough together to keep people like me from jumping off it. I jumped on the railing and starting kicking the slats as hard as I could. I wanted to make an opening big enough for me to crawl through.

Before I could make it through, a couple of the male nurses dragged me off the balcony and took me to the rubber room. They strapped me into a bed and I lay there screaming for hours to let me out. They shot me up with more drugs to stop me from screaming. It was like trying to put out a fire that won't stop burning.

As it happened, I went directly from San Luis Rey to St. Mary's Church for my confirmation. My parents took us to a Mexican restaurant after the ceremony and I remember my father telling me that now I was a man in the eyes of God and the church. My mother gave me a little Virgin Mary medallion and told me to always keep it with me. My father gave me some money and, for the first time I can remember, he gave me a hug.

The day after my confirmation, I ran away from home.

I didn't need a home. I had a whole neighborhood that would take care of me if I needed it. At least I thought that was the case. But the reality was that I was twelve years old and I was relying on other thirteen- and fourteen-year-olds to give me food, money, and a place to sleep. I lived on the streets for a little while. I slept on a mattress that someone had thrown away. There was a carport in the neighborhood that nobody used, so I carved out a space in it for the mattress and slept there at night.

During the day I went to my cousin Roy's house to take a shower, wash my clothes, and grab some food. I'd spend the rest of the day at the beach or hiding out in the canyon with the other truants and some of the older guys who were already up-and-coming gangsters. These were the only people I felt comfortable with. There wasn't anyone telling me to write with my right hand. There were no inspections and sudden fists flashing across my face. These people from the neighborhood felt like the only real family I had. We shared everything—food, dope, guns, girls, advice—and we protected each other. If we had enough to share, we did. And when we didn't, we'd rob it and share it.

But I couldn't hide forever. One day I was out on the street and high on paint fumes. The cops saw me stumbling around like a drunk and took me home.

After a couple of violent arguments, I told my parents that I wouldn't be running away anymore but as far as I was concerned, Fred wasn't my father and I didn't have to listen to him anymore.

I tried going back to school, but I only went there to hang out with some girls I liked, make some dope connections, and make a few dollars selling dope. I'd show up for first-period class and then ditch. After roll call I'd either go to the canyon with the homeboys, go to the beach to sling some marijuana, or hang out at the football field at Jefferson High School. There were a lot of older Posole homeboys there and we'd smoke cigarettes, weed, and eat some Black Beauties.

That Marine who gave us marijuana for mowing his lawn turned into a solid drug connection for me. Roy and I would buy ounces from him, break them down into nickel and dime bags, and sell them in school. I was buying clothes on my own, eating in diners and fast-food places. My mother asked me where I got the money and I told her it was from mowing lawns. She told me to give her some of it so she could save it for me. So I did.

I'd been out of San Luis Rey Hospital for a few months and I was taking the Valium I had been prescribed. But the thing I wanted was oblivion. And this time I was going to make it stick. And before leaving my life, I was going to tell my story.

I had an eight-track tape machine that had recording capability. I went into my room and spilled my guts into the tape. I recorded some music between the farewells. I had eighty-two Valium pills in the bottle. I hadn't been taking them, but they kept refilling the prescription. They were ten milligrams each and I figured that would be enough to do the job. I wrote out a note and swallowed all eighty-two pills. Then I laid back on the bed and waited to die.

3

The Beach

My father came home earlier than I expected and found me almost unconscious. He tried getting me to sit up or move. I wouldn't. My mom came home right around the same time and she was the one that realized I'd just tried to kill myself again. "Listen to the tape," I told them, "and just let me go." No luck with that.

The next thing I remember is being back in the ICU, having my stomach pumped and vomiting.

Living in San Luis Rey was just as crazy as the life I'd been living on the streets. The patients did almost anything they wanted as long as it didn't start any bloodshed or make the staff write out reports.

I was thrown in with child molesters, heroin addicts, genuinely psychotic people who needed massive doses of medication and who sat in their chairs in front of the TV completely zoned out on drugs, and people who just couldn't function for whatever reason. We didn't talk about why we were all there. It was just assumed that you needed to be kept off the streets and medicated.

By that time I'd already had sex with a few of the girls from the neighborhood. As awkward and fumbling as the sex was with girls my own age, I was at least familiar with the mechanics. But at San Luis Rey I got a real education from a beautiful thirty-year-old woman who everybody called a nymphomaniac. I had no idea what that was. But I found out fast what they meant. I knew she was screwing everybody in the building who wasn't too stoned for sex, but at that age, who cared? It was fun.

By the time I was released four months later, I found I was a little calmer in the brain and less manic. I was diagnosed with severe depression, given more pills, and sent back home. The fact that my home was what made me depressed didn't seem to matter.

Once I hit the streets, I started selling and using drugs again. But this time I was a little more organized and businesslike about dealing. Even though I was technically a Posole homeboy, I made it a point not to dress like a gangster. I let my hair grow out to look more like a white boy and less of a Chicano hood. I didn't wear bandanas or Pendleton shirts with just the top button done up. I wanted to pass as what we called a "casual," just a regular non-gang-affiliated kid. The reason was that I didn't want to stand out when I was selling dope on the beach.

San Diego is a big tourist destination. We have great beaches and the sort of beachside towns that attract people from all over the world. Tourists came to San Diego to party and I had the idea that I could help them party as much as they wanted.

That summer, I bought a beach bike, a fanny pack, and a Panama hat, and dressed up to look like a surfer. I was still only thirteen and even the cops, as hip as they are about gangsters, would never single me out as a drug dealer. In the mornings I'd stuff my fanny pack full of weed, acid, PCP, cocaine, pills, or whatever I could get my hands on and cruise the beaches.

These days, everyone is familiar with the term *profiling*. John Douglas, the FBI agent who essentially invented the term, developed the technique and codified it. The truth is, one of the first things you pick up on the streets is the ability to tell friend from foe and differentiate the harmless from potential danger. When I first came across John Douglas's book about profiling in the California prison system years later, I realized all us little homies had been using Douglas's techniques without actually being aware of them. On the streets, and especially in the prison system, profiling individuals is what keeps you alive.

During those long sunny days at the beach, I developed the sixth sense of who I could approach and who to avoid. The Europeans were easy to spot. They didn't dress like us and obviously I could always pick up on an accent. They were the easiest and safest people to approach. And I found out early on that they were in San Diego for the full Southern California experience—the beach, the sun, the girls, and the drugs. This is what they saw in movies and read about in the papers. I saw myself as just another beach life icon. There were the fast-food stands, the umbrella rental guys, the lifeguards, and all those tanned and hard-bodied girls. They were all part of the show and I was the friendly neighborhood dealer. I taught myself to play the part to perfection.

After all, I was just a harmless-looking teen and I learned to develop an approachable and easygoing attitude. I smiled a lot, learned a few phrases in German, French, and Italian for the benefit of my clients, and never pushed hard. I got to actually be friends with a lot of my clients. They'd invite me to parties and I learned how to handle myself around these twenty-year-olds. Those four months hanging around with the nympho at San Luis Rey completely demystified the female gender for me, and I discovered I could approach any girl I wanted and strike up a conversation. I was amazed at how easy it was if you watched the body language, the eyes, and what they did with their hands. The key is to look and act harmless. Which I was. I didn't want to rob or assault them. All I wanted was their money in exchange for drugs.

I was making a lot of money for a guy my age, but I was spending it just as fast. I was on a great ride and didn't think about tomorrow or the next day or next week. The beach and the tourists would always be there if I needed money, so I spent it on clothes and partying with the homies from Posole.

But summer doesn't last forever. Not even in Southern California. The tourists went home, the beach was once again repopulated with the locals, and my tourist market dried up. It was time to go back to school and figure out what to do until next summer.

Compared to the beach life, going back to school was like going to a concentration camp. In retrospect, I realize that I was caught between multiple worlds. There were the full-blown Pee Wee Gangsters with the shaved heads, the Dickies pants, and the bandanas. These were the guys that knew they were going to be gangsters and had pretty much taken all the necessary steps to make crime a career goal. I'd meet up with a lot of them later on in the California prison system.

And then there were the casuals who reminded me of sheep. They shuttled between school and home, did their homework, and never had any fun. And then there was that white world of the beach, the nice houses, and the new cars when the kids turned sixteen. These were the kids that floated through life without ever having to actually face it. They went to school, surfed, partied, and eventually landed a job that kept them floating into middle age. They never had to hustle dope or work on a loading dock or in a warehouse for their money. I envied and hated them at the same time. They had the one thing I was missing: stability.

As that year dragged on, it dawned on me that one of these days I'd have to make some kind of decision. Which world would I join? I could go back to mowing lawns and going to school, and become a sheep. Even though I could read and write above grade level, and mathematics was easy for me, my gut told me there was no future in academics for me. It was boring. I was too manic for that. The white world was out of the question. I wasn't white and the only status my family could claim was a ball-busting Marine gunnery sergeant. Besides, I didn't want to become a *pocho,* or a coconut—brown on the outside and white on the inside. A lot of blacks I met were the same way. The neighborhoods they came from were like mine and "acting" too white made you an outcast.

Eventually, the decision was made for me. Not that I resisted very much. I already had a halfway criminal mentality just from being around the neighborhood. That world is always "Us Against the World" anyway. Slinging drugs and stealing wasn't just tolerated. It was celebrated.

The day I was first sent to juvenile detention camp wasn't much different from any other day in school. I'd sold some marijuana to my cousin Yolanda. Like a fool, she and some of her girlfriends went into the school bathroom to smoke it and they got caught.

I happened to be in school that day and the principal tracked me down and asked me to go to the office. When I got there, Yolanda and all her girlfriends were sitting on a bench outside the office. When they saw me, they all put their heads down and couldn't look at me. Right away I knew this was trouble.

There was a school cop in the office with the principal and the first thing they did was search me. I was lucky that I didn't have anything on me at the time. But they accused me of selling drugs. They said the girls ratted me out. They cuffed me on the spot and marched me out of school in full sight of everybody that knew me. I should have felt humiliated but I wasn't. I took the arrest like a badge of honor. I didn't see myself as a criminal yet, but if they wanted to treat me like one, then fuck it. Make me a criminal. I could handle that easier than being Fred Corona's disappointing son. I was halfway hoping that it would reflect badly back on my stepfather, and he had it coming to him anyway.

4

Gladiator School

By the end of that afternoon, I was being processed into Rancho Del Campo, a minimum security facility for the California Youth Authority. Nobody calls it Juvenile Hall anymore. In our world, it was just YA, for Youth Authority. We also called it Gladiator School.

On the street, neighborhood gangs are like self-contained little families. We look out for each other. If somebody has money problems, needs a place to stay or even a meal, we'll take the last dollar in our pockets to help out a homeboy. In YA, that doesn't exist. At least not to the same degree. If you're in there with some of your homeboys, you definitely associate with them and form a little clique of your own. If you're lucky, you come from a gang that's really deep, a gang that has a lot of active members. Even if another gang outnumbers you in YA, just the fact that you come from a very active gang gives you a certain status. If you come from a gang that has a reputation as being a party gang and not an actively criminal gang, you have no status at all. And you either become a victim or prove yourself as a soldier.

The best of all possible worlds is to be housed with your home-boys and with gang members who are not rivals on the street. In my situation at that time, Posole was not at war with other bigger gangs like Shelltown and Logan Heights. So, officially, I didn't have enemies in YA. But unofficially, the personal beefs between individuals are always a problem.

When you put a bunch of young, aggressive kids who can't handle their lives on the streets in the same building, it's a matter of when, not if, fights break out. Nobody in YA wants to be thought of as a pussy or a guy who can't handle himself in a fight. So people look for ways to prove themselves. Somebody looks at you funny and a fight breaks out. Somebody thinks you cut in front of him on the food line and you're liable to be wearing your lunch and smashed in the head with the tray. The one thing you never want to do is walk away or back down from a challenge. Once you do that, you're forever branded as a guy with no heart. They'll take your personal property, money, or commissary items at will and you'll wear that jacket for as long as you're in that world.

In my case, I didn't have a personal reputation. I was just another kid from Posole who hadn't earned any stripes or done anything to distinguish myself other than sell some dope. And everybody did that, so it didn't particularly mark me as someone to be feared or respected. It didn't take me long to figure out that my lack of status had to change if I wanted to survive in YA. The one thing I did right was not snitch on my dope connections. I didn't rat out the Marine or any of the wholesale dealers I was buying my dope from. That got me a little status.

Just like in the California prison system, the YA system has two sets of rules. There are the house rules imposed by the authorities. And then there are the more important rules established by the Sureno (Southern California gangsters) hierarchy and the EME (the Mexican Mafia). The house rules essentially don't matter. If you break the house rules, all they can do to you is give you more time in custody and fatten up your inmate jacket. Breaking the EME or the Sureno rules, however, is extremely dangerous to your health. And the EME has eyes and ears everywhere in the California Department of Corrections (CDC) and YA. Once you're in one of those institutions, you can't hide from them.

The YA system is basically the farm team for the Mexican Mafia. YA is where a future EME member begins to make a reputation for himself. The carnals (full-blown EME members) are always scouting for new recruits. They enhance their power, status, and money-making ability in the prison system by being able to issue orders to solid, reliable soldiers on the outside and in the prison system. An EME member with a crew of twenty guys who will do what he tells them is a powerful man. If those twenty guys can control an entire neighborhood like Posole or Logan Heights, that EME carnal is the monarch of a kingdom. He literally has the power of life and death. So for a carnal to stay in business and keep the drug money flowing into his prison bank account, he's got to keep an eye out for up-and-coming talent. If you want a career as a criminal, YA is the place where you start making your bones and establish yourself as a soldado.

You have to bear in mind that the EME was established in 1957 by a bunch of YA juvenile inmates who eventually landed in the CDC. The accepted theory is that the EME was founded by a gangster named Luis "Huero Buff" Flores from Hawaiian Gardens in LA County. The EME was formed as a prison gang, and the initial group of EME members were also members of various street gangs like White Fence, Artesia, Rockwood, San Fer, Avenues, Maravilla, and others. At the time when the EME was first formed, the Hispanic population in the CDC was outnumbered by the white and black inmates. The Hispanics banded together for protection against those two racial groups.

One of the first rules laid down by the EME was that quarrels between gangs on the street ceased to exist when members of those warring gangs landed in prison. You were expected to bury the hatchet and let the old beefs die while in prison. This was purely a move for self-preservation. Hispanic inmates can't fight each other and then hope to defend themselves against the blacks and the white inmates. It's that old proverb about how a house divided can't defend itself. That rule is still in effect today. But over time, the EME morphed from an entity for Hispanic self-protection into a violent group that preys on its own Hispanic gang members.

One of the first things I learned when I landed in YA for the first time was that I wasn't allowed to associate with anyone other than Hispanic inmates. This was a hard adjustment for me. On the street, I had Samoan, Filipino, black, and Asian friends. I was mostly blind to race and ethnicity. I hung out with people I liked and got along with and it didn't matter what color their skin was. That changed in YA. As it turned out, one of my best friends on the street was a black guy named Daniel Taylor. He landed in YA soon after I did. When the Surenos saw me hanging with him, I was told to cut him off. He was a tinto (colored) or a mayate (dung beetle) and the Big Homies wouldn't tolerate it.

When you're in custody in the system, there's no such thing as affirmative action, cultural sensitivity, or racial tolerance. The inmates operate entirely on the concept of tribal allegiance. You don't associate outside the tribe. In truth, the Surenos have tolerance for white inmates, who generally operate under the banner of the Aryan Brotherhood (AB). Historically, there's been a mutually beneficial cooperation between the AB and the EME. A lot of white guys grew up in Hispanic varrios and some of them even made it into the ranks of the EME. The best known of them was a legendary white EME member named Joe "Pegleg" Morgan. Morgan, who had an artificial leg, moved easily between EME and AB factions because of the respect he carried in both camps. Despite his artificial leg, Morgan in his prime could never be beaten in handball, a game played like a blood sport in the CDC.

That same level of tolerance is not extended to black inmates. During my time in the CDC, I remember the ACLU suing the CDC to force them to integrate the cell blocks. A lot of politicians jumped on that bandwagon, thinking that they could force black, brown, and white inmates to get along by sharing cells. What these well-intentioned fools didn't realize was that we were criminals and we were running a criminal business with certain rules created to keep us in business. We were already in prison. What sort of punishment could they give us to force us to be nice to blacks? When they tried forced integration, the EME just sent out the call to riot. And we did. The other thing that politicians and the public don't realize is that the Mexican Mafia controls the California prison system. They call the shots. The EME is the control motor of the CDC, not the guards or the wardens.

While the racial aspect didn't appeal to me, I understood it for what it was. Namely, it was solidarity. The EME doesn't want divided loyalties for the simple reason that one day they may tell you to grab a bone crusher shank and kill that black guy in B Yard causing trouble. And if that black guy turns out to be an old friend, you may not jump to it the way you're supposed to. And you can't run a criminal or military organization like that. Your loyalty has to be beyond question. There's no room for sentiment or loyalty higher than what you extend to the Mexican Mafia. Loyalty to the EME comes before God or family.

I may have learned profiling people on the beaches of San Diego. But my real education, the instructional blocks that I needed to stay alive, started in YA. I literally learned how to walk. I watched some of the older guys who were making their second or third tour through YA. Everybody knew that they were headed for prison someday. Some of these guys who were approaching seventeen or eighteen had already been gangbanging for almost a decade. These were the hard cases that grew up worse than I did. They were the real gangbangers.

The difference between gangbanging and just being a member of a gang is that a banger puts in a lot of work. Basically, that means violence. Gangbanging or set banging is the equivalent of going to war with another gang—either a rival Hispanic gang or a black or Asian gang.

Gangs "claim" neighborhoods. And those neighborhoods have clearly defined and clearly demarcated boundaries. They mark their territory with gang graffiti. Unlike our own national borders, gang borders are constantly monitored for interlopers. As a Posole, your side of the street belongs to your gang. But it's entirely possible that the other side of the street belongs to, let's say, the Crazy Mexicans. So, as a solid soldado, you mark your territory with a gang placa (graffiti tag) and the Crazy Mexicans mark their side of the street. If you both respect your boundaries—you don't go selling dope in the other guy's house—everybody gets along. If some homie decides that he'd like to sling dope in the other gang's house or just demonstrate some power, he'll sneak across the street and spray-paint over the other gang's placa and replace it with his own gang's placa. That's not just rude. It's considered a declaration of war. That's when the guns come out and the homies start cruising the neighborhood at night looking for enemies. That's called putting in the work. You're literally on a military mission to neutralize the enemy. And if you catch one of them in the open, alone or walking deep and with or without their weapons, it's fair game. It doesn't matter if he wasn't the guy that painted over your placa. What matters is, he's one of them and they need to be taught a lesson. The pride and honor of the neighborhood is at stake and you don't want to be the guy that tarnishes the reputation.

These guys who had already put in a lot of work for their neighborhoods were the ones that walked and talked like warriors. They were the ones I watched and emulated. They'd shot people and been shot at. In the military they would have been called battle-hardened. And there was nothing false about the way they acted. They were the real deal, the guys with heart, and they ruled YA. And in time, they would come to rule the prison system and eventually entire neighborhoods all over Southern California. That's why it's called Gladiator School. It's basic training, boot camp for future super-criminals.

The staff at Rancho Del Campo was a combination of paycheck collectors who didn't care what we did, well-intentioned but naïve people who grew up wanting to save the world, and those who were borderline criminals themselves who would smuggle in dope and contraband for the right price.

On my first trip to YA, the director was a very decent man who gave us a lot of lectures on living a moral life, avoiding drugs, the benefit of prayer or meditation, and generally doing what he could to keep us from coming back. He realized that the inmates were at the hormonal stage in their lives and needed hard physical outlets. So he was always organizing track meets, ball games, and any physical activity that would burn off excess energy. A teenager tired from running ten miles is less likely to go out into the yard and look for trouble. Thanks to Sergeant Corona, I was already hardened to the point that none of the physical stuff ever got me tired out. I grew up with the physical discipline, and ironically, Fred Corona trying to turn me into a Marine made it a lot easier for me to become a disciplined soldier in a criminal enterprise. I was going to be a hell of a candidate for the Mexican Mafia.

Even though I was affiliated with Posole, I wasn't a banger yet. I hadn't put in that sort of work other than sell dope and share the proceeds with the homeboys. In the eyes of higher-ranking Surenos, not snitching on my dope connections made me loyal to my set but it didn't earn me any serious stripes. You get that by spilling blood. And I still had long hair. But that didn't last long. One day a guy who I think was from Logan Heights looked at me hard and said, "What's with the hair?" That was my order to cut it. I liked my hair long and I didn't want to go full pelon (military buzz cut, literal translation is "bald"). So I had it cut short, but not to the point you could see the skin. Apparently that was good enough for them.

One at a time, they started setting out the rules for me and guys like me. The first thing was I needed to have a weapon or access to a weapon at all times. Those are Sureno rules. In YA and the CDC, that means a shank—some sort of stabbing weapon. I was also told that if a Sureno gave me a weapon, I was supposed to hide it and keep it safe. And, of course, I couldn't snitch to the staff as to who gave it to me if they found it on me. I was supposed to keep my mouth shut, take whatever staff punishment I got, and not rat out another Sureno. That was part of being a good soldier.

I was also told that if I saw a Sureno getting jumped by mayates, I was supposed to jump in and help him no matter what the odds were. If there were ten guys beating a Sureno, I had to jump in even if there was a chance I'd get killed too. That's the way you show heart. That's the way you build up a reputation and earn some blood stripes.

I was amazed at how eagerly I jumped at the chance to prove myself. I jumped in with both feet because I felt like I was finally part of something that wanted me. It wasn't until decades later that I realized why I was so ready to show heart. With my father, I could never do anything to get his approval. No matter how hard I tried, it was never good enough. Ironically, it was easier to get respect from gangsters than it was from a Marine gunnery sergeant. The path to acceptance was the path of the warrior. My father was a warrior in his world. I would become a warrior in my world. In my mind, my world was a lot tougher than his. And I was going to prove it to him.

While I was in YA, my cousin Yolanda came to visit. She told me that it wasn't her who snitched me out to the principal but she knew who did. By that time I didn't care who ratted me out. I was in a place that felt more comfortable than the streets or my own house. I was surrounded by homies whose respect I was slowly earning. I got to know the staff guys that could smuggle in dope and I'd sell it for a small profit and then break off the extra to give to the guys I was close to. Giving a guy with higher status than you free dope was a way of showing them you were part of the clica (clique). You wanted to be one of them and if they thought you were worth something, they'd school you and start to give you some responsibilities and assignments. They became your prison mentors.

I adjusted pretty quick to my new situation. And because my neighborhood didn't have a lot of enemies, it gave me an opportunity to get to know fellow camaradas (Southsiders) from other neighborhoods. You have to remember that we were basically a bunch of twelve- to seventeen-year-old delinquents who couldn't function according to society's rules but still felt we needed to belong to something or prove ourselves in some way. These juvenile facilities were organized to try to do the job that our parents and teachers couldn't do.

I started to clique pretty good with a few dudes and we got pretty close. Probably the same way soldiers clique up in boot camp and on the battlefield. Sleepy from National City and Gallo from Encanto were both from different hoods, but it felt like we were cut from the same piece of stone. We've all had the experience of running across people that you feel you have everything in common with. We laughed at the same humor, liked the same music, and were interested in the same things. Gallo was there for having a sawed-off shotgun and Sleepy was there for gangbanging. We basically became our own crew and we were always together.

One night we were given dining room detail. All we had to do was clear and wipe down the dining room tables. We were clowning around the way we usually do, when all of a sudden Sleepy started arguing with a white guy. Before we could react, the arguing turned into a full-on fistfight. We jumped in on Sleepy's side and other guys jumped in on the white guy's side and it turned into a mini riot.

One of the cooks came out of the kitchen and got on the radio to call for help and started yelling at us to break it up. For some reason, Sleepy breaks off the fight and runs out the door. Not knowing why he did that, Gallo and I followed him out. We ended up near the school, still pumped up on adrenaline and wondering why Sleepy took off.

We were there for less than a minute when Sleepy says, "Fuck this. Let's blow this pop stand." I don't know how or why, but it seemed like a really good idea at the time. And just like that, we went from just doing our time and programming (being good inmates) to "let's bust out." It was clearly reckless and there was no purpose to it. But at the time, we were so bonded together that we felt we had to support each other no matter how crazy the idea was. It was a deeper brotherhood than I had ever felt to that time. Years later, Gallo and I would end up as cellies (cellmates) in Soledad Central prison. I'll get to that in time.

5

The Ones That Got Away

We knew we couldn't just walk out. We needed a plan. We figured if we're going to do this, we'll do it better than anyone else had ever done it. Rancho Del Campo was a juvenile camp with no fences and it was only three miles from Tecate. And Tecate is a border town—half in the US and the other half in Mexico. We knew that a lot of other inmates had escaped but they were all caught within hours. We figured we would be the ones that got away.

Our first plan of action was to dump the jail clothes we all wore so we wouldn't stick out in public. Next, instead of taking the highway to Tecate, we would hike over the hills into Mexico, make our way back to Tijuana, and then find a way back across the border into San Diego.

We knew that when they found us missing, they'd alert the local cops, the Border Patrol, the California Highway Patrol, sheriff, and any other law enforcement they could think of. So instead of leaving camp, we decided to break into the camp woodshop and lay low until all the excitement calmed down. In retrospect, it was a good idea. There we were in the woodshop while all that chaos of cops and camp counselors were out there uselessly beating the bushes for us.

Around two or three in the morning, when we didn't hear any more commotion outside and we were pretty sure they'd all gone to sleep for the night, we made our way to the clothing room. When you're processed, they take your street clothes, box them up, and put them in storage until you leave. So we had a lot of clothes to pick from.

When we finally picked our clothes from the dozens of boxes we searched through, we headed out of camp. You have to picture the fact that Gallo and I were thirteen years old. Sleepy was fifteen. And we're hiking into the hills in absolute zero visibility because we couldn't find a flashlight. We could hear rattlesnakes getting alarmed as we walked by. And we knew there were scorpions out there. And every few steps the thick brush was scraping our skin and clothes. We walked as best we could until dawn started breaking.

When the light was bright enough, we could see a roadway down a very steep hill. We started running toward it because we wanted to make the road before too much traffic built up and the cops would be out looking for us. As luck would have it, Sleepy trips and lands hard directly into a patch of cactus. He starts screaming because he's got cactus thorns all up and down the front of his legs. He looks like a mess.

Gallo and I help Sleepy pull out the thorns we could see and then Sleepy pulls his pants down to get the ones we couldn't see. It took about three hours to finally get most of the thorns out of his skin. By this time, of course, the traffic on the road had picked up considerably and the chances of getting caught were growing.

We made it to the road and eventually a truck pulled over and Sleepy tells the driver that we're going to Tijuana. The driver says he's only going as far as Tecate. That was good enough for us. We had to get off the road and he was the best chance we had.

The three of us were exhausted and wished the ride were a little longer. But it was only a few miles to Tecate, and before we had a chance to catch our breath, we were standing in the middle of a dusty street in Tecate, Mexico, wondering what our next move would be. We felt good that we actually made it farther than anyone else had ever made it from Rancho Del Campo. But we still needed to get back to the streets of San Diego if we really wanted to stay under the radar.

Gallo and Sleepy found some pay phones and started making calls. We needed to find someone who could come down there and give us a ride back to the US. After a while Gallo hooked up with one of his homegirls who could give us a ride but she didn't want to drive into Mexico. She'd pick us up on the US side of Tecate. So now we had to cross back into the US on foot.

We didn't have that far to walk because the border crossing was right there in town. But we were nervous as hell as we approached the border checkpoint. We were smart enough to get our stories straight in case the border agent started asking questions. Which of course he did. The first was "Where you guys going?" We told him the truth: "San Diego." Then he asked where we were coming from. Sleepy said we were coming from visiting his uncle in Tecate.

Then the agent asked for IDs. We didn't have any, of course, because all that stuff was back at camp. So he called another agent and they split us up and took us into three different rooms to see if we could keep our stories straight. We did, but we got betrayed by Gallo's underwear.

They told us to strip down so they could check us for weapons or whatever. Sleepy and I were smart enough to change into underwear we found in the storage room. Gallo had kept his issued underwear. Sure enough, when he took off his pants, there was the big C.D.R. (Campo Del Rancho) stamped on his boxers. The agent made a call and was told there was a BOLO (Be On the Lookout) for three teenagers that had escaped from youth camp.

The agents cuffed us up and we sat in a room until that night. A van came to pick us up and we were driven back to camp. When we got there, the place was locked down for the night, so they put us in the Program Office and told us to get some sleep. They would take us to Juvenile Hall in the morning to face escape and burglary charges, for stealing the clothes.

We were awake all night even though we were worn-out from not having had any sleep the night before. The next morning, they cuffed us up. I was cuffed to the arm of a wooden bench. Sleepy was cuffed to the other end of the wooden bench. They cuffed Gallo to a metal chair across from us. At breakfast time, they sent in this giant, goofy white guy to bring us some food. We could see right away that this kid wasn't too smart. But he was like six feet two and weighed about 240 pounds. He was really sympathetic and said that he felt bad for us. We could see that he was for real and a little soft in the head.

So we tell him that if he really feels that bad, he should help us out. He says he doesn't know what to do. I tell him he should kick the wooden arm of the bench I was cuffed to so I could move around a little. Sure enough, he takes one mighty stomp and breaks the arm of the bench. And I'm free. He does the same thing to the end of the bench that Sleepy is cuffed to. And Sleepy is now free. But the chair that Gallo is cuffed to is made of metal. Even with his size, there's no way he can kick metal apart.

We start looking for something to cut Gallo loose, but there's nothing in the room. But as we're looking, we can see through the glass into the next office and notice that somebody had left a set of keys on a desk. There was a cuff key in the set. So we tell the goofy white kid to go back to the kitchen and just pretend that nothing happened. We promised we wouldn't rat him out. He was nervous as hell but went and did as he was told. As soon as he leaves, Sleepy kicks the door in and I go grab the keys and unlock Sleepy's cuffs. They'd taken our shoes the night before, but they were still there in the next office, so we grabbed them too.

Apparently, the door we kicked in was wired, because as soon as it swung open, the alarm sounded. We ran out and immediately crawled under the building because we knew all hell would break loose. Sure enough, here came the counselors stomping into the room we had just been cuffed up in and we could hear them talking through the wooden floor. "Dammit, the little bastards got away again."

As one of them was cursing, the other one got on the camp intercom and issued orders to lock down the whole camp. "All inmates report to your dorms." We stayed huddled up under the building and we heard the sheriff show up and radio to all units about our escape. That lasted for a few hours, but by noon, the camp was off lockdown when they didn't find us and everybody started reporting for their normal duties—school or work.

By this time we'd been under the building for five hours and we were hungry and thirsty. The only guy we saw walking around was this kid named Huero who came from Sleepy's neighborhood,

National City. We knew he was nowhere near being a good soldier. He was sort of a nerd and we didn't hang around with him, but we were starving. Plus, we wanted to get some intel to see what the cops were doing and where they were doing it. Sleepy calls out to him from under the building, and when he finally gets his attention, Huero yells out at the top of his voice, "What the hell are you guys doing under there?" We tell him to lower his voice. If he kept talking that loud, he'd bring the whole camp down on us.

Right away he started preaching. He told us everybody's looking for us and that we should give ourselves up. We said we would eventually but we were hungry and thirsty right now. We knew he worked in the staff living quarters, so we told him to go in there and bring us back something to eat and drink. A few minutes later he came back with sandwiches, popcorn, and sodas. And again he told us to give up. We told him we were thinking about it but right now we needed to eat and get some sleep. We were exhausted. He promised not to rat us out.

After a while the three of us actually were dozing and didn't hear the work recall alert over the intercom loudspeakers. They told everyone to get back to their dorms. What finally woke us up was a sheriff's deputy shining a flashlight into our eyes and another one holding us at gunpoint with a shotgun. "Don't make a move. Just relax."

The opinion we had of Huero was justified. The guy was not a camarada, a soldado, or anything close to being a real homie. He was a rat and told the counselors the minute he got a chance. In a way, we were relieved it was over. We were exhausted, still hungry, and we needed a shower. We were taken directly to Juvenile Hall and were now charged with destruction of state property, two escapes, and the burglary charge for stealing clothes. The three of us caught another six months and this time we had to do it all in Unit 100 in Juvenile Hall. No more camp without fences and dorms. We spent our time in cells.

I did close to a year in YA. When the day came for release, the staff took me to the door and just said, "Go out there and behave."

I was fourteen by this time and I didn't go home.

6

Power Boosting

I had names of people on the street I'd gotten from the older guys in YA. When you're in that world, you survive by connections and allies. If you have any kind of status, that information gets out there and you're welcomed wherever you go. I knew I wasn't going home and I asked them if they knew people I could go live with. If I had no status, they would have ignored me and thrown me away. Instead, they gave me the names, addresses, and phone numbers of people on the outside who could use me. I was told by my homeboy Chato that he had a sweet setup for a place to stay, dope connections, and the chance to make some money. Chato and I grew up together in Oceanside since we were babies, and our mothers had been good friends since they were practically babies too. That's how far back we went.

Before I got to Chato, I hooked up with a neighborhood girl named Tiny. She was a runaway like me, so we started hanging together and eventually we went to see Chato. Chato said that an apartment in his building was empty and that Tiny and I could live there. We broke into the place and slept on the floor for a while.

Tiny and I would go around stealing anything that wasn't nailed down to furnish the apartment. We even robbed her mother's house. The building already had some squatting runaways like us, so we didn't have any trouble with the neighbors. We were all in the same boat.

A month later, Tiny and I were having sex in the apartment when the landlord of the building came through the door. She was showing the apartment to a couple. The three of them backed out of the apartment, and the landlord right away wanted to call the cops. I stopped her and told her that I was paying rent to a guy who came by once a month. I told her I was paying $375 a month. It was a lie, of course. We were living there illegally for free. On top of that, the place was full of the stuff we robbed from Tiny's house and other places—jewelry, clothes, food, and a couple of guns that Tiny's mother had around the house.

As if that wasn't enough, Tommy Garcia and I had just broken into a pawnshop one night and we took mostly clothes and bullets. We wanted the guns too, but they were locked up behind bars and in big safes. We were selling the clothes and the ammo to buy food, furniture, and drugs. When the landlord went off to call the cops, Tiny and I grabbed everything we could and took off. We left behind a lot of stuff plus a .22-caliber rifle that Tommy and I had stolen from a house. Weapons and drugs go together because sometimes you have to make deals with people you don't know. In the dope world, there's always the danger of getting ripped off. You have to have weapons because you can't go crying to the cops that somebody stole the dope you were trying to sell. So you have to be responsible for your own security. Otherwise you'll end up broke and dead.

Tiny and I bailed out of the apartment just in time, because a half hour later, five police cars pulled up to the building and found the stolen rifle, some dope, and a lot of the clothes we stole from the pawnshop.

Tiny and I dumped what we couldn't carry into trash cans and took a Greyhound bus to San Diego. We had the name of a guy who ran a shady sort of hotel in San Diego. He called it Pops Treetop Garden. As long as you paid him five dollars a night in cash, he didn't care who you were or that I was fourteen and Tiny was thirteen or you were Jack the Ripper or John Dillinger. We had our own room, but we had to share the shower and bathroom with a couple of other "guests" at the Garden. Pops knew that we were runaways, but all he cared about was the five dollars a night.

Pops would pay me for odd jobs around the hotel. And he got Tiny a job as a waitress at a diner that his friend owned. We lived like that for a couple of months, but I knew it couldn't last forever. By that time the cops had a warrant out for me for burglary and possession of firearms. Tiny had some sort of paperwork out for being a runaway. Tiny's mom, I found out later, was a clerk in the San Diego court system and she had a lot of her cop friends looking for us.

I wasn't getting any information about how close the cops were to getting me and I was running out of money, so I called my mom to see if she could give me some cash. She told me the cops had been to her house and were looking for me. And Tiny's mom had also been to the house and she wanted to charge me for kidnapping and rape. She was convinced that her precious daughter would never have robbed her own mother's house if it wasn't for my evil influence. She had no idea that Tiny was as out of control as I was.

My mom asked me where I was staying. I thought she wanted to know so she could send me some money. Like a dumbass, I told her. The next morning, around 7:00 A.M., I was asleep on the bed. Tiny had already gone to work. And then the cops showed up. They found a stolen .45-caliber pistol under the bed and a bunch of stolen property. They put me in the police car and we went to get Tiny at her work.

They released Tiny to her mother's custody and I was getting ready to face kidnap and statutory rape charges in addition to the burglary and weapons beefs. A few days later, Tiny's mother sent her to be examined by a doctor and she was told that she was pregnant. Her mom came to me and said that, as the father, if I signed the abortion papers, she would convince the cops to drop the kidnap and rape charges. So I signed the papers and Tiny got her abortion. They couldn't prove that the .45 was mine and they couldn't trace it as stolen, so that charge was dropped too. I managed to avoid going back to YA. In a perverted way, I really wanted to go back there. Instead, they released me to my mom who, in my mind, was nothing more than a rat and a snitch. That sort of ended any relationship I had with her for years.

Tiny's mom was afraid Tiny would run away again, so she put her in a group home for runaway girls. About a month later, I made a date to go see her and snuck her out of the group home for a few hours. By that time, Tiny wasn't the same Tiny I'd known. The abortion changed her completely. It's that Catholic thing. We took a walk through a cemetery, we had one last round of sex, and I never saw her again. Before I left, she said she was tired of running and she was intending to turn her life around, go back to school, and become a normal person. Nothing about that experience changed me at all. I knew where I was going and it wasn't school or the military or a warehouse job. I didn't trust anybody. What my mother did was out of concern and love, and as mad as I was, I couldn't stay mad at her. Still, the bond between me and my crimies was way stronger than what I had with my own family. I was going to become a gangster and the rest of the world could go fuck itself.

I looked up people I met in YA and we started seriously stealing and boosting anything that was lying around. We stole a Honda three-wheeled off-road bike right off the dealer's lot in broad daylight and sold it. We broke into a school at night and stole power tools from the shop classes.

We did a lot of what we called Power Boosting. They were like mini invasions or smash and grabs. I'd go into a clothing store and look around while one of my crimies would hang out near the door with a gun. I'd grab as much clothing as I could and blast out of the door. If anybody tried to stop us, the gun would come out and stop anybody chasing us.

I started hanging out with a heroin addict named Santos. He and his girlfriend were boosters like me and we robbed a lot of stuff. Through Santos, I met a crazy girl named Bonnie. She was a homegirl from Sherman and she was the kind who would do anything for money or a cheap thrill. She'd had a lot of boyfriends who were now in prison and she'd tell me stories about all the people they used to rob, the cars they stole, and the dope they ripped off from dealers. She wasn't just bragging. What she was doing was seeing if I had the same pair of balls that her former boyfriends had. She was basically daring me to do the same. Or worse. Like a fool, I decided to do worse.

I went back to selling dope on the beach just as a sideline. By that time, PCP hit the streets and I was selling lots of it. This was also right around the time when I first tried heroin. I took it almost on a dare. I didn't want Bonnie to know that I hadn't done it before, so when she offered it, I took it like I'd done it a dozen times.

That first shot was pure heaven. I'd never felt so good. I could see right away why people get instantly hooked on it. I remember getting a little nauseous. But after that passed, it was pure bliss. I knew I'd found the perfect drug. I started doing it every few weeks and I started heading down that addiction highway until some of my homies found out.

Gangsters are fairly tolerant of drug use. Pills, liquor, and pot are pretty much acceptable for partying and having fun. But when it comes to heroin, even the hardest EME criminals draw a line. From experience, homies know that a heroin addict, a tecato, is ruined as a solid warrior. Once you're hooked, you're a liability. You'll sell out your mother and rat on everybody you know just to get high. So one day, some of my homies took me aside and basically beat the crap out of me to teach me the life lesson about heroin. I didn't completely stop doing heroin, but I kept it under control. Every once in a while when I wanted to shut everything out and take a break, I'd use heroin. But I was careful not to let anyone know about it. I didn't want to wear the tecato jacket. I had a career in crime to think about and I couldn't let heroin sidetrack me.

One of the biggest robberies I remember committing at that time was in a Macy's department store. We planned it with what we thought was military precision. Our target was a bunch of fur coats. We knew from doing a recon that the fur coats were attached to the racks with steel cables. We also figured out the fastest way in and out of the store and where to park the two getaway cars. We knew a girl named Linda who said she could help us unload all the coats in one big move.

So four of us figured out a plan. I went in with bolt cutters. I had one of my crimies standing guard with a pistol, just in case. And we had two drivers ready in two separate cars. We had Linda standing by in her neighborhood, ready to hide the fur coats and unload them.

That afternoon, I boosted twenty-seven fur coats from Macy's and had them sold to Linda's friends less than an hour later. My cut was $3,000. I was sixteen and that was more money than I'd ever seen in my life. Who the fuck needed school, a bullshit job, or an education. This was living. Fast easy money, dope, girls, and the thrill of the robbery. I was absolutely hooked on the gangster life and I was damned good at it. In the gang world, kids that age aren't supposed to be making this kind of money and pulling crazy daylight burglaries in front of God knows how many surveillance cameras. We were off the charts. And we were also stars. We were earning status and the girls were all over us. I found out real fast that the badder and ballsier you are, the more the homegirls want to fuck you. Something about being with gangsters just made them want to fuck you more.

It was odd, the girl that snitched me out to the principal tracked me down one day and basically asked me to take her virginity. She wanted to be with a badass and I would have been a fool if I didn't go for it. That's how crazy the shit gets on the streets.

After all the crazy boosting, the fur coats, the three-wheeler, and dealing at the beach, I finally got arrested for stealing twelve pairs of Levi's from a Miller's Outpost. It was a stupid move and I should have been a lot more careful, but I was so drunk with my own self-importance as a criminal that I got sloppy. I thought I was invincible. I was still underage and I went back for another tour of YA.

By this time, I had a solid reputation as a criminal. Although I hadn't shot or stabbed anyone, I had a rep for being absolutely fearless. Daylight smash and grabs? Boosting a motorcycle right in front of the dealer? A $3,000 take for ten minutes of work? Yeah. I was a star.

I walked into YA with a swagger I didn't even have to think about. By now it was natural. It was part of me. It was the walk, the way you carry yourself, that first broadcasts to everyone around you that you're not somebody that can be pushed around.

I was still wearing my hair longer than most of the soldiers. Right after I landed in YA, Tommy was sent there on some beef or other. We looked at each other, hugged each other, and I finally divested myself of any pretense of being anything other than a criminal. I went to the barber and had him shave my hair. Samson got weak when they cut his hair. I went the other way. I was a bald-headed gangster, a pelon, and I no longer cared who knew it. I was now ready for bigger crimes, more status, and more violence.

7

Surenos Don't Stoop

After spending my first time in the juvenile system, I developed a perverse taste for that kind of life. I felt like a young tiger who finally tasted living flesh and develops a taste for blood. The blood in this case was the camaraderie I felt for all these guys from different areas. It felt exciting and it was a novelty in my young life.

They respected me and we were down for each other. In almost every significant way, it's the same experience that soldiers have in war. It's the brotherhood of the foxhole. Although I loved my homeboys and they were there for me as well, there's that old saying that "you'll never be a hero in your hometown." What I found was that I could go into any neighborhood and be recognized as a respected Sureno.

There's a cruising boulevard in San Diego called Highland Avenue in National City. Sleepy, the guy I escaped camp with, was from National City. Gallo, the other guy on the escape, was from Encanto. So when we cruised either of those places, I'd run into their homies. And as soon as I introduced myself with my Nite

Owl street name, the normally reserved and suspicious gangster attitude melted away. "Whoa, you're *that* Nite Owl from Posole? My homeboy told me about you." And the waters would part, the doors would open, and I was immediately accepted. Dope, pussy, a place to hang out and stay if I needed a bed for the night or a week—it was all just offered up based on nothing but my reputation and the respect I earned while in juvie. In retrospect, juvie was the beginning of the end for me. I have no idea what would have happened to me if I hadn't had that kind of reception on the street after getting out of the juvenile system.

Naturally, my appetite for acceptance just got bigger. I realized that my irrational acts of hoodlumism (a new word going around at the time) were actually being watched and monitored by people I didn't even know existed.

I spent the first few months out of juvie basking in this new-found respect and it sort of pushed me to punch up my résumé with even bigger acts of antisocial behavior. The one area that I pushed open was shooting dope. That was a stupid one. By that age I'd been using drugs—legally and illegally—since the age of eight. I naturally smoked weed, Sherm (PCP), drank beer, and when I was kicking it with the homegirls, their favorite of Thunderbird wine mixed with Kool-Aid.

Getting high to have fun is one thing. Getting high to support a habit is officially graduating into a whole new world. The irrational motivation to shoot heroin has nothing to do with money or the simple necessity of making a living on the street as a criminal. You're now serving a whole new demon—the heroin, meth, or coke demon that will make you take the sorts of chances you would never take as that cool, methodical criminal.

When you're high, you're in a cloud of indifference mixed with invincibility mixed with paranoia mixed with—let's face it—bliss. Nothing seems impossible or impossibly stupid. Rob a dope dealer? "No problem. Show me where he's at." Break into a house or a crowded store where they may have something worth stealing? "Cool. Just keep point for me. If they chase me, start blasting. The car's around the corner."

And I couldn't believe the sex that came my way whenever I was holding and giving away dope. I was a porn star. I remember once being locked up in a motel room with two girls for two solid days. I don't think I wore clothes once in that forty-eight hours. We were loaded on meth and heroin and we literally partied like our very existence depended on it. Until we ran out of dope. That's when the second demon comes into your world and reminds you that you're human after all and that money is finite and the time comes when you have to pay for your sins. It's the coming down and the withdrawals. This is the monster lurking in the syringe and when he comes screaming into your brain, it turns into a war for your soul. And most people lose the war at the first battle.

I'm convinced that most girls selling their bodies on the street do it to support a habit. The monster will make you steal from your own family. I've seen young women make their kids go hungry by either spending their money on dope or selling their food stamps at a discount to get dope.

I started becoming reckless and taking chances that just didn't make sense had I been in my rational mind. I mean, who walks into a crowded department store flashing a gun, grabbing as many clothes as he can, and daring anyone to try to stop him? The answer is me.

Here's the thing, though. I never let the heroin, coke, or meth get the edge on me. I was disciplined enough to know where the line was. And I was smart enough to know that the shot callers would put a tecato jacket on me that I'd never be able to shed. So as hard as I partied, I never got hooked.

But the dope was my demise at this point in my career. I was convicted of shoplifting when in fact I could have gotten an armed robbery charge. That's how I found myself back in custody and headed for the California Youth Authority. This is state time and one step down from prison. And this is also the place where all the rules change. And this was also the only way I was going to kick the habit and slay the monster. This is where the Big Homies keep an eye on you and give you structure. If you screw up here with them, you're marked forever as useless to them and you're just another throwaway that they can exploit and use any way they want.

The first stop was Norwalk Southern Youth Correctional Reception Center (SCRC). It's the place where they send delinquents like me from all over Southern California. This is where they evaluate you for medical issues, mental problems, and where they basically try to see what kind of badass or mental case they're dealing with. For me, it was my next big opportunity to do what business and corporate types call networking. It was a chance to meet new camaradas from Los Angeles, Long Beach, Ventura County, Venice Beach, and the San Fernando Valley.

In the world of Surenos who want to make crime a career, friendships made here often lead to lifelong associations and sometimes to lifelong feuds. This is where the future leaders, Big Homies and shot callers, all came from. Let's remember that the original founding members of the Mexican Mafia prison gang met each other in these reception centers as young men my age. And they did more to change the face of organized crime in California than the Italian mob could ever hope to accomplish on the West Coast.

At that time, the gangbanger cholo attitude had just started to migrate from the varrios into mainstream culture. Even though it wasn't until 1988 when Dennis Hopper directed and released *Colors* that, suddenly, the shadow existence us gangsters were living was on movie screens for the whole country to see. The movie got really close to the truth, and while it wasn't as ugly as real life, it gave the general public a taste of what was happening under their noses. It was to us what *Goodfellas* would become to the Italian mob two years later. Having spent time with some of the Italian mob bosses in places like Sandstone federal prison, I got the idea that they thought their movie was as close as anyone could have gotten to the truth of their organization.

At Norwalk SCRC, we started seeing white, suburban kids showing up dressed like us, trying to act like us, and wanting to be one of us. Most were sad imitations, but just the fact that they were emulating our culture was putting ideas in our heads. Like maybe we were a bigger deal than we ever thought we could be.

In Norwalk, I was officially starting to be schooled in Sureno politics. Now keep in mind, when we say Sureno politics, what we actually mean is Mexican Mafia politics. Just like in the movie, the Italians rarely call themselves the Cosa Nostra. They use the goodfellas shorthand to indicate the existence of an entire world of criminals. It's the same thing with Surenos. Nobody tosses that word *Mexican Mafia* around lightly. The code word is *Sureno*.

We had six buildings in Norwalk and each building had an official Sureno Rep. These Reps were the shot callers for each unit. And there was a hierarchy in each unit. There was Prez (short for *president*), Vica (pronounced "veesa," a corruption of *vice president*), and Third Man. It was their job to educate you in the South Side mannerisms. We had to absorb the culture as laid down by the shot callers. First and foremost, you had to stick up for your own people. That means Surenos stick together against everyone else. The other thing is that if we had beefs on the outside with rival gangs, the beefs would be suspended while in the facility. Sureno unity in any institution was way more important than local gang fights. We were told to bury the hatchet and deal with whatever problems we had after we got on the outside.

Surenos had to walk a certain way. No shuffling of feet, no downcast eyes, no stooped backs. We walked like warriors surveying the battlefield after a victory over the enemy—shoulders back, head straight forward, and a swagger. We owned the facility and everybody had to know it just from watching us walk. We couldn't eat or drink anything with blacks.

Our clothes had to be clean, sharp, and on point. The Reps even told us how to carry our cigarettes. Back then, we all smoked Camel nonfilters and they only came in a soft pack. We were told to crease the corners of the soft pack so as not to crush the cigarettes when we put the pack in our pockets. Why? Because they wanted it that way. It was like the Army telling you to put military folds on the blankets. You had to be squared away in every single thing you did, from the pack in your pocket to the appearance of your room. If you failed in certain areas, you were reprimanded and checked. Too many reprimands and you started carrying a reputation as an unreliable Sureno. No career advancement for you.

It may sound crazy, but I came to know and love the structure. Frankly, it wasn't much different from the discipline of the Marine master gunnery sergeant who raised me and drilled me on making beds and doing things the military way. But instead of being constantly critical, the shot callers were complimenting me on being a model Sureno. By the time I finished my second stint in YA, I was appointed as Vica in my unit. A title. That was worth more to me than a hundred "attaboys" from the outside world.

Part of the program at Norwalk was determining how dangerous you were to society and where they'd send you. Since I had the escapes from camp on my record, going back there was out of the question. I would be going somewhere "behind the fence," where escape was harder if not impossible. The charge of felony shoplifting that landed me in Norwalk, coupled with the escape risk, was enough for them to send me to the Ventura Youth Correctional Facility in Camarillo.

Camarillo is just north of the San Fernando Valley in its own little valley. Geographically, it's a great place to live. There's still a lot of farmland and agriculture. And the weather never gets too hot or cold because it's right on the coast. But the facility where I'd be going was, even then, legendary for being mismanaged and abusive. They had isolation cells—like the junior versions of the SHU (Security Housing Units) of adult prisons like Pelican Bay. This despite the fact that Ventura was considered a medium security facility.

To begin with, Ventura was a coed facility. To me, that's just asking for trouble from the start. You have to wonder what brainiac thought mixing up delinquent males and females in the same place was ever a good idea.

In a lot of ways, it was like a crazy fun-house-mirror version of the worst college you can imagine. For one thing, we were allowed to wear our street clothes. We didn't have uniforms. And we went to school every day in mixed-gender classrooms. And just like school on the outside, girls would fight over guys. The guys would fight each other to get the attention of the girls, and everybody was always looking for a place to take a girl who was more than willing to be shown a good time. It was a festival of adolescent raging hormones mixed with drugs and criminal attitudes.

Officially, sex was forbidden. Imagine trying to enforce that rule when you're managing a bunch of delinquents. So, officially, when some of the girls would get pregnant, we'd call them Immaculate Conceptions. The girls would never admit to having sex. And the boys would never cop to it because it would land them in the hole. And the staff would give up trying to get to the truth because a pregnant female was just a reminder that they weren't doing their jobs.

Part of the program in Ventura was that you were assigned a job. They had jobs in the kitchen, groundskeeping, cleaning up the classrooms, the library, and the housing units. They also had jobs "off campus," working out in the free world. I got lucky enough to land a job at the infamous Camarillo State Hospital. This is the main Southern California hospital reserved for the criminally insane. Again, you have to wonder who came up with the brilliant idea of sending a bunch of criminally inclined teenagers into a hospital full of people who were criminally insane.

Every afternoon at one thirty, a vanload of us was driven through the town of Ventura to the hospital. When we got there, we were given our assignments and briefed on the safety rules as well as the security limits they put on us.

The hospital had a cafeteria where the hospital patients could buy burgers and fries and other kinds of junk food. Some of the more reliable patients were given little envelopes of cash so they could buy their food. After gaining their confidence, we would clip some of that money out of their envelopes and use that money to buy drugs right there at the hospital.

This one time, I had eight Black Beauties on me that I'd just bought. The irony of me being in custody because of drugs, and then being sent to a place where I could buy all the drugs I wanted, was lost on me at the time. But that was the system then and I don't know if it's changed much since. It was a day I was working in the kitchen with a guy named Dave. He was a young guy around twenty-four years old who was a hired civilian who had gotten a job at the hospital. Dave was a very cool guy who never treated us like rising young criminals. He gave us free food and sort of treated us like younger brothers.

This one day, he was looking really tired and worn-out. I asked him if he was feeling okay and he said he was but that he'd been up all night after going to a Santana concert in Ventura. He said he'd gotten fucked up on liquor and dope and he was dragging his ass. He said he'd do anything to get rid of his hangover. I asked him if he thought some Black Beauties would straighten him out. "Fuck, yeah," he said.

We kept working together for a little while, but when I had a chance, I snuck into his office and left three Black Beauties under a pile of papers. Before I left, I told him to go check in his office and we went back to our units.

The next day, after breakfast was over, he caught my attention and said he wanted to talk to me. For a second I was panicked. I thought he was going to turn me in. He asked where I got the pills from. I denied everything and claimed I didn't know what he was talking about. Then he looked at me for a long while and said,

"I'm not going to bust you. I just want to make sure you're not setting me up." I finally convinced him that I wasn't doing that. I told him he was very cool with all the inmates and we thought he was a friend. Then he said, "Go check the cleaning supply room. There's something in the paper towels." I went there and found a small manila envelope. I looked at him. He smiled. I took the envelope and went back to my unit. Once I was back in my cell, I opened the envelope and saw three joints. I smelled one, and sure enough, it was weed.

The first thing I did was break one in half. I had to look out for my boys Grumpy from Culver City and Shorty from Verdugo. These were my go-to homies. Even though we were from different varrios, we all looked out for each other.

I also had this neighbor in the cell next to mine. He was a white guy with red hair and he had an amazing resemblance to Ralph Malph, the character from *Happy Days*, the TV show. By this time, my family had been stationed to Hawaii and I wasn't getting any family visits and not much mail. "Ralph" apparently figured this out and was always telling me stories about his family and constantly trying to set me up with his sister.

I sent the last of the weed to one of the homegirls from my neighborhood. She was serving eight years for a robbery and an attempted murder charge. I figured she could use it. That's the way it is in prison and YA. You're all in the same miserable boat, so if you can make one day pass a little nicer for someone else, you do it. Or at least, that's how I operated. Pot was my comfort drug since I was twelve and I figured they would all appreciate a taste of it.

The next day, when I saw my opportunity, I pulled Dave to the side and thanked him. He just laughed and asked if I enjoyed it.

"Hell, yeah," I said. Then I asked him if we could work out some sort of deal. I didn't know if this was some kind of test or not, but he asked me where I got the Black Beauties. I told him I couldn't tell him because I didn't want to get anybody in trouble. "Just like I wouldn't tell anybody where I got the weed," I said to him. It was the simple truth. It was the safest and best way to operate. You don't go blabbing about stuff that doesn't need to be blabbed about.

That's the hook. If you can earn someone's trust so that they know you have their best interests at heart, then you build their confidence and a relationship of trust. He realized I wasn't giving up my pill contact and so he felt enough trust to try me out. I explained to him that I had a source of cash and maybe we could work something out that would benefit both of us. I guess I was learning the art of the deal. Both parties walk away with something they each want and neither is trying to burn the other.

He asked me how much I wanted. Remember this is around 1979 and 1980. Weed was being sold in "lids" and a lid was measured by the thickness of one finger. A finger lid cost ten dollars. Two fingers was twenty dollars, and so on. These days, especially with the arrival of legal medical marijuana, you get a tiny ziplock bag for between twenty and fifty dollars, depending on all sorts of factors.

I had to admire him for the fact that he was giving me straight street prices. Most people in his position, knowing that I was in an institution and couldn't shop around for a better deal, would have jacked me up for as much as he could get. Dope in prison can go for double or triple the street price simply because of the scarcity of supply. Simple economics. I've known corrections officers to this day who boost their salaries by tens of thousands of dollars per year just selling cigarettes in prison. Same goes for cell phones and other "items" that are scarce in prison. But Dave wasn't a hustler or out to make a fortune selling weed to teenagers. I had a sense I reminded him of a family member or a close friend, because he always treated me right.

I gave him my twenty dollars and the next day he brought me a fat, two-finger lid. It was actually more than I paid for. Needless to say, me and my close boys became extremely popular in Ventura and we were invited to all the social functions. Every Friday they held inspection of all the units. The unit with the highest score was allowed to hold a social. If it was a girls unit, they could invite any boys they wanted. If it was a boys unit, they could do the same. So for the next four months, we, the ones who were holding, were invited to every social that the girls won. They weren't big affairs. They served Kool-Aid, cake, and there was music and usually a movie after that. We provided the party favors. The party favors guaranteed us special favors with the girls, meaning that we'd all get laid.

Dave and I got along so well that it got to the point where if I wanted to see a particular girl, he'd arrange to have her brought down to the kitchen supposedly for an interview for a job in the kitchen. Of course, once she got there, the girl and I would sneak off somewhere and screw like rabbits. One of these girls, Kitty from Eighteenth Street, became my girlfriend for the last four months that I was there. After I paroled, we stayed in touch and I drove up from San Diego to pick her up when she was released. All in all, my time in Ventura was very easy time.

I think it was too easy. The truth was that I had no fear of going back. My time there showed me that I could continue to get high, get as much sex as I wanted, expand my network of friends and allies, and get taken care of by the state without having to hustle for every nickel or meal. It was that lack of fear that once again landed me in prison. Ninety days after being released, I was arrested for a parole violation and I was back in Ventura.

I realize now that I was already becoming institutionalized. Being in prison wasn't much different than being on the street because prison was becoming second nature to me. It was just the way I lived. This was my normal. I adapted to prison and street without breaking stride and I just didn't care anymore one way or the other. And that easy geographical and emotional transition from street to prison just makes it that much easier to commit crimes. We weren't offered any alternatives once we went behind bars. The system just recycles inmates like aluminum cans. From my point of view, the prison system is a business to keep the corrections officers and the whole prison enterprise on the receiving end of government spending. The people running the institutions don't care whether you come back or not. In fact, if you asked them hard, I'm sure most of them would rather have you come back so they can keep the money merry-go-round moving, increase the size of the staffing, build more prisons, and keep the government union plans fully funded. There is no incentive in the system to educate inmates so they can be in a position to fend for themselves once on the outside. Inmates are money in the bank.

8

A Chance in Hawaii

After I was released from Ventura, I wanted to be paroled to my uncle in San Diego, but the YA would only allow me to parole to my parents. And so I was going to live with my parents in Hawaii.

Even though I really missed them while I was in jail, so much had passed between us that I knew it was going to be next to impossible to find some way of getting along. For one thing, I was no longer that troubled kid they saw when I left for YA. In every way that counted, I had a thug's mentality. I was a lot harder now than when I went away. I'd been schooled by the system and by older gangsters. I'd fired guns in anger and been shot at. I'd robbed people at gunpoint, stolen property out of crowded department stores, ingested enough drugs to kill several horses, and the only people I respected were those with similar or bigger criminal backgrounds.

After the plane landed at Oahu airport and the plane doors opened, the heat and humidity blasted me. The sight of my family made me break down and cry. Their OP floral shirts flapping in the breeze, they were insanely cute, as innocent as angels, and they were smiling, jumping up and down in their flip-flops as they saw me. For a glorious, brief, shining moment I forgot I was a thug, I forgot I was on parole. I was helpless as this enormous wave of emotion swept through me. My tough-guy dam broke. I cried, they cried. We hugged like we would never let go and stood there for a very long time blubbering and happy. Maybe there was a chance, I thought.

Although my father wasn't there because he was deployed to the fleet, there was another person at the airport that day with my family. An absolute knockout named Jasmine. She had green eyes, an amazingly happy disposition, and a body that made heads turn. By the time we'd gotten to the car, my mother warned me—actually, she made me swear—not to go after Jasmine, who she considered a good friend of the family. Jasmine's husband was also a Marine and they lived in the same base complex as my family. My dad was a good friend of her husband.

I came to find out soon enough that the rest of the families in the base housing complex didn't have the scruples that my mother imposed on me. They called the complex Sodom and Gomorrah. In Oceanside and at Camp Lejeune, we had lived off base in our own home. In Hawaii, we lived on base in what could be called garden apartments. On the island the general feeling among the families was that this posting was an elaborate form of an extended camping trip. There was a lot of socializing going on, especially with the men, like my father was at the time, off with the fleet for two months and the women and children left behind on base to entertain themselves as best they could.

I couldn't have gotten a better reception when we reached the house. I had my own room, and my mom had bought me a lot of island clothes—OP shorts, floral shirts, flip-flops, drawstring pants, and dock loafers. Coming from YA, where the uniform of the day was khaki pants and Pendleton shirts, this was a strange transition for me. But not an unwelcome one. On base, I'd be just another Marine brat instead of an inmate. After I changed, my mom made a massive meal with all my favorite food for a welcome-home feast. Honestly, nothing had tasted this good in years. My mom is an amazing cook and I ate until I could barely move.

A few days later, my mom said that she was going to the Staff Club just to socialize and hang out with the other Marine wives. She said that Jasmine was coming and asked me if I wanted to go with them. She said the drinking age was eighteen, and since I was old enough, she told me I could drink but not to overdo it. I'd been a regular drinker and doper for years, so it was a little funny to hear my mom talk to me like I was a teenager fresh off the turnip truck, but I promised I'd keep it under control.

I'd been locked up for eighteen months at this point and I was ready to do some partying without the fear of being reported by the staff, obeying a curfew, or hitting on whatever girl I wanted to without being punished for socializing after lights-out.

Before we left, I went to my sister's room. She was twelve at the time and I asked her to show me what people were dancing like those days. Sure enough, she put on a record and showed me. Ultimately, it wouldn't matter if I could dance, glide, or stumble around like a lame mule. I didn't know it, but I was about to land in the middle of a swinger's paradise.

When we got there, the first thing I noticed was that the women outnumbered the men by about four to one. Most of the men in those units were off with the fleet, and their wives were making the best of being fleet widows. My mom, innocent as she was, introduced me to her friends in an effort to just get me decompressed from institutional life. The way she saw it, I needed to acclimatize myself to the outside world, and hanging around with other families in our situation would go a long way toward getting me readjusted.

We were only there about an hour when a blond twenty-eight-year-old that my mom introduced me to earlier asked my mom if I could drive her home. "I'm too drunk to drive and I don't want to take a chance. Can your son drive me?" My mom says sure. "But you come right back, mijo. Don't go wandering away."

I drove her home and walked her into her apartment to make sure she didn't fall or anything. We literally barely got through her front door when she was all over me like a cat in heat. Remember, I was eighteen at the time and she was a married woman of twenty-eight. It didn't seem to matter to her. I didn't leave until twelve thirty that night and made my way back to the club. I'd been gone for hours. By the time I got back, my mom was a little tipsy but she wasn't so tipsy that she couldn't figure out what had happened. I drove her and Jasmine back home feeling like I'd just landed on Fantasy Island, where every wish I wanted was fulfilled.

For the next few months, I literally did not do much more than go to the club, troll for women, and score. And the odd thing is, I didn't have to do much trolling. The women were as bad as I was. I was going home with a different Marine wife almost every night of the week. It got so bad that my mom finally had to step in and tell me to stop it. A lot of the women's husbands were in the same company that my father was in. And if it started getting around that Fred Corona's son was banging their wives while they were on fleet duty, there could be a lot of trouble for my dad, their wives, and the whole unit. It actually got to the point that it got boring. Not the sex, but the monotonous repetition of doing the same thing night after night.

After a few months of this, I'd started getting friendly with Ropati, this Samoan kid who lived next door to us. He was the same age as me and we were together so much that people started thinking we were brothers. He started teaching me Samoan and I started teaching him some Spanish. He, naturally, knew how to surf, so he got me to the point where I could stand on a board and do fairly well. I taught him how to lift weights. It wasn't long after we got friendly that we fell into a routine that would have been the envy of every eighteen-year-old in the world. Or even Hugh Hefner.

In the mornings we'd go surfing. The afternoons we spent at the base gym working out. We'd go home, eat, take a nap, and by the evening we'd be at the Staff Club or the base golf club. Honest to God, sometimes we were both hitting two to three girls a day. This was paradise. I had three girls I was seeing regularly. One was a twenty-year-old Hawaiian punk rocker name Kahleo who worked at the base PX (Post Exchange). She had a knockout body, crazy-colored hair, and she sang in a punk band.

Then there was Heather, a really cute white girl with brown hair who served drinks at the Staff Club. She was really possessive. And then there was Tammy, a petite blonde the same age as me whose favorite pastime was getting naked at the beach. Tammy and I would meet in the morning and go down to the beach. She'd tan while Ropati and I surfed. After that, Tammy and I would find some secluded spot in the bushes and spend the early afternoon having sex. After that we'd go swimming to wash the sand off places where sand shouldn't have been.

This brief period really was the best time of my life. I was carefree, happy, and for the first time I felt like I could put my past behind me and start fresh. I was so optimistic that I even went down to the recruiting office and tried to join the Marines. When the recruiter got to the part in my résumé about being a convicted felon, he made a face and said it would keep me out of the service. "Come back when your dad is back from fleet duty. We might be able to do something." Honestly, it was a big disappointment. I wanted to join, hoping that the experience would wash off all the bad and make me into a new person. Meanwhile, I continued my playboy lifestyle and waited for my dad to come home. But by the time he did, my life would be heading in a completely different direction. I'm fairly certain I wouldn't be where I am today if the Marines had taken me that day. But those are the breaks.

Her name was Chou. She was a Japanese girl with short black hair and skin as smooth and cool as polished porcelain. She had intensely black eyes that seemed to run about a mile deep, and I literally fell in love with her the first time I saw her. She lived a house down from us. The very first time I saw her, she was wearing tan shorts, a white spaghetti-string blouse, and white sandals. She was carrying towels and walking with a little boy about three or four years old. My heart almost stopped.

The very next day, Ropati and I were working out in my backyard when that same little boy I saw her with came ambling up to us. He asked me, "What's your name?" I told him and he took off running the way he came. Five minutes later, he comes back and asks me, "How old are you?" I asked him, "Who wants to know?"

"My auntie," he said.

"Well, why don't you take me to her," I said, "and I can tell her myself."

He took my hand and led me to her house, which, as I said, was only one house over from ours. I noticed all the shoes at the front door, so I took mine off and went into the living room. From the kitchen I heard a female voice ask, "What did he say, Justin?" So I yelled out to her, "Why don't you ask me yourself?"

She was startled, of course. And a little embarrassed. But when we saw each other we started laughing. A feeling shot through me that I've only ever felt three times in my life. This first time was with Chou. Then with my wife (my daughter's mother), and then with my Carolina Cardinal, someone who isn't part of these confessions. I've never as completely and thoroughly given my heart so freely as with those three women.

Unfortunately, none of them ended with happily-ever-after. Each of those relationships ultimately fell apart and I became a harder person. They helped drive me along the road to the person I am now—guarded and genuinely frightened of giving myself completely to anyone.

For the next few weeks, I courted Chou in the most chaste way I knew how. We behaved like a Gidget movie. Picnics at the beach, surfing, snorkeling, bowling, going to movies, and all the conventional rituals that were alien to the way I'd been relating to women. A lot of the time I brought my little brothers with me so her nephew, Justin, would have someone to play with. I spent all my time with her and ignored everyone else. Even my best friend, Ropati, had a hard time getting my attention. She had a powerful spell on me that, in fact, made me want to be a different person than the one I was.

The day came fairly quickly when she wanted to stay home and watch TV one night. It was a night of revelation for me. We made the most intense love I'd ever experienced. It was deep and, if there is such a thing, magical. We could not get enough of each other.

A few weeks later, I realized that I'd abandoned my best friend, Ropati, and cut off virtually everyone else in my life. We saw each other constantly. She was the first thing I thought of when I woke up in the morning and the last thing I thought of at night.

My mother pulled me aside one day and told me that I should be careful and not get Chou pregnant. I guess she saw the extremes that I lived by. I was either banging every woman on base or thoroughly besotted by this beautiful young woman. There was no middle ground and I can see now how that was the way I lived my life. No half measures. No halfhearted commitment. It was all or nothing.

I don't know if my mom's warning was a jinx, but one day Chou told me that she had missed her period. She thought she might be pregnant. A lot of men dread to hear those words and a lot more start heading for the door. I was thrilled. The notion of having a child, marriage, starting a life together, filled me with joy. I wanted this more than I realized. She asked what I wanted to do. "I want to be with you forever," I told her. She hugged me and started to cry. At first I thought they were tears of happiness. Then she dropped the bomb and said that she had lied to me. She wasn't eighteen years old. She was only sixteen. Naturally my heart sank.

We talked some more and I told her that I loved her and that I wanted to have a child with her and that I would love the child in a way that I had never been loved. I was happy and ready to commit myself to spending the rest of my life with her and the baby. It was probably immaturity on her part, but she said, "Let's run away." That's something I know how to do really well. I've been running away my whole life. But this time I didn't want to run away. I was getting along with my family for the first time I can remember. I actually felt like I belonged there with my family, her, and the baby. Why would I want to run away? This is the world that I was looking for.

I knew that my dad and her brother-in-law would both be back from fleet duty in a few weeks. So I told her to just hang on for a little while. When they got back we would talk to them and put everything on the table. We were in love, she was pregnant, and we wanted to get married.

In the meantime, Chou and I went to my house to tell my mom. It came as no surprise to her. She smiled at Chou and me. They liked each other and I immediately felt hope that this situation might work out after all. But my mom, practical down to the bone, asked Chou if she'd been to the doctor. She said she had not seen a doctor yet but that she was never late. My mom gave me the keys to her car and told me to take her to the clinic to make sure. Chou and I with her nephew, Justin, in tow went to the clinic where, four hours later, they confirmed that she was pregnant.

We agreed that we wouldn't tell her sister until after my dad and brother-in-law got home. We went to my house and showed my mother the paperwork from the clinic. "I knew this was going to happen. I warned you, mijo," my mom said. Then she tells Chou, "I guess I'm going to be a grandmother, mija," and she gave Chou a big hug. She also gave us some more advice.

"You need to tell your sister because I don't want to be part of any secrets. And you better tell your father as soon as he gets home next week. He's looking forward to seeing you, but this is the kind of thing that you have to tell him yourself."

Then my mom continued on with the realities and responsibilities of being a parent and that we'd better start thinking about the future. It was all good, sound advice and I honestly had every intention of following it to the letter. I was glad my mom didn't get angry or excited. I guess it was the fact that she'd been in Chou's situation when she was pregnant with me and she put herself in her shoes.

I walked her home and we agreed that she would wait until her brother-in-law came home to break the news. I told her that I would look for a job right away and start saving up money for when the time came that we'd live as a family. The carefree playboy days were obviously over, but I didn't regret it for a second. I was happy beyond words. I didn't need other women. I had Chou and that was more than enough for me. I don't know if it was naïve on my part, but I produced these bright pictures in my mind of the three of us starting a life together there on the island. I'd work, she'd be home with the baby, keep house, and we'd live a normal life with all the simple pleasures. No more drugs. No more stickups. No running wild.

Whenever I put my mind to it, I never had a problem getting a job. I genuinely like working and at the end of every day of work, I do get a huge sense of satisfaction from accomplishing something. I guess it comes from the work ethic that my father instilled in us at a young age. We always had chores, and whenever my dad did things around the house, he made me help him and showed me the value of doing things for yourself. Whether it was hanging a screen door or working on the car, he had me at his elbow, schooling me on how to do things the right way. I never properly thanked him for that, but that ethic served me well on both sides of the law.

A few days later, I had a job running a forklift for Hawaiian Sun Products, a company that made fruit juices, preserves, and chocolate-covered macadamia nuts. In those few months after I landed in Hawaii, my dad would come home to find that his son had a job, had gotten his girlfriend pregnant, and was starting to drink every day. I think I was feeling the pressure of responsibility weighing on me, but I'd have a few beers every night after getting home and then a few more. I didn't see any danger in that. I knew I could control it. I'd done it with all sorts of drugs, including the big monster of heroin.

On the day my dad came back from fleet duty, we left the house at 8:00 A.M. and drove down to Pearl Harbor. I was driving my mom and Jasmine to the arrival of the fleet. We went to a place assigned for the military families and we watched as they towed the carrier and the rest of the support fleet into port. There was an impressive ritual of disembarkation where the Navy thanks the Marines for their service on this latest deployment and the Marines reciprocate.

When that was over, all the sailors and Marines come down the ramp to their families. My mom and dad hugged for a long while and then when he saw me, the both of us started crying. My mom too. Then he pushed me away from him and realized that I was actually taller than him. "You've grown up, guy," he said. Then he hugged me again. That was always his word for me. When things were going well between us, it was either "guy" or "kid."

I helped collect all his gear and start driving us home. My mom tells me, "Go ahead and tell your dad what's going on with you.

He's going to find out anyway, so he might as well hear it right from you."

"Well, sir," I started and gave him the capsule version of my situation. For my entire life, I always addressed my father as "sir." We were just brought up that way. In fact, it wasn't until decades later and after my final release from federal prison that he told me I could stop calling him sir.

Instead of addressing me directly, he asked my mom who Chou was and was her father in my father's company. My mom tells him and it turns out that her brother-in-law was in the motor pool of my dad's company. My dad thought about all this for a minute and then he sort of chuckled. He rubbed my head and said, "You need a haircut, kid."

I told him I had a job but that I wanted to get married and join the Marines. He said we'd talk about it when we got home. When we got home, I called Chou and told her to come over to meet my father. Apparently, the atmosphere at her house was completely different. Her brother-in-law and her sister went completely ballistic. Her sister was telling her husband that Chou had been seeing an eighteen-year-old boy who had just gotten out of jail and that she'd been sneaking out of the house at night and basically painting a very bad picture of me and Chou. Chou said she was frightened and that she still wanted to run away. I told her we might not need to do that. She told me she'd call me later.

Around 11:00 P.M. that night, Chou called and said she was coming over. We sat in the living room talking about how differently our families had taken the news and what we were going to do, when my father came into the room. He must have heard us or something. I introduced them to each other. My dad was gracious and nice to her, but he said it was late for her to be up and sneaking around her family. He said all this in a very nice way. He also said that we had taken on the responsibility of bringing a life into the world and we should start acting like adults and not sneak around like kids. He offered to support whatever decision we made, but we'd have to do our part for the sake of the baby. He then asked Chou how old she was. She put her head down and said, "Sixteen."

"You didn't tell me she was underage," he said to me.

I told him I didn't know. "She told me she was eighteen and only told me the truth after she got pregnant." He told me to walk her home and make sure she got there safely and we'd talk some more about it in the morning. As I walked her home, I told her that everything would be okay. My parents would help us take care of things. My parents, in fact, were ready to help us get our life started.

9

Baby

The next day, Chou told me her brother-in-law and sister wanted to talk to me. She met me outside her house and said, "Don't say anything about the baby." When we got inside, they were very formal and reserved. They sat me down and asked where I was from, what I did for a living, and what goals I had in life. This was some kind of warm-up for what was to come. Then they asked how Chou and I met and what my intentions were. Chou jumped in and answered for me. Then they asked how old I was. I told them. "You know Chou is only sixteen, right?" I said I knew that now but I didn't know it at first. They asked what we intended to do for the future. We both told them that we were in love and wanted to take our relationship as far as it would go. They said that we were too young to be making these kinds of decisions that would affect the rest of our lives. Besides, we'd only known each other a few months and it was way too soon to be making life decisions. Finally they said Chou and I could continue seeing each other as long as we respected the rules of the house and didn't go sneaking off in the middle of the night. They wanted everything between us open and aboveboard. That was fine with us. But we never told them about the pregnancy. And that knowledge became like a cloud over us.

But I still knew, no matter what happened, that I was going to take care of her and the baby and I was committed to forging a normal life for the three of us. Over the next few weeks, I took her regularly to the clinic for checkups and prenatal care. I continued working at the warehouse and trying to save every nickel I could for our future. But a few weeks later, I got a call at work from Chou. She was crying and almost hysterical. Her sister had found some of the vitamins and literature that the clinic had given Chou on teenage pregnancy and how to help ensure a healthy delivery. They had gone ballistic again and were now insisting that Chou should get an abortion. I told my supervisor that I had a family emergency and had to go home.

By the time I got there, all hell had broken loose. Chou's sister was at my house yelling at my mom. She said she was going to call the police and have me charged with statutory rape. My mom told her that Chou had lied about her age and at this point, there was no use in assigning blame. Chou and I were both responsible for this situation and we should all start thinking about what's best for the baby and its future. By this time, my father and Chou's brother-in-law had come home. We were all in the house and Chou and I sat there holding hands while the adults went back and forth on what should happen next. Her sister said that Chou was going to get an abortion and that she was going to college and entering a profession. She wasn't going to waste her life having a baby at that age and miss out on all the opportunities that a smart sixteen-year-old was entitled to. I told them that I wanted to join the Marines and marry Chou. But her family wasn't listening to me. My parents' priority was the baby. They wanted to make sure that the baby would be taken care of. Her family didn't give a crap about the baby. They wanted her to abort. Period.

For some reason, her family decided that from now on, we couldn't see each other unless it was in the presence of one of our family members. No more going out on dates or picnics. I was working every day, so the only time I could see her was at night in her living room with either her sister or brother-in-law present. The circumstances didn't matter to me. I just wanted to be with her. Chou was so petite that after only a few months she started showing a belly. Sometimes we'd be at my house under "parental supervision." She still wanted to run away, but I told her that I wasn't making enough money to do that and take proper care of her. We'd go to my room for some alone time and we'd lie there just holding each other and I'd talk to the baby. I never wanted anything more in my entire life than that baby. We were still crazy about each other and we both wanted the baby.

It was in January of that year, 1981, that I was at work and got another devastating phone call. It was Chou. She was crying so hard that I could barely understand what she was saying. She said that she had started bleeding and they had taken her to the hospital. The doctors had decided to induce labor because it was the best chance they had of saving the baby and making sure that Chou would be all right.

I left work around three thirty in the afternoon and I had to take two buses to get to the hospital. An hour and a half later I arrived to find her sister and brother-in-law in the hall outside her room. They said I could go in and see her. The sight of her tiny little frame in that hospital bed made me cry. She was pale and her lips were chapped and she was barely coherent. I hugged her and asked how she was. She said she was in pain but that she'd be okay soon. Then we both started crying. She told me we should have run away together and gotten away from her family. A few minutes later she fell asleep and the doctor came in and told me I had to leave.

I didn't want to leave, but I couldn't stand being around her family, who I knew were blaming me for everything. Around seven that night I got a call at home from Chou. She was crying again and the only thing she could say over and over again was, "The baby is gone. The baby is gone." I wanted to use the car to see her, but my dad wouldn't let me have it. He said there was nothing I could do right now and the best thing would be to wait until she got home the next day. They were going to release her because there hadn't been any complications to keep her there. Chou told me to stay home because they'd given her painkillers and she was about to sleep.

I told my parents that the baby was gone and they were almost as devastated as I was. My mom cried and my dad did what he could to make me feel better. I was falling apart. I was angry and heartbroken. I didn't know how to deal with this. It was tearing me apart. I had my heart set on starting our family. And now it was all yanked away from me.

The next day after work, I went to the mall and bought flowers and a teddy bear for Chou. When I got home I called her, but her sister said she was asleep. I didn't want to hear that. I went over there anyway. When I got to the door, her brother-in-law stood in my way as if to keep me from going in. I didn't have to say anything to him. He took one look at my face and said I could go in but only for a minute.

She wasn't asleep at all. She was in bed crying. I held her for a long time. Then she said, "When you came to see me in the hospital holding my hand, the baby was already coming out of me. I didn't want to tell you. So I pretended to go to sleep. When you left, I went into the bathroom like they told me to do and the baby was hanging down between my knees. I could see the little hands and feet." Then she burst into hysterical crying. And she says over and over again, "If only I hadn't seen the baby. If only I hadn't seen the baby."

It was a boy.

I lay in her bed that night holding her and the both of us crying and sobbing. I could sense even through her tears that something had changed in her. Something I'd never be able to name or understand. I wanted to lash out. I wanted to hurt something or someone. But who do I blame? Me? Her? I blamed God for taking my son and I swore that I would pay him back. Chou didn't want me to leave, so we lay there until we fell asleep. Later that night her sister came in and woke me up. She said it was time for me to go home.

When I got home, my parents were still up waiting for me. They both gave me a hug and told me to go get some sleep. "Things will look better in the morning," they told me. They weren't better the next morning or any time after that.

Chou started to withdraw from me and it looked like she was withdrawing from the rest of the world as well. Whenever I tried to see her, she broke into tears. I tried to be as gentle as possible with her, but she refused any sort of attention from me. She wouldn't let me touch her, physically or in any other way.

She went back to high school and I continued to work at the warehouse, but we started drifting apart. She rarely answered her phone. And she never seemed to be around when I knocked on her door.

I began making friends at work and started spending time with other people I met off base. My mom had a group of friends she played Bingo with and when they would go camping, they invited me along. And through them I met even more people. It was inevitable that Chou and I would see each other on the street, but it was no longer the same sweet, innocent Chou that I knew. She seemed detached and almost robotic in the way she moved and talked. I tried a few times to talk to her about what had happened and see if there was some way of getting back together, but she cut short the conversations with excuses that she had to go somewhere or had chores to do. We would never be able to get past what had happened. It was over and I don't think I ever fully recovered from it.

After a few weeks I met Amanda, a California girl who was going to college in Hawaii. She worked at Baskin-Robbins in the afternoon and we took the same bus to go home. Soon after we started dating, she asked me if I wanted to move in with her. She was living with two other people in Honolulu, which was close to the university. I didn't really feel any strong impulse to move in with her, but living almost next door to Chou was becoming harder and harder for me. It was an excuse to get out of that neighborhood and try to get my life restarted. The relationship with my parents was better than it had ever been and I didn't want that to end, but I felt I had to get out of there or I'd drive myself half-crazy every time I saw Chou's house and thought of the son that I lost. I was angry all the time and maybe the change of housing and some new people in my life would help put the whole episode out of my mind.

Unlike Chou, Amanda was more of a party girl. After work and school, we'd spend the evening either tangled up in lust or cruising the beaches drinking or getting high on whatever we could get our hands on. She knew a lot of the locals and I had a lot of friends from work, so there were always people around for us to party with. Some of the guys I knew from work had access to a lot of marijuana, this being Hawaii and the home of the fabled Maui Wowie. She introduced me to a guy named CJ. He was half-black and half-Hawaiian and he had a connection for both LSD and cocaine. Whenever we could afford it, we'd track down CJ and score.

As it turned out, CJ and I got to be really good friends. And it wasn't long after I met him that he asked me if I wanted to help him sell dope on the beach. Just like in San Diego when I was younger, the tourists were the prime market for what we were selling. We sold it at the beach and at the International Market in Waikiki. Combined with my connection for marijuana, we became a one-stop retail outlet for anything that a tourist looking to get high could possibly want—acid, coke, bud, you name it, we had it, and in large quantities. It wasn't long before we were making $700 a day each. That paid a lot better than pushing a forklift around a warehouse.

I quit my job at the warehouse and went full-time into dealing drugs. Amanda and I bought a VW Karmann Ghia and she pretty much gave up going to classes. When we weren't on the job selling drugs, we were high. Even though I no longer worked at the warehouse, I made sure to stay in touch with Gilbert and Chris, the two guys at work who had the major marijuana connection.

During the day, CJ and I would split up and work the beaches and the markets. At night we'd hit the nightclubs. There was a punk club called the 3D, a disco called the Red Lion, the Jazz Cellar (another disco), and then there was the Enlisted Men's Club at the Army base. I stayed away from the Marine clubs. After a few weeks of regular night calls at these places, the bouncers got to know me. All I had to do was give them a little payoff and they'd let me in. They'd also let me know if there was anyone around that looked like they could be a narc.

Naturally, when you're in a club and you've got a lot of dope, you become a very popular guy. And I was. I was meeting and banging all sorts of girls from everywhere in the world. White girls, black girls, foreigners and mainlanders, and people from Europe. I remember spending one memorable night with an amazing blonde from Sweden in a hot tub on the roof of her hotel, frying our brains out on acid and screwing like rabbits until the sun came up. I was back in paradise. I'm still eighteen at this time and I'm making more money than my father, having all kinds of sex with beautiful women, and not a care in the world except making sure the drug supply kept flowing. By this time, Amanda was beginning to complain that I wasn't spending enough time with her, but I told her we weren't married and we weren't attached at the hip. We were just out to have a good time and it was going to stay that way.

By the time summer arrived, CJ showed me another hustle that he had going. We went to Kuhio Avenue and rented a hotel room. Once we had the room, we went up and down the avenue letting all the prostitutes know that we had a room available, where it was, and how much it would cost them to rent from us by the hour. We already knew most of these girls anyway from selling them dope. Now we were sort of providing them with a safe place to turn their tricks. One of us would stand outside the door to make sure that the johns wouldn't get mean or refuse to pay. We weren't pimps exactly because they kept all the money they made. They would just pay us ten dollars per trick for the room and whatever safety we could provide. We also sold them and their tricks dope if they wanted any. And it worked great.

As trust developed between us and the girls, they started treating us more like family than business partners. One girl in particular, an absolutely stunning, tall Chinese girl named Rashia, was always after me to "buy" her. She'd come up behind me, put her hand on my crotch, and ask me, "When are you ever gonna spend some money on me, baby?" It's not that I was still innocent or shy around women, but this girl was so stunning, so traffic-stopping beautiful that just being three feet away from her left me tongue-tied, intimidated, and stuttering like a fool. And the more tongue-tied I got, the bigger the kick she got out of it.

The "trick pad" business we were running took off in a huge way. Pretty soon we were renting two and three hotel rooms at a time. A big part of our success is that we treated the girls right. We didn't abuse them, shake them down for money, and ask for free sex. It was just a business with us and I knew that if we just kept treating the girls with a certain amount of respect, they'd keep using our trick pads. When it got to the point that we were making $2,000 a night each, we decided to split the chores. One of us would work the trick pads at the hotels and the other would hit the nightclubs and sell dope. We pooled our money to buy the dope and, just like the girls, CJ and I didn't try to screw each other over. It was straight-up business. With things going from bad to worse between me and Amanda, I moved out of her apartment and moved in with CJ, who had an amazing condo on Kapiolani Boulevard right by the canal. This wasn't some rathole. It was luxury living for the well-heeled people who could afford it.

It amazed me at the time how quickly I went from wanting to be a Marine, get married, and have a family, to falling back on my evil ways of dealing drugs on the street. I was back in my comfort zone. Whenever I wasn't too busy, I went to visit my parents. They aren't fools and they can tell that I'm up to no good. I don't have a "job," but I'm driving a new car, wearing great clothes, and seem to have all the money I need. I was a little sheepish going over there, but I really did miss them and my little brothers and sister. In spite of their fears, they let me take my siblings out to eat, to the beach, and spend money on them buying clothes and things they wanted.

On one particular afternoon visiting the family, I ran into Chou on the street. It was an awkward meeting and while I regretted it later, we went to the beach that day and had sex later that evening. But it wasn't the same. It was more mechanical and completely stripped of the passion we once had for each other. It left me feeling empty. Later I found out from my sister that Chou had hooked up with a girl from Alabama and the two of them had gotten a reputation as a couple of tramps. They banged any Marine that got them drunk and showed them a good time. I felt devastated. I thought of how different it all could have been and it just made me harder.

PART TWO

EDUCATION

10

Big D's Tickets

I was living the party life and, inevitably, the party has to end. One day CJ told me that he was too wired from the night before to sleep so he was going to the International Market to sell some weed. I told him I was going to sleep and we'd hook up later in the afternoon. I was with a girl named Linda at the time who looked almost like a twin to Valerie Bertinelli. She was frequently approached on the beach or on the street by people wanting to know if she was Valerie and would she give them her autograph. Soon after we fell asleep, there was a loud knock on the door. It was one of the street dealers we knew named Kalani. He said, "CJ just got busted. He had a fanny pack full of coke, weed, and acid. He got busted selling to an undercover cop."

I woke Linda up and told her to start making some phone calls for me. While she was on the phone, I started throwing everything in the house into a big plastic bag. We had sheets of acid (one hundred hits per sheet), an ounce and a half of cocaine, and about two pounds of weed. Plus, there was about $12,000 in cash in the condo. I took the bag with the cash and lifted up a ceiling tile. I stashed the bag over a heating duct. We also had a .380 semiauto pistol, which I stuck in my waistband. I took the bag with the dope and left the condo.

We were living on the seventh floor. There was a six-feet-three-inch, 350-pound pimp on the sixth floor named Big D. He ran between three and four girls on the street. Big D and I always got along, and a few times in the past, CJ and I got one of his girls out of trouble. Her trick didn't want to pay, so we stepped in and convinced the guy to pay. Big D even bought all his dope from us. I went to Big D's apartment and told him the story and that I wanted to stash the dope with him in case the cops came to our apartment. He said no problem and took the dope, except for the coke, which I kept with me. My plan was to get the cash from the apartment and go bail CJ out.

By the time I got upstairs, Linda had found out that CJ was being held at Honolulu PD and they were going to transport him to the county jail on Sand Island. As Linda and I were getting ready to go, the phone rings and it's CJ. He was already in the county jail and told us that they were holding him for drug trafficking and they set bail at $500,000. He told me to stay put and that he was sending his brother to the condo to pick up his stuff.

I knew CJ's brother and knew enough about him that I didn't trust him. He was in the Army, stationed at Fort Shafter. And even though he was a user and occasionally bought some of the girls we knew, there was something about him that made me feel like I needed some backup if he was coming over. Linda had a brother named Tom who was about six feet two inches, a very buff surfer and at the same time he was a heroin user. He was at the point of being addicted and I knew he'd do anything for heroin. I told Linda to tell him we'd give him some dope but he needed to come over right now. The minute he showed up, I took him downtown to Hamburger Mary's. It was a local gay hangout where I sold a lot of dope, everything except heroin, that is. There was a guy there who sold heroin and we tracked him down. A guy named Scott owned the place and he was forever hitting on me and saying that he'd give me whatever I wanted if I became his boyfriend. Although he was usually kidding, at the same time he wasn't. It didn't matter. I knew I was never going there and he knew that I would never switch teams. He knew Linda anyhow and most of that bantering was friendly. Scott would put on an air guitar contest once a week and Linda and another girlfriend of hers had won the contest three separate times in the past. It got to the point that it was cheaper for him to pay Linda and her girl-friend to just host and entertain during the air guitar contest, so he paid the two girls to do just that.

The guy we were looking for was named Spider. We found him, bought our heroin, and went back to the apartment. Within a few minutes, Tom was cooking his fix and had tied off. I hadn't done heroin in years by this time. Since hitting the island and long before, I kept it to coke, acid, and weed. But watching him made me remember the rush. I asked him if I gave him some coke, could he cook up a speedball—combination heroin and cocaine. He said sure.

I gave him the coke and went into the living room to Linda. She was watching a new channel on TV called MTV. They showed nothing but music videos. I wondered at the time if anybody would ever sit in front of the TV and watch nothing but music videos all day. I guess history proved that people would. A few minutes later, Tom calls me into the bedroom. He asks me, "Are you sure you done this before?" I told him not to sweat it. I just asked him to help me tie off and find a vein. He was a pro. He found a vein right away and shot about 30 cc of speedball into me. The first thing that hit was the cocaine. I got this mean rush and then my ears started ringing. Then the heroin kicked in and I started staggering. I got dizzy and had to sit down. I'm rushing from the heroin with a warm feeling and then it got ugly and I had to throw up. I run to the bathroom and puke my guts out. I'm floating and at the same time I'm throwing up. Linda comes into the bathroom to see what's wrong and I told her I was fine. I brushed my teeth and went back to the living room. But by now I'm nodding out. She asks what's wrong again and I told her I was just a little sick.

By now it's three thirty in the afternoon and CJ's brother hasn't shown up yet. So we continue chilling out and waiting. Tom is such an idiot that he keeps giving me these knowing smiles and winks. All he was doing, of course, was making Linda more suspicious. He behaved like a teenage girl trying to keep a secret and at the same time doing everything he could to give it away.

It's almost time to go to work, but I have to wait for CJ's brother. So I go downstairs to Big D's apartment and I ask him if he could send one of his girls to rent a room for the night. I gave him a hundred-dollar bill and told him to tell the girl to get a fifty- or sixty-dollar room and for her to keep the change.

A few minutes later, I get a call from CJ again and he says he's been booked and is going to need money. I tell him there's no problem with the money and he says that his brother is on his way right now. He tells me to help his brother pack up his stuff. "Are you coming back?" I ask him.

"I don't think so," he says. "At least not for a long time."

I asked him if he wanted me to keep the business going and he said yes. He said his brother would tell me about that.

When his brother showed up shortly after that, he walked in with a giant attitude. I wasn't having any of it, so I had to verbally check him. Right away he pulls in his horns and pretends nothing happened. We went into CJ's room and started packing. Then he asked me, "Where's CJ's money?"

"You mean me and CJ's money, right?"

"You wouldn't have no money if CJ hadn't put you to work," he said.

So here it comes, I think to myself. He's going to try to punk me. I told him to hold on and I'll go get it. I went into the living room and told Linda to go downstairs and see if he had come with anybody else. I wanted to know if this guy had brought a backup guy with him.

I took Tom back into the bedroom with me and told CJ's brother, "Me and CJ hustled together to earn that money. I was going to give you his half so he could have it. But now I don't trust you since you're trying to punk me for my half. So tell CJ I have his money and I'll hold it for him until he gets home. So as for you, fuck you. Take his stuff and get the fuck out of here."

There's no hiding the fact that I was dead serious. He looked at Tom and then grabs all CJ's stuff. Tom and I help him. By this time, Linda has come back and tells me that the guy is alone. So we all grab something and take CJ's stuff to his brother's car. Before he leaves, CJ's brother looks at me in what was supposed to be a threatening way and says, "I'll be back."

I say that's cool. "I have no place to go and I'll be right here."

After he took off, I told Linda that we were going to stay at her place for a while. She was living with her brother and another roommate. We packed up some of my stuff and got it into the car. I went to Big D's apartment and asked him for my bag back. He gave it to me and I told him I'd be staying at Linda's place for a little while. Just to show my gratitude, I broke off some dope and gave it to him as thanks.

When we got to Linda's place, I met Jay, another California transplant surfer dude. Jennifer, her other roommate, was there too. By this time I'd known Jennifer for a few months. I first met her at Hamburger Mary's, where Linda and Jennifer would do their sexy air guitar show and just clean house. Jennifer was nineteen, blond, about five feet eight inches, mesmerizing emerald-green eyes, and a body that would qualify her for a Victoria's Secret catalog or a *Sports Illustrated* cover shot.

I told Linda that I had to go to work. But first I had to go to my parents' house way across the island. I told her where the trick pad was that night and she should meet me there later and help me run it. She said okay, but she asked me if I could take Jennifer to a place she needed to get to. It was somebody's apartment. I said okay but we had to move. Jennifer and I got into the car and she realizes that we're going back to my apartment. She asked why. I asked her if she could keep a secret. She looked at me a while and said, "That depends." I told her that I didn't trust Tom and I didn't trust Linda not to tell Tom everything she knew about me and my business. I told her I had to go back to my place to get some money.

We went back to the apartment, where I stopped at Big D's again to get the key for that night's trick pad. We went to my apartment where, before opening the door, I pulled out my .380 just in case someone was there. I didn't need to worry. The place was still empty. I pulled out a chair and moved the ceiling tile in the kitchen out of the way and pulled out the ziplock baggy with $12,000 in it. By now, I totally have Jennifer's undivided attention. I told her I was going to take the money to my parents' house and asked if she wanted to come along for the drive. She was up for it.

When we got to my parents' place, I told them I was just there to pick up some clothes. I went to my old room, took $2,000 for walking-around money, and left the remaining $10,000 hidden in the room.

I have to admit that I was attracted to Jennifer from the first day I met her. I mean, who wouldn't be. She was gorgeous, she had none of the attitude that often comes with great beauty, and she didn't seem to mind living right at the edge of the illegal world. She knew what I did for a living and I think it actually made me more attractive to her. Later on, after I took her to California with me, my grandmother gave her the nickname of La Muñeca—The Doll.

On the ride back, we start talking and she made the startling admission that she'd always been attracted to me. But because she was a friend of Linda's, she never let on. I told her I felt the same about her. We went to the trick pad to make sure we were ready for business, but before we hung out the shingle that night, Jennifer and I had sex in the trick pad. Afterward, she said that we should be together. I totally agreed. But right now, things were up in the air. Chances were that I couldn't go back to my apartment. Linda for sure wouldn't have us under the same roof. We agreed to keep our secret between us for now and she would try to work something out.

The next few weeks, things limped along as usual. Except now I'm using more and more heroin with Tom and Jay. And I'm sneaking around with Jennifer. Then one night, Tom asked me if

I had my pistol with me. By this time, Tom and Jay had been helping me with the trick pad and with selling dope. I asked him why he wanted the pistol. He told me that he was tired of dealing with Spider, his heroin connection at Hamburger Mary's, and wanted to take him down.

I told Tom I wouldn't let him have the gun but if he needed help with Spider, I'd like to go along with him. We were all at the mall selling dope, and Linda was there as well. And she piped up and said she wanted to go too. I told Tom to go set it up.

About an hour later, Tom called and said that Linda and I should meet him at her house. When we got there, Jay was also there. Tom set it up with Spider that Spider would come by and take Tom to Spider's house to buy a quarter ounce of heroin. Tom needed $500 as "show" money that indicated that this was a serious buy. Linda, Jay, and I waited in the car. When Spider showed up to pick up Tom, we followed them at a distance to make sure Spider wouldn't see us following them.

When they got to Spider's house, I parked on the street and waited. About ten minutes later, Tom came out of the house and told us to come in. When we got in the house, we saw that Spider was tied up on the floor, wearing just his underwear. Spider was cursing at us and yelling that we were going to be in trouble if we did this. We searched the whole house, but all we came up with was a little bit of cash, some junk jewelry, and some weed. No big score. Tom grabbed Spider and slapped him around a few times, asking him where the heroin was. Spider held out for maybe ten seconds before he told Tom, "It's in the kitchen." A minute later, Tom came out of the kitchen with a chunk of heroin about the size of a baseball. Heroin! A big chunk of it.

We grab the heroin and go back to the trick pad. We break it up equally and we each walk away with a nice payday. Linda and I went back to her apartment while Jay and Tom went off to do whatever they did. About an hour later, Tom calls and tells us that Jay is in the hospital. Somebody beat him up really bad. His face was completely swollen, he had broken ribs and a broken arm. Tom said this was payback for having ripped Spider off for his dope. When we went to see Jay in the hospital, he told us that we'd all be killed if we didn't give back the dope we stole. Jay and Tom want to give it back. But Linda and I say no. I told them that even if we did give it back, they'd probably still kill us just to teach us a lesson.

The first thing I thought of was getting off the island. I went to Big D and asked him for his advice. He told me he had a couple of airline tickets to California if I wanted them. I told him I did. Linda and Tom said they had an uncle in Waipahu who had some kind of criminal connection and they went to see him to try to straighten the mess. I couldn't count on that. I needed to leave. I grabbed whatever stuff I had at Linda's place with the intention of going back to the condo. As luck would have it, Jennifer was at Linda's place as well. She already knew what happened and she says that if I'm leaving for California, she wanted to come with me. The condo was paid through the end of the month so I still had the key, so we go there to pull together whatever I had left there. While we're packing, Sherry, one of the girls, came up and told me that Big D had the tickets. Jennifer and I fell asleep because we'd been up all night and we were crashing bad.

Later in the day, Sherry and another girl woke Jennifer and me up and told us that Big D wanted to see us right away. We clean up fast and go down to see him. Big D looked worried and a little scared. Not for him but for us. "You fucked up," he said. "Spider was selling dope for the Tanakas." The Tanakas were Japanese mobsters, probably Yakuza, and they wanted either the dope or the money back. Big D said he couldn't help me anymore, that I was on my own. He said I should buy those tickets and leave the island as fast as possible. For some reason I can't remember or explain, Jennifer and I had done acid that morning and we were tripping hard.

We went back to the condo to gather up what we could. We called Linda and Tom but got no answer. Jennifer then suggested we go to her mother's house. Her mom was a cool lady according to Jennifer, but she didn't like hard drugs and didn't want them in the house. We decided to do whatever drugs we had left, loaded up the car, and headed to her mom's house.

When we got to her mom's house, I realized where Jennifer had gotten her looks from. Her mom, Amy, was about five feet four inches and exquisite in every detail. She had light brown hair, smoky gray eyes, and a golden, tanned skin that looked like it had been polished. A lot of people thought she looked like Jane Seymour, the actress. A real knockout.

Just like Jennifer had promised, Amy was a very cool lady. A thirty-six-year-old free spirit that had managed her affairs well enough that she owned a couple of condos in Waikiki and another condo in Las Vegas. She'd been married a few times and the real estate and financial support were part of the divorce settlements. Amy didn't have to work and what she basically concentrated on was keeping herself looking great and having a good time. Jennifer had an older sister named Tracy who was in Hollywood trying to become an actress. She also had inherited her mom's good looks. And there was a younger brother they called Speedy who was spoiled rotten.

After I unloaded my stuff, Jennifer and I went into the living room, where Amy was entertaining a male friend of hers. They were both drinking and I could see that Amy was on her way to being drunk. After a few minutes, Amy's friend looked at me and asked if I had any weed on me. Jennifer looked at me and nodded and said that I did. I broke out the weed and we spent the rest of that afternoon and night getting stoned.

The next morning, Jennifer and I woke up naked in her bed. This was the first time we'd spent the night together and she was all snuggly and affectionate. Then she dropped a bomb.

"My mom asked me last night if you have ever had a mother-daughter three-way before." I couldn't believe what I was hearing. This was one wild family.

"No," I told her. "But I'm ready to try anything once."

Jennifer slapped me on the chest.

"Yeah, I know you guys. That's why I'm glad we leave for California in a couple of days."

We fell back asleep and woke up around noon to the sound of Amy and her son. I got up to go to the bathroom and ran into Amy wearing a tiny pink kimono that made it clear she had nothing on underneath. Amy asked me if I still had some weed. I told her I didn't but I could get her some. I called my friend Chris back at the warehouse and asked him if he had anything. He always did. So I told him I'd be over there later. I had to go to my parents' house to get the rest of my and CJ's money, and Jennifer said she wanted to come along. Amy asked me if I knew how to ride a motorcycle. I said I did and she offered to let me ride her big Harley. So Jennifer and I went to get the weed first and then rode to the base to my family's house.

When I got to the house around two that afternoon, I knew

CONFESSIONS OF A CARTEL HIT MAN

from my first look at it that I no longer belonged there. Something had changed in those months that I'd been there and the changes weren't for the better. I felt like a visitor who had overstayed his welcome. I didn't tell my mom I was leaving the next day. But I did call Ropati. He came over and we talked in my room for a while. I told him I'd gotten my ass in a crack and that I needed to leave. We hugged and I didn't know at the time that I would never see him again. A few months later, Ropati had gotten himself a huge drug habit and he died of an overdose.

I said good-bye to my brothers and sister and my heart sort of broke not knowing when or even if I'd ever see them again. The life I was living was unpredictable and literally anything could happen without warning when you get yourself involved in drug dealing.

That night, Jennifer, Amy, Speedy, and I went out to dinner and got a little tipsy. When we got home, Amy wanted to go out to a club. Jennifer and I were getting up for an early flight in the morning and needed to get some sleep. So we volunteered to "babysit" Speedy. Knowing she probably wouldn't see me in the morning, Amy came over and wished me good-bye and a good flight and wrapped her arms around me to give me a kiss. This was not an innocent kiss. She was trying to taste what I had for lunch—right there in front of her daughter. "Okay, Mom," Jennifer said. "Leave my boyfriend alone, please." Although she tried to be playful saying this, she was definitely not amused. I always wondered what would have happened if we hadn't left the next day. Probably none of it would have turned out well. Crazy, but not at all well.

11

Circus Circus

I slept most of the flight from Hawaii to Los Angeles because I'd smoked a ton of weed before getting on the plane. When we landed at LAX, I rented a car and drove south toward Oceanside. I was planning on surprising my grandmother. She was living in my parents' house while they were stationed in Hawaii and I knew she had plenty of room for me and Jennifer.

This was Jennifer's first time in LA and she was as excited as a puppy in a bacon factory. We got to Oceanside around ten thirty that night and just for fun I cruised the old neighborhood while heading to the house. As luck would have it, I saw a car with my homeboy Chato in it. I told Jennifer, "Watch this."

I pulled in front of his car, stopped, and got out yelling a lot of shit. "So what, brah. You looking for a beef?" This was Hawaiian street slang for "You want to fight?" The truth is I probably looked like one of the many Samoans that lived in Oceanside. We had a lot of them, especially on the East Side. The last time they'd seen me, I was Nite Owl, the homeboy with a shaved head, khakis, and

Pendleton shirt. I now had my hair below my shoulders and was wearing a floral shirt, drawstring pants, and dock loafers.

I'd jumped out of the car acting like a maniac and Chato and two other homies got out ready to smash me. Before they get close enough to do some damage, I yell out to them that it's me, Nite Owl. They stop, take a hard look, and a moment later we were hugging and laughing right there in the middle of the street. They were on their way to see some girls who had a bottle of Sherm (PCP) and they were getting ready to party for the night. It was made from embalming fluid, and back then, there was an epidemic of PCP all over the country. I introduced them to Jennifer and told them that we were on the way to my grandmother's house but I'd call them later and meet up. We got to my grandmother's around 11:00 P.M., and needless to say, she was extremely surprised to see me. I introduced her to Jennifer and told my grandmother that Jennifer and I were on our way to Las Vegas to stay with her family and we'd only be staying with her for a few days. She said we were more than welcome and put us up in my uncle Manuel's room.

The next day my grandmother wanted to know if my parents knew where I was. I told her they didn't. Then she asked if Jennifer's parents knew and I said that her mother knew. That's when she laid that *Muñeca* handle on Jennifer. A doll. She took an immediate liking to Jennifer, and Jennifer seemed to like her as well.

After eating, Jennifer and I went driving around the neighborhood looking for Chato. I ran into a bunch of other homeboys who, after being blown away by the way I looked, were happy to see me. The news had already gotten around that I was back and that I was looking "funny." We found Chato at his mom's house and there were some homegirls there as well. One of the homegirls lifted the long hair on my head and said, "You need a haircut, Nite Owl." I looked at her and said, "Shave it. Cut it all off." She did. I was transformed once again, blending into my environment like a chameleon.

I told them that I was on my way to Las Vegas to visit Jennifer's family. Robby, one of my homies, asked if he could go along with me. He said he knew some people there. So I said okay if his car worked. He said he'd have it tuned up and ready for the drive.

I ran into another homeboy named Frankie who had started doing tattoos while I was gone. So I asked him to touch up a cross tattoo I had on my arm. Jennifer was fascinated and told me she wanted to get a tattoo as well. She decided to get a tattoo of a heart on her butt with her name and my name on it. Frankie obliged and before we knew it, there were like a half-dozen homeboys standing around trying to grab a peek at Jennifer's outstanding ass.

The next morning, I turn in the rental car and wait for Robby to show up. We hit the road around eleven thirty in the morning but didn't get to Las Vegas until eight thirty that night. We had to stop a lot of times for Jennifer's benefit because she'd never seen any of the desert between LA and Las Vegas and she wanted to see everything. We checked into Circus Circus and went looking for someplace to eat. Jennifer called her mom and told her we were in Vegas and then called her uncle who lives there. We continue walking around and Jennifer's good looks get her noticed. One guy came up to her and told her to stand next to him while he played blackjack because he thought she would bring him good luck. She looked at me and I shrugged my shoulders and walked away to let her decide. I didn't know from gambling, luck, or what people did in Vegas. She went over and stood next to him and sure enough he wins a couple of hands and hands her a $100 chip. She came up to me and said that he was now offering her $500 to go up to his room with him. I was upset but didn't want to show it. I wanted her to make the "right" decision without influence from me. I wanted her not to want to go on her own. Which is kind of ironic because when she first met me, I was basically in the prostitution business, even if it was in an unconventional, tangential way. I didn't run girls, but then again, I wasn't exactly a pure innocent when it came to prostitution. So I told her to do whatever she wanted. So she went.

Robby and I played a few more games and waited for her. She came back thirty minutes later with the cash and said that all he wanted was for her to get naked and give him a massage. She didn't have to "do" anything other than the massage. I just listened and didn't say anything. We finally got around to getting something to eat when we went over to the MGM.

As we walked through the casino, this guy at the bar calls Jennifer over. He told her that he was with the band playing in the lounge and they were on a break. Then he asks her if she'll take $1,000 to go up to his room with him. Like I said, she was a gorgeous nineteen-year-old girl with the body of a goddess and I think that people in the casinos naturally assumed she was a prostitute. No matter, she went ahead with that guy up to his room. I was upset but determined not to show it. I was under the impression that we had a relationship and should have, at the very least, a minimum level of fidelity. But I guess she felt otherwise.

She left with the guy, and Robby and I went to Circus Circus where he met a local girl. She told Robby that she had some weed and did the two of us want to party. Her girlfriend worked as a cocktail waitress at some other hotel. The four of us went to my room and got massively stoned. I ended up in the bathroom having sex with the cocktail waitress while Robby got nasty with the other girl on the bed.

When we were done, the four of us went back to the casino to get some drinks. We ended up in the kino pits drunk and with the two girls hanging all over us. A little while later, Jennifer shows up, sees the girls, and gets really mad. "Who the fuck are these two?"

I told her they were just a few friends we just met. The cocktail waitress took a long look at Jennifer and said, "Is this your girlfriend? She's really pretty. Maybe we can have a threesome." Jennifer flipped out and began yelling at the cocktail waitress. When they realize that this isn't going well, the two girls collect their stuff and walk off.

Jennifer took a small jewelry box out of her purse and threw it at me. There was a wedding band inside. "I used the money I made to buy you this. I thought you wanted to get married. I'm ready to do it. Are you?"

My nineteen-year-old pride made me say, "You think I'm going to marry a girl who sells her body. I loved you but you were too quick to make a fast buck by selling your ass. Now you want me to marry you? You're crazy." She stalked off, calling me a user, among other things. I was worn-out. I went back to the room drunk and high on weed and passed out.

The next day, I started piecing together the events of the night before and it took me a while to figure it out. I started looking for her in the hotel but she wasn't there. Then I checked the hospital, the local jail, juvie—and nothing. Finally I called Amy, her mom, in Hawaii and Amy told me not to worry. Jennifer had gone to see her uncle and he'd bought her a plane ticket back to Hawaii. She was already in the air, apparently. Her mother didn't seem upset with either me or Jennifer, and Amy just told me to call her in a few days and that Jennifer and I would work it out. I was devastated. I took out the ring and looked at it. What the hell had I done? Was she totally normal trading sex for money so she could buy me a ring or was I totally normal for thinking that a woman shouldn't do that?

I told Robby what happened and his response was "Fuck it. Let's go back to the hood." So we left Vegas before noon and got to Oceanside that evening. Somehow or other we ended up at my homeboy Boogallo's house who was there with a bunch of other homies. They asked about Jennifer and I told them she had to go back to Hawaii. There was a lot of dope around so we all got loaded and I eventually landed back at my grandmother's completely stoned and stumbling around.

I called Amy's number four days later and talked to Jennifer. She said that I'd hurt her and started crying. I tried to calm her down and told her I still had feelings for her and she shouldn't have left. Then she said that if I came back to Hawaii, she would buy me a ticket. I agreed. But I asked her to give me a couple of days to get some things straightened out in Oceanside. I was stalling. I didn't really know what the hell I wanted and being loaded all the time made it harder to figure out.

That night I was invited by a homegirl to come see her in Vista, which is near Oceanside. I went there with a couple of other homies. Eventually, someone broke out a bunch of Sherm and I ended up naked in a room with a couple of twins, also naked, having crazy drugged sex. I had the $500 ticket to Hawaii that Jennifer had sent me. And for some reason, I asked the two girls if they wanted to go to Hawaii with me. They both jumped at the chance. So I took out the ticket and said that I'd cash it in, buy a bunch of Sherm with it, sell it at a profit, and then we'd all be able to go to Hawaii. It was absolutely crazy. I was out of control again. I spent the money buying Sherm, getting loaded all over the varrio, and spent every nickel I had left, including all the money that CJ and I had made in Hawaii. Within a few days, I found myself in county jail facing burglary charges and a bunch of parole violations.

12

Small Fish, Big Ocean

I was still on Youth Authority parole, so some of the older home-boys in county jail told me that I should ask the judge to send me to Chino prison (an adult facility) on a ninety-day observa-tion. When I came back from that, they would probably put me on adult probation and probably let me go. This was sound advice because it would reduce the amount of time I'd spend in jail. But this was adult jail and at the time, I didn't quite know what I was getting into.

When I went to court, I brought that issue up with the judge and they agreed to send me to Chino for the ninety-day observa-tion. So by March of 1983, I was in Chino West Yard for my 90-Op. As soon as I arrived there, I found six homeboys from my varrio. It was like going back to the neighborhood. Anyone who's ever been there knows that Chino West is wide open. Anything and everything you could want was available there. I was shown around by my homies and told that a Big Homie named Benny from Pico Rivera was running the place. I start working right away. My homies Sapo and Johnny from Logan Heights did some burglaries from other inmates for cartons of cigarettes and then sold the cigarettes for weed. Another homie named Mando was getting cocaine and heroin from the outside and we started helping him sell that.

One day I got up early and went out to the yard. I spotted Benny and some of his LA homeboys, so I went over to them to say hello. "Come over here, little homie, and have a seat," Benny said. "What are you doing up so early?" I told him that my homeboy Mando was going on a visit and he needed me to hold something for him. That was because they always search you before and after a visit.

"You better make sure you put that up somewhere (put it someplace safe) because something's about to go down and we might get locked down."

No sooner than he finishes saying this, a guy came running out of the cottage toward us. Benny waves him off and tells him to run to the other side of the yard. The guy follows Benny's direction and runs off. A few seconds later, another guy comes running out of the same door. This guy is covered in tattoos. He's also covered in blood from about ten different holes all over his chest and his arms. He runs out asking Benny and our group, "What's going on?" Benny told him to get lost and not to come our way. So the bleeding guy staggers off toward Control and the alarms start to go off.

In a few minutes, they had cleared the yard and sent everybody back to their dorm. What had happened was that the two guys had a beef on the outside and they couldn't get it worked out. So the Big Homies let them settle it. One guy caught the other guy slipping and stabbed him with a shank. The yard did get locked down, but it was such a minor event in the course of prison life at that time that lockdown only lasted until after lunch.

By that time, Mando had finished his visit and I was waiting for him to give him back his property. He breaks off some of the dope I was holding for him, we got high, and then Mando decided to go pay his respects to Benny. He asked me to go with him. When we went to see Benny, Benny said to Mando, "Your little homie handled himself like a champ this morning. He didn't panic or anything." Mando put his arm around me and said to Benny, "Yeah, this little homie has been around and he's got nuts." That blew my head up more than anything I could remember to that time. After that, I was invited to play dominoes with Benny and Mando.

A little while later, I was working out with Georgie Castaneda from Vista. Mando was on another visit and some guys came up to us and said, "I think your homeboys are going to get into it with the tintos (blacks) over by the canteen." So Georgie and me shoot over to the canteen, and one of the San Diego homeboys, Chivo from Imperial Beach who was on crutches because he broke his leg in a soccer game, is arguing with this black guy. The cause of the argument was that the black guy had cut in line in front of him at the store. As soon as we get there, the two of them start fighting and within seconds every Hispanic in the yard is beating on every black they can get their hands on. Naturally, the gun tower fires a round into the ground. With that first shot, everyone standing is down on the ground, facedown and laying still. The second shot would not be fired into the ground but into whoever might still be fighting.

I landed next to this black guy who was still yelling, talking shit, and spitting at me. I got up and started beating on him and people are yelling at me to "Get down. Get down." But I was blind with rage and I paid no attention to them. Then other people get up off the ground and start fighting again all over the yard. But oddly enough, no further shots were fired from the gun towers.

The COs finally swarmed the yard and I found myself held down by three of them and my hands cuffed behind me. I was taken to the Program Office, where they had eight small cages and they put me in one of them. They put Chivo in a cage next to me and they put some black guys in some of the other cages. The guys on visits were walking back to their dorms and Mando sees me in the cage. "What happened?" he asked. I told him what I could get out. And laughing, he said, "See, little homie. I can't take you nowhere without you getting in trouble." Then he said, "You're missing out. I hit it big-time." Meaning that the person that visited him just smuggled in a huge stash of dope.

We got sent back to Central and placed in Palm Hall, which is the hole for Chino. They put us on the third tier on the East Side. As soon as we arrived, a huge black guy covered with tattoos came over to me and Chivo.

"Where you fools from and why you back here?" he asked.

I looked at Chivo, and Chivo told him, "We're from San Diego. Is there any raza (Hispanics) here?"

The black guy laughs and says, "I am raza, fool. They call me Ziggy from Wilmas (Wilmington, a city in LA County). And this is my homeboy Farmer." This other giant Mexican guy appears. Wilmas is a Hispanic gang and I'd never come across a black Sureno. This was a revelation.

Chivo and I introduce ourselves and tell him what happened. They tell us that they're the tier tenders and for us not to worry. We would be in good company. They went on to say that the Big

Homie, Wino from La Rana, is downstairs from us. La Rana is a gang. The brothers are all Mexican Mafia members and run all the drugs in the San Pedro, Wilmington, and Torrance areas of Los Angeles. Over the course of their criminal careers, they became nearly legendary for their ability to maintain a high level of control on the streets and in the prison system. Having a big name dropped like that on me and Chivo was like saying that John Dillinger and Al Capone were living downstairs from us.

The black further said that when we went to classification committee, we should tell them that we wanted to be released into the Southern Yard. He also said that when the COs gave us our copies of our write-ups (the specifics of our violations), we should send the copies to Wino.

When we got our copies we dutifully obeyed and sent them to Wino. I knew from experience that the COs always embellish the write-ups to make the inmates look worse than their actions actually warrant and put them in more trouble than they actually deserve. So it was no surprise that they accused me and Chivo of "inciting a riot" with the blacks and that we refused to comply and get down after several warning shots from the tower.

If there had been more than one warning shot, I never heard it. I guess I was too busy fighting. By the time Chivo and I got back to the yard, we were welcomed back as heroes. We conducted ourselves like warriors and followed the Mexican Mafia orders to stand up for our own kind against the blacks or anyone else that attacked a Sureno.

When my ninety days were up, they sent me back to the San Diego County Jail. I was expecting to be put on adult probation and leave the jail that day or very soon afterward. But I saw that the judge was carefully reading my observation report and the look on his face wasn't promising for me. When he finished reading, he looked at me and said, "Well, I guess you've found a new home." He sentenced me to sixteen months in state prison. This was it. I was finally in big-boy prison and doing big-boy time.

I spent another month in San Diego County Jail and then was sent back to Chino. Being that I had already gone through the observation and screening process in Chino, my case was already done and I was designated to go to Soledad State Prison in Central California. Soledad is where George Jackson was housed and from where he wrote his revolutionary book *Soledad Brother: The Prison Letters of George Jackson*. Jackson was a Marxist, a member of the Black Panthers, and cofounder of the Black Guerilla Family (BGF) prison gang. The BGF is still in existence as a prison gang and is the Mexican Mafia's primary antagonist within the California prison system.

When I arrived in Soledad in 1983, Soledad was the place where Sirhan Sirhan, Robert Kennedy's assassin, was housed. Also in residence was Gregory Powell, the man who killed an LAPD officer (Ian Campbell) in the infamous Onion Field murder case.

On the bus ride from San Diego to Soledad, we stopped in Vacaville State Prison to pick up some passengers and drop others off. They had me in a cage by myself all the way up front. That was because when I went back to Palm Hall from San Diego County Jail, I was still sentenced to solitary confinement from the "riot" in the yard that I had supposedly started. So being in the cage was like being in solitary on the bus. They also added points to my record. And that meant that instead of going into a drug rehab program, I was endorsed to Soledad and into maximum security housing.

So while I'm sitting in the cage, in comes my homeboy Eric

Flores getting on the bus at Vacaville. "Hey, Big E. What's up, homie?" "Nite Owl," he says. "What's up, baby boy?" He found a seat close by and we start exchanging gossip. Where am I going? Where have I been? When I told him I was going to Soledad, he says, "Me too." We agree that we'd try to cell up together when we got there. Eric and I went back a long way. He was older than me and he helped me out when I was a youngster running around in the streets in Oceanside. We were so close that one time he and his girlfriend, Liz, had wanted to adopt me or at least make them my legal guardians. I lived with him for six months before I was busted for the burglaries that sent me to YA the first time.

When we got to Soledad Central, they put us both in O wing for orientation. They put us in the same cell and we both settled down and started catching up on each other's recent history. He asked me about Mando and I told him that Mando had landed in a drug rehab program at another prison.

Around 6:30 P.M., the CO comes to the cell and asks us if we want a shower. We both do but neither of us have shower shoes. We were in transport and all we had were the prison-issued boots. The thing is, you don't want to go into a prison shower without some kind of footwear. Shower shoes are a must because the showers aren't all that sanitary and you can pick up all sorts of diseases if you go in there with bare feet. Since we didn't have shower shoes, Eric and I decided to wear our boots into the shower. We looked sort of ridiculous and we knew it and were laughing about it.

All of a sudden we both clam up and get real serious. There were three other guys in the shower with us. They were all Mexicans and their tattoos identified them as Nortenos. This is the Northern California Hispanic prison gang—the eternal enemies of the Surenos. The Mexican Mafia (Surenos) and the Nuestra

Familia (Nortenos) have been feuding since the early 1970s. Lots and lots of blood has been spilled by both parties, and to this day, it hasn't stopped. It's an eternal war that has lasted close to fifty years with no indication of it ever stopping.

The Nortenos are tensely checking us out. Eric and I are outnumbered and we're mentally getting ourselves ready to fight for our lives. We can feel the hatred pouring out of those guys. Then one of them calls out, "Hey. Nite Owl. Is that you?" I look hard at the dude. Then I recognize him. "Yeah, Rock," I said. "It's me." I told Eric to be cool. Rock (his real name was Pascual) turns and talks to his guys very quietly. They look at us as he's talking. And then they turn away and continue on taking their showers. Then Pascual yells over and says, "Nite Owl. It's all good. We're just gonna take a shower and pretend that this never happened, okay?" I told him it was okay and that it was good to see him again.

We showered in peace and went back to our cell. Eric is dying to know. "What the hell was that all about?" I told him that Pascual and I were on the same fire team when were at the Mount Bullion Fire Camp in Youth Authority. I told him we'd become friends being on the same team and that we got along really well. I knew that if the situation was reversed that I would do the same thing. Give the guy a pass. But in either case, it was dangerous for him and it would have been dangerous for me. Eric didn't have to explain it, although he did. "The dude's a Norteno, little homie. Whatever friendship you had was cool in YA, but here in the joint, we're at war. We got a pass this time. But from now on, we have to be on our game." Eric and I both knew that we were outnumbered and probably they could have taken us apart. But the code says that you neither ask for nor give a pass. Ultimately, Eric and I would have rather taken our lumps from these guys than have the Big Homies find out that we didn't charge in to fight those guys even if we were outnumbered and had our asses handed to us.

We only stayed in O wing one more day. After that, I was transferred to B wing and Eric went to G wing. I was put in a cell with a guy from Maravilla (a street gang from Los Angeles) named Sniper. He was doing a lot of time and he'd already been at Soledad a number of years. When I went to the dayroom for the first time, I ran into a lot of Surenos from LA that I'd met throughout my career. They told me there were a lot of homeboys from San Diego but they were in other wings. Then I heard my name called out. I look over and it's this giant of a guy holding a broom and smiling a mile wide. "Hey, Nite Owl. Is that you?" It was my cousin Manuel Zarate. He was huge and built like a truck. Although I didn't know him as well as I did his brother Peter or his sister Patsy, who actually used to babysit me when I was a kid, Manuel was a sort of legendary figure on the streets because of his size and the amount of heart he had for the gang. He had a great reputation in the prison system as well. He had a deep, booming voice. So big that they called him Foghorn. So when he called out to me, everybody in the dayroom looked our way. I walked up to him to shake his hand and he throws me a huge hug.

"Come here, cabron," he says. "We're family, fool."

He asked me where I was living and I showed him. He looked around the cell and saw that I didn't have anything in the way of luxury or convenience. "I'm working right now so I can't bring you anything. But I'm gonna move you to my wing. I have a pad for you. In fact, you know him. Gallo from Encanto."

I couldn't believe it. It was David "Gallo" Dominguez. The guy that I escaped Rancho Del Campo with years ago. And I'd be celling with him. Manuel goes into my cell with me and says, "Here." He pulls something out of his pocket and hands it to me. "Sell some for your canteen items and smoke the rest of it with your little buddies out there. I'll be back later to check up on you and you should be down in my wing by tomorrow." Then he tells some of the Surenos within earshot in the dayroom, "You fools keep him out of trouble. This is my little Primo and if he gets in any wrecks while he's here, it's your ass." They took this good-naturedly but I wondered how genuinely afraid they were when they said, "Don't trip. We got him." He gave me a big hug and he said, "I promised Grandma Lupe I would keep you out of trouble, so don't fuck up." I told him I came up with big Eric and he said he knew. I grew up with the Moreno family.

My Big Homie, Chapo Moreno, was a legend in the gangster world. He was killed by an off-duty cop from Arizona. Chapo and my homegirls Lucy and Vera were coming back from Braw-ley, California, in the late 1970s. They were hitchhiking and they got picked up by this off-duty cop. But they didn't know he was a cop. During the ride, this cop kept hitting on Vera, who was Chapo's girlfriend. This guy is making a real pest of himself until Chapo got good and tired of it. He had the guy pull over on some pretext or other and when they got out, Chapo grabbed the guy and threw him into the trunk of the car. They drive back to the hood and they stopped under a freeway overpass. Chapo yells at the guy through the closed hood, "Thanks for the ride." Lucy felt bad leaving him there, so she opens the trunk and the guy apparently had a gun back there in the trunk. As soon as the trunk lid goes up, the guy shoots Lucy directly in the head and kills her. Then he turns to Chapo and unloads the rest of the ammo into him. He then turns to shoot Vera, but the gun is empty. So he cuffs her and waves down a bus. He tells the driver that he's an off-duty cop who has been kidnapped and just shot his kidnappers. Chapo died in Vera's arms and she was never the same after that.

The cop walked away from it all scot-free and never even saw the inside of a courtroom or a jail cell. Chapo's murder left Jessie Moreno with a bitter heart and he became this beast in the neighborhood. He spent the rest of his life going in and out of jail. Later on, he was indicted in a federal case and was sent to federal prison, where the EME made him a brother. Then one day, Jessie just retired because he didn't want to spend whatever time he had left with hatred in his heart and constantly on the warpath against enemies real or imagined. To my way of thinking, he'd put enough work into the EME as any three or four brothers put together.

After my cousin Manuel leaves, I call Sniper over and show him the weed. It was about five caps. A cap is the cover of a ChapStick tube and in the joint we use the cap as the universal measure for dope. Sort of our own system of weights and measures. Back in my day, a cap of weed would buy you a whole carton of cigarettes. Sniper says he'll ask around to see who wants some. In the meantime, we roll a joint and smoke it. After that, I made some coffee and watched some TV while Sniper went out looking for buyers. After all was said and done, we got a can of Bugler tobacco; a bunch of hygiene stuff like deodorant, soap, shampoo, hair pomade; Top Ramen noodles, chips, soda, and a can of tuna fish. And I still had enough left over to smoke with some of the Surenos in the dayroom and a whole joint for me and Sniper to smoke in our cell later.

After dinner, Manuel came by and he's got Jessie Moreno with him. Jessie and I hug for a long time and he says, "I knew your ass was gonna end up here." Jessie starts talking about the old days and he told Manuel the story about him and his old lady picking me up on the streets where I was living and putting me in his car. They took me somewhere and parked. He got out and ten minutes later he came back and stuffed a huge wad of money in my hand. "Don't say nothing," he told me. I don't know where he got the money, but I found out later that a bank had been robbed in that neighborhood. I wasn't about to question the Big Homie. I was only a fourteen-year-old kid. We went on talking about ancient history in the varrio and then Manuel asked me if I sold that stuff. I told him I did and bought a bunch of canteen stuff with it. Then Manuel hands me another cap and says, "Don't be giving these bums a free ride." He meant the camaradas, the guys who weren't made EME members but were basically their eyes, ears, and fists. Then he asked me if I had called our grandmother yet. I told him I hadn't. He said tomorrow we'd go to the yard and make sure that I called her. They both gave me a big hug and left. This was fairly typical in prison. Our guys, the Surenos and especially Surenos who were family members, looked out for each other. If we'd hadn't been in prison, this was the sort of conversation anyone would be having on the outside. They just came by to make sure I was squared away, that I had toilet articles for my health, and that I stayed in touch with family.

The odd thing is that I was never scared going into prison. There are countless books and movies about how terrifying prison is and how people are constantly in danger and so on. The truth is that prison is full of killers, misfits, and dangerous people and shit was always jumping off, but I never remembered being scared. To me, it was more exciting than it was scary. Maybe the big difference is that I literally had nothing to lose. I had no children, no girlfriend of any consequence, and I'd been on my own since I was thirteen. I knew I was a small fish in a big ocean and if I wanted to survive, I'd have to learn to swim with the sharks. Killer sharks.

13

The First Order of Business

I had to see my case manager for orientation. She asked me about what kind of work I wanted to do. I told her I wanted to work in the body shop. Then she mentioned school and I told her I wasn't interested. Then she asked me if I had any family in the prison. I didn't know how to answer her. If I said yes, would she have me transferred someplace else in the prison? So I just asked why she wanted to know. "Because I understand you have family here that want you to move to their unit. But I just wanted to make sure that this wasn't someone setting you up and you find yourself with some problems." That kind of stuff happened a lot in prison. So I told her that my cousin Manuel Zarate was here and I wanted to move close to him because we hadn't seen each other in a long time. She nodded and took notes. In short order I was moved into F wing and put in cell 250 with my old homeboy from YA camp, Gallo. This was a real trip. It was like old homie week.

After I got settled in, I went to visit Manuel in his cell, who was putting a tattoo on Jessie Moreno's chest. Manuel then slides me a key to his cell. Back in those days, you were allowed to have a key to your cell to keep your stuff from being burglarized while you were at work or out in the yard. Manuel is a very talented tattoo artist and there are hundreds of guys all over the place with his ink on them. He was putting a giant tattoo on Jessie's chest. It was the last known picture of Emiliano Zapata taken before he died. It was coming out really nice. Then Manuel asked me if everything was going okay and I said it was. Then he told David (Gallo), "Take him to the yard so he can call home. And tell Grandma that I said hello."

I can take a hint, so David and I leave them to their work and we catch the next "unlock" to the yard. In Soledad, it's laid out in one long corridor with wings coming out on the sides. And every hour on the hour they have movement. When they unlock the access doors, people can then move from one cell to the other or to different wings. Inevitably, people do sneak into areas where they're not supposed to be, either to kick it with their homeboys or sometimes to "put in work." And the "work" is never pretty. It just means that someone is going to feel some pain or maybe worse.

Sometime after that, I saw the craziest thing I ever saw in all my time in the prison system. We were out in the yard sitting in the bleachers and just socializing. There was a crazy black dude walking around, talking to himself. We knew he wasn't right in the head because he was always getting in trouble for doing the dumbest stuff. He was actually harmless. Just a little touched in the head. But this one day we noticed him carrying a blanket to the yard and walking toward the wire fence right under one of the gun towers. For some reason, the gun guard didn't notice him approach and didn't notice when the black guy threw the blanket over the razor wire at the top of the fence and started to climb over.

We looked at each other. "Is this really happening?" We couldn't believe the gun guard didn't see this. He was probably asleep.

So the black guy goes over the fence and lands between the wire and the wall and he starts walking as casually as can be toward the other gun tower. The second gun guard sees him and apparently gets on the phone to call the first gun guard, because all of a sudden the first gun guard starts yelling at him over the bullhorn. We're watching this getting more dangerous. The black guy keeps walking and yelling shit back up at the two guards. At one point he flips them both off. Finally, one of the guards fires a round from his Ruger Mini-14 into the ground near the black guy. It doesn't work. The whole yard hits the dirt, of course, but this black inmate just keeps walking. Then the second guard lets go with a shotgun round into the ground. That doesn't do any good either. And now we know it's coming. The first guard hits the black guy and he goes down. But he rolls over, gets to his knees, stands up, and keeps walking. And then he starts jogging. The guards then start pouring fire into him until he goes down and doesn't get up. A perimeter vehicle finally shows up and they cuff him up and put him inside. We eventually found out that he'd been hit five times and he died in the hospital while they were operating on him.

A few days after my interview with the case manager, I got a "ducat" (an "order") to report to the auto body shop. The shop was located all the way at the other end of the long corridor in an area they just called Industries. To get to it, you had to go through two metal detectors and a full strip search.

When I got there, I realized right away that the instructor must have given up any hope of teaching years ago. There was nothing going on there at all. A couple of guys were working on a VW Bug. A few guys were playing cards, others were sleeping, and everyone else was just hanging around entertaining themselves in whatever way they wanted.

At the time, I had a homeboy named Boxer from Avenues. Avenues was one of the biggest gangs in Los Angeles. They'd been around since the end of WWII and their neighborhood included places like Highland Park, Cypress Park, Montecito Heights, and most of that area northeast of downtown LA. They were deep and they had a few of their guys that eventually became brothers in the EME. Many years later, in 1995, Avenues became the center of national attention when some of their street soldiers killed a three-year-old girl named Stephanie Kuhen. Late one night she was riding in the backseat of her parents' car. They were coming back from a ball game or something and apparently they got lost on their way home. They turned into an alley on Isabel Street just where a bunch of Avenues gangsters were hanging out. The Avenues guys thought that they were being rolled up on by a bunch of enemies from Highland Park, another gang in that neighborhood. So they grabbed their weapons and started shooting into the car. Stephanie was killed.

When that story hit the papers the next morning, it started making news literally all over the world. They called it the Wrong Way Shooting. A few days later the world media was crawling all over Avenues territory looking for a story. The detectives at Northeast Division of the LAPD who were assigned the case were getting calls from as far away as China and Russia. It was a story that wouldn't go away. In fact, a few days later, President Clinton mentioned the Kuhen homicide in a speech he made about guns, violence, and the gang problem. Clinton promised the country that things like the Kuhen murder would not happen again and he promised to provide enough federal money to put an additional 100,000 police officers on the streets of the nation. That one murder literally woke up LA and its citizens to the existence of the Mexican Mafia and its influence on the streets.

At any rate, Boxer and I had met when we were in B wing and we had gotten to be friendly. Not real close, but friendly enough that we spent eight hours a day in the body shop trying to find ways of amusing ourselves until the end of our shift. One day, Boxer comes in and says we got some work to do. He said we needed to make some "pieces" (prison knives, also known as shanks). Nobody needed to tell me that when the order for shanks comes in, it meant that the orders came from way up in the EME food chain. They were either expecting trouble or were about to start some trouble. We had to work fast because someone was going to come by later and pick them up. We had to be careful, of course, because making weapons could land you deep in the hole. We started looking around the shop and found a nice piece of steel about an inch wide, a quarter-inch thick, and about three feet long. We took the piece to the band saw and cut it down to pieces about seven inches long.

Boxer started working on the grinder, shaping the shanks into sharp knife points. He told me to keep an eye on the office where the instructor spent all his time and on the other inmates. They didn't need to know this. Not that they'd rat us out, it just wasn't any of their business. Of course, running a two-horsepower industrial grinder isn't exactly quiet, and making a three-foot-long shower of sparks isn't very easy to hide or camouflage. But Boxer was working fast and about a half hour after he started, he handed me a sharp shank and asked me if I wanted to make one for myself. I said, "Fuck, yeah." So he takes point and I spend the next fifteen minutes grinding the hell out of the steel until I got it looking like a knife, complete with a nice handle so it'll fit right in your hands. I showed him the finished shank and he whistled. Nice job.

We clean up our mess and Boxer wraps three finished shanks in a shop towel and two pieces of unworked stock in another rag. I asked him why he didn't finish the other two and he said they could store them in somebody's cell until they were needed. If they didn't have an edge, they weren't considered shanks, just contraband that didn't earn you any time in the hole.

After the shop rags, Boxer wraps them really tight in a plastic garbage bag. Just before lunch, another homie came in with the paint crew and Boxer gave him the shanks. Later on, Boxer explained to me how to smuggle contraband like that through the prison. What happens is that one of the inmates, on orders from a shot caller, places a work order to paint something in the building. The paint crews are given their paint cans, tools, and so on. When the piece needs to be transported, they drop it into one of the five-gallon paint cans and from there it gets delivered to whoever ordered the shank. This was prison education for me. These are the lessons that make you a valuable and efficient soldier behind bars. Getting stuff done on time and without fuckups gets you noticed. It's really no different than a business or the military. The management is looking for self-starters and people who can think on their feet. The workers are looking for a pay raise, promotion, and a little more power. And while the EME wants and recruits hard guys who can take care of the physical and violent side of the business, they also want people to be smart enough to know when to back off from a violent confrontation if it means achieving a more important goal.

There was, for instance, the time I was actually checked and mildly punished for letting things get out of hand when I should have been smart enough to see the big picture and avoid trouble.

Part of our daily routine was working out in the yard, or playing ball, or anything physical to release tension and be able to sleep well at night. One Friday night I had plans to meet up with a bunch of guys my own age at the dugout of one of the two baseball diamonds Soledad had at the time. Every little faction in the prison had their own "space" somewhere in the yard and for the most part, people avoided entering other people's spaces. One of our guys had gotten some Sherm (PCP) smuggled in a week earlier and our plan was to hang out and smoke it. The way it went was we'd dip a menthol cigarette into the liquid PCP and pass the cigarette. Dip again and then pass it around again.

After we finished smoking, somebody decided we should go for a stroll around the track field. Prison rules said that you couldn't walk in a group of more than four inmates. That was considered a gang. There were a lot of us there that night, so we broke up into groups of three and four. It was all very casual and none of us were looking for trouble. Some of us would have visitors that weekend and they were looking forward to that.

As we went around for the fourth time, a group of Nortenos were playing ball and a hard hit on the ball sent it rolling our way. One of the Nortenos goes running after it and bumps into one of the guys in our group, Danny. Maybe because we were high or there might have been something else involved, but instead of just blowing it off, Danny gives the guy shit and says, "Watch where you're going, punk." The Norteno turns and tells Danny, "Go fuck yourself." The Norteno had a red bandana sticking out of his pocket, so Danny grabs it away from him, pulls out his lighter, and tries to set the bandana on fire. As he's doing this, he's giving the Norteno shit and calling him a buster. That's short for "sodbuster." One of the ways of insulting Nortenos is to call them farmeros (farmers), wetbacks, or sodbusters because a lot of them were raised in the northern rural agricultural parts of California. For their part, the Nortenos call Surenos Surats, implying that Surenos are all snitches and rats.

When the other Nortenos on the baseball diamond see the bandana being burned and the shit going back and forth, it literally cleared the benches. They swarm out to us and we naturally wade into the fight. We fought for over two minutes, which is a hell of a long time. The gun towers naturally come to life, but because it's dark and they can't see very well, they hold their fire. When they finally hit their lights, everyone in the yard scattered like roaches when the lights come on. Because of the low light, none of the gun guards got a good look at who was fighting.

The administration naturally locked down the yard. But because they couldn't identify anybody to do an investigation, they didn't know if this was a minor beef between individuals that got out of hand or a major war that was about to start or the preamble to something even bigger. So out of an abundance of caution, they locked down the whole prison for the entire weekend until people cooled off. And that lockdown was what got me and some of my close homies in trouble with the older guys. Visiting days were suspended that weekend and that got everybody pissed off.

Visiting days are really important for a number of reasons. One is that this is where most of the dope is smuggled into the system. It comes in with wives, girlfriends, moms, little kids—you name it. And dope in prison means cash flow and influence and power. And there were the more humane reasons as well. Inmates want to see their family and sometimes the family has to make a lot of plans to, say, leave LA, drive up to Soledad, get a motel room, and spend money doing it. So yanking visiting day like that at the last minute disrupted a lot of inmates and their families. And, of course, there was the intelligence network that also needed a constant flow of information to function properly. Visitors meant fresh and relevant information from the outside world. If some wiseass in Pacoima or Logan or Lancaster wasn't paying his taxes or obeying orders, the Big Homies in prison needed to know this and issue orders to "correct" the situation. And a lot of that information came through on visiting days.

Fortunately for me, my cousin Manuel had the "keys" to the yard at the time. That meant that he was representing the desires and the orders of the EME, even though he wasn't officially an EME member, or a carnal. As the key holder, he had final say on the nature of the punishment we youngsters would be getting.

Believe it or not, Manuel had us go over to the Nortenos and apologize to them for starting the fight in the yard. While that might sound out of character for a couple of vicious prison gangs, it was actually sound foreign policy. In prison, the first order of business is "business." That meant drugs and money. Long-standing beefs and occasional skirmishes could be dealt with eventually, and it was smart guys who knew how to hold their water and wait for a time and place when necessary violence disrupted the business as little as possible. In addition to a very hard lecture by Manuel, I also got a mild beating in my cell, but that beating had so little behind it that Manuel and I ended up laughing while he was in the middle of punching me. It wasn't really my fault, but for a guy like me who was held in higher regard and respect than the other guys my age, it was my responsibility to have tried to calm matters on the spot as they happened. I was supposed to "know better," but at the time I let the situation get out of hand.

Before I knew it, my eighteen months were up and I was paroled. When I got back to the barrio, I found that I'd acquired a whole new level of respect. I'd been to the big house and carried myself the way I was supposed to and proudly carried not only the Sureno flag but also my barrio's flag, which lent a sheen of respect to all the homies in that area. I gave everybody in the barrio news on how Jessie was doing, what Manuel was up to, and all the gossip and information I picked up in Soledad. Manuel had life at the time and when I wrote this, he had spent thirty-five years in prison. He spent twenty-five of those years in the SHU (Security Housing Unit) in Pelican Bay, the ultimate supermax prison in the state of California. Frankly, I couldn't understand how he didn't go crazy from being in prison all that time. It was hard for guys like me to see these guys locked up for so long and not be able to do anything for them. But when you're a fuckup like I was, what could I possibly do for them? If there is a God, I hope there's a place in his heart for those dudes and he forgives them for whatever put them there. Maybe God will give them a tier-tending job in that big pinta in the sky.

14

Mainline

As I said, getting out of Soledad prison gave me a new status in the barrio. I represented the neighborhood and came home like a soldier returning from a tour of duty in a combat theater. It's funny how things change. The homegirls want to give their pussies. The dope dealers want to reel you in by giving you that "first one" for free, knowing that once you're strung out and pulling burglaries and robberies, you'll be spending your money with them.

And the homeboys, of course, will give you "props," a level of respect, because you've earned your place in the hierarchy. It's crazy because this is all we lived for.

Anyhow, one thing I had a hard time with was making parole. I mean, I would rather just send my parole agent a pair of tennis shoes and a note saying "Catch me if you can" than show up to his office every week and give him an excuse to violate me; my pee was always dirty and I didn't have a job. Dope was always in my life—either selling it, or shooting it up, smoking it, or moving it by the kilo.

So it wasn't long before I found myself back in jail with a three-year sentence and on a bus to Folsom Prison. It was the mideighties and Folsom had an average of 350 stabbings and thirteen murders per year and some of the most violent criminals in the state of California. It was headquarters for the Mexican Mafia, the Aryan Brotherhood, Nuestra Familia, and the Black Guerilla Family. Just as I got there, the warring prison gangs had declared a "peace treaty," so the mainline was open.

When you get off the bus at Folsom, you're lined up under a pavilion in front of the Program Office. Then you come into R&R (Receiving and Release), are stripped out, and given a bedroll. They tell you to go up some stairs and have a seat on the benches until your name is called. These benches are on top of the captains' and lieutenants' offices. They're like bleachers looking onto the yard and there are sharks of all colors there, looking for who is getting off the bus. Lucky for me I see a homie from Carlsbad, Gato (Gilbert Alcarez).

I yell, "Gato, what's up, homie?"

He looked at me and did a double take. He says, "Nite Owl?"

I said, "Yeah, Big Homie, it's me."

He asked me if I was okay and how much time did I have. I told him three years and he says, "Okay, I'll let everyone know you're here."

After he's gone, they call my name and I go into the office. Sitting behind the desk are a couple of heavyset cops with big mustaches. One is a captain and the other is a lieutenant. They ask my name and number, and when I told them, they asked me who I run with. Growing up, I was always told if a cop asks you if you run with a gang, you deny it. So I don't know how to answer these two. The captain looks at me like I'm retarded and asks,

"North or South?" I shrug my shoulders and he just puts on this dramatic sigh and says, "Look, I'm going to house you. Do you want to get a cell on the mainline or should I put you in PC (protective custody)?" I say mainline. So he asks me, "Where you from?" I told him San Diego.

Then he says, "Okay. This is the South. See how easy that is. Building 2, Fish Row cell 523." And out I go. When I leave the office, I'm met outside by my homeboy Wizard from Logan Heights and my Big Homeboy Juanon Flores. Juanon was a gangster too and he was doing twentysomething years for robberies and had been down about eight years already. The homeboy had juice in the yard, which I would find out real quick. Anyhow, we all hug and they ask me where I'm going. I tell them what cell and they say, "Okay, don't trip, we'll be getting at you."

So they walk me to my building and Fish Row is up on the fifth tier, so it's five flights of stairs. Ain't no elevators here. Once I find my cell, I find it's already occupied by someone, so I come in and the dude is a short stocky guy from LA. He's from a barrio called Fifth and Hill, which was mostly Hondurans and Salvadorans. In fact, this was before they had MS-13. Anyway, he introduces himself as Marciano and I introduce myself. The cells are small—five by eight feet—and there are two bunks, a toilet, and a sink and that's it. He's got the bottom bunk, first come first served, so I set myself up on the top bunk and settle in.

He asked me where I came from and I told him Chino. Then he asked how much time did I have and I told him three years. Then he says, "You look real young. How old are you?" So I say I'm twenty years old. He shakes his head and says, "You're just a youngster." But he said it in a derogatory way. I noticed the dismissive tone but I didn't make any comment.

Then he told me he just got out of the SHU and that he was back in prison for two years for stabbing someone. I told him that was cool with me and I asked what the SHU was like. I let him go on about what it's like in the hole. I spent time in Palm Hall, so I'm pacifying him, giving him that old "I respect you because you're older and have been around," but in the back of my mind, I'm thinking the guy is a little too arrogant for my taste. So his story is going in one ear and out the other.

First impressions are always the biggest influence. Then comes instinct, that gut feeling. Prison is the best educator when it comes to "street smarts." When I first came to the joint, the homies always said, "Look, listen, and learn. Keep your mouth shut, don't volunteer your opinion unless asked, and never raise your hand for something unless it is personal." These were survival skills. If you paid enough attention, then you made the right call.

Anyhow, after Marciano gave me his attitude, we went to sleep. The next morning we got ready for breakfast and they released us for chow. As we're walking down the tier, I hear my name called out. "Nite Owl." I turn around and it's an older homie from Shelltown, Bobby Colmenaro. He catches up to me and says, "What's up, fool? How long you been here?" We knew each other from the county jail and I was good friends with some of his homeboys from my juvenile days. When you're in prison, you only have two sides, the North and the South. The Hispanics will hang out with people from their area because they have a lot more in common. Anyhow, we go to breakfast and come back, then the processing starts. You see the nurse, psych, case manager. While I'm sitting there on the benches waiting my turn, I meet a couple of dudes from Orange County. Chapo from Stanton and Eddie Munster from Santa Ana. We talk about how good the breakfast was and Eddie, "Monstro," asks me how old I am. I told him I was twenty and that I'd turn twenty-one in February. They both say, "Damn, you're young. What are you doing here?"

We talk until our names are called, then about lunchtime we head back to our cells. After lunch, I'm laying on my bunk when this dude comes to my cell. He's pushing a broom and he asks, "Who's Nite Owl?" I say me, and he looks at me and asks, do you have any homeboys here? I say my homeboy Juanon. He says, "Okay. Hold on." And he goes back down the tier and in about five minutes comes back with a box. And it's a nice-sized box, because he has to hold it with both arms and it's filled to the top. He says, "Juanon sent you this."

He hands me sweatshirts and bottoms, thermals, a beanie, socks, books, magazines, soup, coffee, sugar, tuna, candy bars, packs of Camel cigarettes, a can of Bugler tobacco, soap, shampoo, deodorant, and hair grease. I mean, basically everything I need to stay comfortable. I ask him, "Do you want anything? A pack of smokes?"

He says, "Nah. I'm all good. You enjoy." Then he takes a bundle out of his mouth and hands it to me.

I ask him what it is and he says, "I don't know. It's yours."

If he had said he knew what it was, then that would mean he went through it; that's taboo. You don't go through someone else's shit no matter what it is. Because if it's tampered with, you're responsible. So I tell him, let me check it out and I'll get at you. He says, "Don't trip. Your homie took care of me."

Well, I'm set. And I have some weed too. So I tell my cellie Marciano, let's smoke one. We smoke a pin joint and have some coffee. I ask him, "If I give you a joint, will you let my homeboy Bobby come smoke one with me, and you smoke one with his cellie?" My cellie agrees, so at dinner I tell Bobby and he says, "Hell, yeah!" So when we get back to Fish Row, Bobby runs to his cell for his toothbrush and comes back to my cell. We smoke one and start joking around. Bobby is a real character. We become really good friends later and end up running around a little on the streets, but that's in the nineties. Anyhow, I shoot Monstro a book because he asked if I had any reading material and I shoot him some cigarettes and a joint. Me and Bobby stay up pretty late telling "war stories" and joking.

The next day after breakfast, we switched back and my cellie Marciano comes home. I can tell that he's really upset, so I ask him what's up. He says, "Don't ever ask me to do that again. That dude was stupid and he doesn't even speak Spanish." I just brushed it off. I know this dude has some kind of "macho complex," so I don't pay any attention. So I get into one of my books. I love to read. Well, a couple of days go by and my cellie isn't talking to me. I told Bobby about my cellie being pissed off, but Bobby just says, "Fuck that dude. We'll be on the mainline in a couple of days, so it doesn't matter."

About a day later, my cellie takes a mirror and looks up and down the tier to see if there's anyone out there. Then he turns to me and says, "Hey, cellie, you got a minute?" So I climb down off my bunk and say, "What's up?" He says, "You haven't said anything to me in a couple of days. You got a problem with me?" Well, here it comes. I knew this dude thought he was a badass or whatever, but the last thing I'm gonna do is let him bully me. I don't care what he thinks he is. I tell him, "Look, you came back from the homeboy's cell all bent out of shape, then you weren't speaking to me. So I just let it go. But I'm not bashful. If you had talked to me, I would have talked back, but I don't have a problem with you. Do you have a problem with me?"

Then he gets in my face and says, "Yeah, I do, morro." Which means "youngster" in Spanish.

Marciano got in my face and I let him have it. I pretty much had him and the guy was all up against the bunk holding on. I could see he was bleeding from a cut above his eye. And he's not fighting back. But then I notice that my T-shirt is wet and I look down and it is covered in blood. I look at his hands and he's holding a razor blade. So I grab him by the elbow and he slices my forearm. I then put him in a wrist hold and start kneeing him in the ribs. He manages to cut me again, on the thigh. So now we're locked. I'm holding him by the wrist and my other arm's around his neck.

Just then the cop bangs on the bars and yells, "Fish Row, prepare for chow." Oh, shit! This is how I'm going to start my time at Folsom Prison. I can just see it now. The cop has to unlock each cell, then go back and slide the bar. In my head he's gonna get to our cell and see us and all the blood and set off the alarm. The gunner on the catwalk is right in front of our cell. He's gonna shoot us. I'm tripping, so I tell Marciano, "Look, I don't want to get caught. Throw that shit out the cell and we will clean up and deal with this after lunch." He says, "Fuck that. You're gonna keep fighting if I throw this out." So I promise him I'll stop and he tosses the blade out the bars.

I get to the mirror and check my face and I've got a nice slice from my ear to under my chin. I take off my T-shirt and start washing up. I get the blood off me, then I snatch the sheet off my bed and start cleaning all the blood off the floor and walls. I flush the sheet and T-shirt down the toilet. I put toilet paper on my neck wound and forearm. The cop comes by our cell and unlocks our door but doesn't notice anything. My cellie has a lump and a cut above his eye and a fat lip, but other than that, he's cool.

The cop yells, "Fish Row, step out for chow," and racks the bar. We come out and my cellie is gone. I wait for Bobby but I don't say anything. We go down to the chow hall and get our food. Me and Bobby are at the same table but I don't see my cellie. Eddie Munster is one table over and he's calling me, "Hey, youngster." So I turn to look at him and he asks me do I have a cigarette for him. That's when I hear Bobby behind me say, "What the fuck happened to your face?" I tell him, "Nothing. I cut myself shaving." He says, "Yeah, right. That was your cellie, huh?" I tell him yeah, but I say I got it covered and for him not to trip. Bobby is pissed off and starts looking around. "Where is that motherfucker?" he says.

We get up from the table and I give Monstro his cigarette. Then Bobby tells me, "Fuck that, homie. We're gonna kill that motherfucker." He stops and grabs my chin and looks at my face and asks if I'm okay and do I want to go to the hospital. I tell him that I'm good and all I want is to just kick that dude's ass. Bobby laughs and says we're going to do a lot more than that. He tells me that when we get to the tier, "I'm gonna knock that fool out. Then I'll grab his arms and you grab his legs and we're going to throw him off the tier. That's five stories up. There's no doubt what's going to happen after that."

Bobby is moving fast and I'm just trying to keep up. When we get to the fifth tier, Bobby stops in front of my cell and says, "Be ready, little homie." We wait a couple of minutes and then here comes

Marciano. But he's not alone. He's with another guy, who has his shirt off and is covered with tattoos. The guy has a push broom.

So Bobby tells me, "We get the guy with the push broom first."

Bobby squares off, but the dude with the push broom puts up his hands and says, "Whoa, whoa. Hold up. Who got in a fight?"

Bobby tells him nobody got in a fight. "That motherfucker cut my little homie."

The guy says, "I know, I know. Let me check it out." So I show him my face, then I show them my arm and thigh. Bobby is pissed. He grabs Marciano, and the other guy tells him, "Look, the carnals already know about this, so that's why they had me come down here and tell you to leave it alone for now. They'll talk to you when you come out."

Bobby is still hot. He keeps his hold on Marciano and puts a finger in his face and tells him, "This ain't over, son of a bitch. It's on, punk." Bobby tells me to get my stuff and that I'm coming with him.

"Fuck that," I tell him. "I'm not going to let this punk run me out of my cell."

Bobby puts his arm around me and says, "Stay down, little homie. You sure you going to be all right?" I say yeah I'll be okay. So he tells me to stay on my toes and that he'll see me in the morning. Then Bobby tells Marciano, "You better not do anything stupid, puto."

Bobby hugs me, and Marciano and I go in our cell just as the cop racks the bar. We wait for the cop to come lock our door, then I get up and say, "What's up?"

Marciano says, "You heard what they said; we can't do anything. We have to stay cool until we get off Fish Row." Then he says, "Look, that slice on your arm was meant for you, not your barrio."

The slice he was talking about happened to cut through a tattoo I have with my neighborhood and he's worried my homeboys will take it as disrespect to the hood. Then he says, "I give you my word I'm not going to do anything. Do you give me yours?" So we shook hands and settled in.

The next day after breakfast a cop comes by and tells both of us to pack up. We're heading for the mainline. I'm kind of nervous. I mean, you hear so many stories about Folsom and I know these dudes don't play.

15

I Want to Kill Him

Folsom is no longer like it was in my day. In fact, I don't even think it's a real prison anymore. I heard it was a tourist attraction with actors playing the part of convicts. Anyhow, we get downstairs and Chapo from Stanton and Eddie Munster are down there. I don't see Bobby anywhere, so I'm kind of just standing there alone when Chapo comes up to me.

He says, "Hey, little homie, the Big Homie Monstro heard about what happened between you and your cellie. In fact, we seen his eye." He kind of chuckled at that and then says, "Whatever happened in your cell stays there. Don't bring any of that shit out on the line because the homies aren't having it." Well, two big revelations are made here. First, Eddie Monstro is a brother! Who knew? Second, they think it was just a cell fight.

So I tell him, "Hey, Chapo. Tell Monstro I got nothing but respect for the Big Homie, but I can't let this go. That dude cut my face. I'm going to be scarred for life."

This was true. I still have that battle wound.

He says, "What are you talking about?"

149

So I show him and it's funny how everyone I showed this fresh wound to would just wince and ask was I okay. I show him my forearm and thigh and run down how the whole thing happened.

He says, "Hold on. The homie didn't know all that, so wait here."

He goes over and starts telling Monstro. By this time they're moving us from 2 Building to the laundry. We walk through 5 Building, which is a trip. This is the oldest part of the prison. It's literally all granite rocks, and doors made from steel perforated with inch-wide round holes. It's where the old hangman's gallows used to be. We walk out of the building and cross the yard, past the chapel, and go between 1 Building and the chapel—an area known as blood alley. Then we enter the laundry room. By this time, Chapo had told Monstro what happened between me and Marciano.

Chapo says, "The homie didn't know that fool cut you. He wants to talk to you." So I walk over to Monstro and he says, "I told Chapo to tell you to let that shit die on Fish Row. But he said you told him, 'Chale, what's up?'"

So I gave Monstro the rundown and showed all my cuts. And after, he says, "So what do you want to do?"

I said, "Pay him back."

Monstro looks at Chapo and says, "This youngster has got nuts. Not only did he not run to the cops, but he also doesn't go to the hospital to get stiches. And now he wants to pay this dude back." They start laughing and Monstro asks me, "What you gonna do, little young buck? You gonna kill him?"

I puff up all five feet seven inches of my frame and tell him, "Yeah. If I can."

Monstro gets serious and tells me, "Okay. Look, when we get done here, we're going to our housing unit. They're going to ask you do you want to stay in your cell or go to the yard. Tell them go to the yard and don't show anyone else these cuts. I'll find you and we'll talk, okay?"

After we get issued our clothes and our bedding from the laundry, they take us to our units. I'm put in 3 Building on the fourth tier. And guess who is housed right down the tier from me. Yup! It's Marciano. Anyhow, the cops ask me if I want to go to the yard or stay in my cell. I say go outside. It's a trip because there's only one way in or out and that's through 5 Building unless you're in the chow hall. Anyhow, when I get outside, I see all kinds of homeboys from San Diego. There's about fifteen or twenty dudes there and I know most of them.

They're all fucking with me, saying shit like, "What you doing in the big house, fool? Don't you belong in Juvenile Hall?"

All that hazing comes to a halt all of a sudden when Monstro and Chapo come calling and I have to take a walk with them. We go over to the bleachers in front of 1 Building and Monstro introduces me to two guys. A tall, slim older guy who talks in a whisper and a shorter, athletic-looking guy who is friendly looking.

Monstro says, "This is Kilroy and the homie Alfie. Tell them what happened and show them your cuts." So I go through all that again and they say, "So what you want to do?" I look at Monstro and he nods his head.

I say, "I want to kill him." They all look at each other and start to laugh. Then they ask me, "Are you sure, youngster, this is what you want?" I got a little frustrated because I thought they were making fun of me.

Then Kilroy says, "Okay. Let us talk and we'll call you in a minute."

While they're talking, I go over to where my San Diego

homeboys are and I hear, "Oooh. Check out the little homeboy. I didn't know you was so important." They're still busting my balls.

Finally, Juanon shows up and he says, "Come here, homie." He gives me a hug and tells me, "I haven't seen anyone from the barrio in almost ten years. I wish we could spend some time together, but I already know what's going on." He asks me, "You didn't tell any of these fools anything, did you?"

I told him the only people I spoke to were Monstro, Chapo, Kilroy, and Alfie.

So he says, "Good. Look, I talked to the Big Homies and asked them if you could get off on the yard. They said no. They want it done on your tier. It's not to leave your tier. Somebody is gonna bring you a piece tonight." Then he asked me, "Can you do this, homie? Have you ever done a hit before?"

I looked at him and just said, "I got this." He puts his arm around me and walks me over to Kilroy and another brother, I can't remember his name, and says, "He's ready."

So Kilroy tells me, "Look, you do what you got to do. After this, I don't want no more fighting with your cellie shit. It's not right that he cut you like that, especially since you didn't have a weapon. But I don't care what differences you have with your cellie in the future. The next time you come to us, okay? Now, when you get done up there, you drop the piece off the tier, you got that? Drop it over the rail. Someone on the bottom tier will pick it up. Don't forget. Have you ever done this before?" And I looked at Kilroy in the eye and lied to him. "Yeah, I've done this lots of times."

That evening after dinner I'm sitting in my cell watching TV with my new cellie, a homeboy from the LA area that's got three life sentences. He's been down for seventeen years already and he says he's got kids older than me.

A while later, this big, bald guy covered in tattoos comes to our cell and asks, "Who's Nite Owl?" I told him I was him. Then he asks, "Where you from?" I say San Diego. He asks to see my face. I show him my cut and he pulls a manila envelope out of his pants that was tucked under his shirt. He says, "Give me the envelope back."

I looked inside the envelope and there were a couple of porn magazines as well as a ten-inch-long steel shank that looked like it had a real nice point on it. I asked him if I can have the magazines as well, but he said they were already spoken for by someone else. "But maybe, after tomorrow. If you're still here." I can't remember his name but he was from Toonerville, a neighborhood in Northeast Los Angeles. I was with a couple of his homies in YA. Then he tells me that the homeboy next door is "gonna help you. So when you come out in the morning, look for your neighbor and he's going to help you, okay?" I tell him okay and he wishes me good luck. He takes off down the tier, pushing his broom.

Me and my cellie look at the piece and it feels huge. My cellie says, "You're gonna have to put a handle on that." So we tear one of my sheets into one-inch-wide strips and he shows me how to start at the end and work your way down, wrapping it real tight. Once I got the handle on it, I started practicing with it. It was actually too big for me, but I tell myself I'm gonna get this done and make my homeboys proud of me. I don't get much sleep that night. I'm tossing and turning. I've never really done this before. I mean, I've had my share of fights. And on the streets I used sticks and bats and stuff. But I've never actually engaged in hand-to-hand combat to the death. Which was what this was going to be. Kill or be killed. I had never had to do this, but I didn't want to be another young punk who was too scared to handle his business. I've been a survivor all my life, fending for myself ever since I was thirteen years old. So I can do this. Then I'll have the respect of the homeboys and the brothers.

The next morning I'm groggy from lack of sleep, but I get up, wash up, and get ready. My cellie wishes me luck and then the cop says, "Fourth tier, prepare to step out for chow." He racks the bar and I come out looking for my neighbor. I walk in front of his cell and he's standing there. He asks me where Marciano is and I indicate that he's down the tier. But I don't see him. So we wait and the tier is starting to clear. So he says, "Go down there. Maybe you'll catch him slipping and still in bed." So I walk down to Marciano's cell and there he is in his boxers, washing his face. I go in his cell and he doesn't notice me. I pull out the knife and bring it down hard in the middle of his back. I hear him lose his breath. And then he turns around, so I raise the shank above my head and bring it down again. But he catches my arms by the wrists and we're struggling face-to-face, locked in deadly battle.

We're looking at each other eye to eye and then he gives and the knife comes down and catches him in the forehead. Blood squirts out and sprays me in the face and up my right arm. He breaks away from me and staggers out the cell. I go chase after him but he collapses in front of the cell next door. I remember what they told me to do with the piece and throw it off the tier. So I back into the cell and pitch the shank like a horseshoe. And wouldn't you know it, with my buzzard luck it hits the top rail and bounces back on the tier with a loud clank. I go to reach for it so I can throw it over, but with all the commotion from Marciano and the loud clang from the piece, the gunner on the catwalk is on me! He sees me and fires a round from his Ruger Mini-14 into the ceiling. He yells, "Freeze, motherfucker. Don't you touch that." The catwalk is only about ten feet from the tier and I'm looking down the barrel of his rifle and I can see the dude is shaking. "Put your hands on the rail and don't move, motherfucker." So I don't take my eyes off his hand on the trigger and place both hands on the rail. This dude is shaking like crazy. I don't know if he's hungover or crazy but I don't want him accidentally pulling the trigger. So I tell him, "Relax, dude. I'm not going anywhere." He just says, "Don't move." By this time I can hear keys running down the tier. I'm not taking my eyes off this gunner for shit. He tells the responding cops, "There's a knife on the tier. I got him reaching for it." So I take my eyes off him now that we have company (and other witnesses). I look down the tier and there's about twenty cops heading my way. A sergeant pulls out a handkerchief and picks up the knife. I can see it has hair and blood on the tip.

The sergeant whistles and says, "That would get the job done, huh?" I see other cops putting Marciano on a stretcher and I got a cop putting cuffs on me. He looks at all the blood on my face and arms and asks me if I'm okay. I say, "Yeah, I'm good."

I've got three cops and the sergeant escorting me and we go out and pass the chow hall. I see everyone on the grill and my homeboy Juanon is there. He gives me a thumbs-up and he says, "Stay down, little homie." I'm taken to R&R and the cops take the cuffs off me and tell me to strip out. I get undressed and they're checking me out, when the lieutenant asks, "What's that?" I say, "What?" and he says, "Those cuts on your face, arm, and thigh. They're a couple of days old but they're still fresh. Did he do that?" I say, "I don't know what you're talking about." I was so caught up in the hit that I forgot all about my wounds. They take pictures of my injuries as well as my hands that were covered with Marciano's blood. Then they take me to the nurse, who looks at my cuts and says that they should have been stitched up when I was first cut. But she said the cuts were healing and it was too late to stitch them. "Just keep them clean and you should be all right," she said. They put me in a red jumpsuit and they cuffed me back up. They escorted me to 1 Building, which is where the SHU is located. I'm then processed and taken up to the fourth tier and put in cell 417.

The cell is small as they can get away with. There's just a bunk, a sink, and a toilet. I can reach out and touch both walls at the same time without having to fully extend my arms. My elbows were still slightly bent. The cell is exactly three paces from the front to the back.

I'm in there about thirty minutes when I hear a bang on the wall to the right. I say, "Hello," and I hear someone say, "Hey, come to the bars."

So I sit at the end of the bunk and ask, "What's up?"

He says, "Here," and a hand appears from the next cell, handing me a yellow piece of paper. I take it and read and it says, "My name is Johnny Haun. They call me Johnny Rotten. I'm a Wood from Oakland. What's your name and who you run with?"

I whisper that I don't have a pen or paper. So next thing I know, here comes his big mitt with a pen and a few sheets of paper. I write back and tell him my name and nickname and that I'm a Sureno from San Diego. Then he writes, "Good to meet you, Nite Owl. You got a couple of homeboys here from San Diego." He yells out, "Hey, Willie." Someone upstairs yells back,

"What's up?" Johnny says, "You got a homeboy that just got here."
The guy from upstairs says, "Okay, I'll get at him later." Then he
says, "Hey, homie. Make a line."

I say okay, but my voice cracks because I have cotton mouth
from all the action that morning. Willie and Johnny both laugh.
So I clear my throat and ask my neighbor, "Hey, Johnny, how do
I make a line?"

He says to hold on. I go to the sink and drink some water to
get some fluid back into my mouth. He bangs on the wall to get
my attention and I see he's holding a mirror about four inches by
four inches in his hand. He's looking at me with it and I can see
him too. He's got long hair and a beard and he says, "You ever
make a fishline?" I said no, because I never had to make one. Not
in Soledad. Not in YA. Nowhere. I always just waited to come out
if I had something for someone. Anyhow, he's looking at me and
asks, "How old are you?" I tell him and he says, "Aw, this is your
first time." I say no it isn't, but then we hear a cop walking down
the tier so he says to hold on.

The cop comes to my cell. It's a female corrections officer. She
asks me, "Are you Corona?" I told her I was. Then she says, "I
have a 115 write-up for you. Do you speak English?" I told her I
did. "I have your initial 115. You're receiving a write-up and being placed in Ad Seg (Administrative Segregation, solitary confinement) pending a hearing because you were involved in an
assault on an inmate with a weapon. How do you plead?" I told
her, "Not guilty."

She says, "Okay, someone will be appointed as your investiga-
tive officer. He or she will help you with your defense." I say okay
and she gives me a copy of the write-up. I sit on the edge of the
bunk and read it. It basically covers everything that went down

that morning. It also mentions the cuts I have. But all that isn't news to me. What stands out to me is the date. It says, "On 2/8/85 you were placed in Administrative Housing Unit Folsom." It's February 8. My birthday. With all the drama in my life the past couple of days, I forgot all about my birthday.

16

The Hole

I hit the wall and tell Johnny, "Hey, I'm not twenty anymore. I'm twenty-one. Today's my birthday." Then I show Johnny my write-up. Well, this is something like what the song says. "*I turned twenty-one in Folsom doing a program in the hole.*" Or something like that.

Johnny reads the 115 and gives it back; he also gives me a book and some magazines and says, "My show is about to come on. I'll talk to you a little later."

Me and Johnny eventually got to be good friends. In fact, he starts calling me mijo, which means "son" in Spanish. I eventually see him when he comes out to the yard and the dude is big. I mean, six feet seven inches, so who am I to argue about him calling me mijo.

I meet the tier tenders for our tier—Gus from Pomona and Mumbles from Oceano. There's a couple of guys that I already knew—Jessie Maldonado (Spooky) from Hawaiian Gardens and Chente from Eighteenth Street East Side. I was in YA with both of them. Me, Spooky, and Baby Ray from San Fernando were road dogs in SCRC Norwalk. I got to meet my homeboys Willie Boy from Lomita 70s and Spider from Logan, who later became a brother in the EME. Things weren't so bad in the hole once everyone found out who I was and why I was there. Although my first day in the yard I was pulled up by one of the Big Homies, Chuy from Varrio Nuevo Estrada. He told me to walk with him. He's got this big handlebar mustache and is covered in tattoos.

He says, "Look, I know why you're back here. And we don't play that shit back here. I hear Marciano is gonna be back from the hospital and he's gonna be on our yard, so you guys leave that shit alone, all right, or else you have to answer to me." And then he says, "Marciano is a friend of mine. And I'm thinking if he had just killed you, he wouldn't be back here again, he just got out the hole. Just so you know, I'm not taking sides. I just want that shit to stop."

I say okay and I shake his hand. And wouldn't you know it, they put him in our yard.

I'm not getting any mail or money from anyone. My parents are still in Hawaii and every now and then, my grandmother sends me five or ten dollars, bless her heart. But other than that, I'm hustling for whatever I need and to be honest, I don't need much. The food was pretty good and my neighbor Johnny was a vegetarian, so he would shoot me chicken, fish, and, believe it or not, every once in a while some steak. This is prison steak so it's not filet mignon or Kobe beef but it was beef.

I was the tier winemaker. I was holding three big shanks for Johnny that no one knew about. Johnny even showed me how to put them behind the toilet into the wax ring, then mold toilet paper and soap and put it in place of the caulking. I learned how to make real good fishlines out of nylon string from the elastic band on our boxers, so I was always making lines for everyone.

Then one day our tier cop comes to my cell and he's got a cart with him. I've been there about six months already and he says, "Your property is here." And he starts handing me my sweats and thermals and all the stuff that Juanon had sent me the first day I got to Folsom. He also says, "When I go down the tier and rack the bar, you can come out and get this." He shows me a thirteen-inch black-and-white TV set. Don't laugh. It was 1985 and I don't care how long color TV has been around but I was just grateful to get any kind of TV. Up until then, Johnny had made me a long earbud and I would sit at the edge of my bed and watch his TV through a mirror with my arm sticking out through the bars.

A couple of days later, Juanon shoots me a kite making sure I got everything, and saying how proud he was of me and that I should let him know if I needed anything else. A kite is a note written on a piece of paper.

Time goes by pretty good. I mean, I'm young and it's a funny thing about us humans, but we learn how to adapt, so eventually it doesn't even seem like I'm in the hole. I stay busy, go to the yard for one and a half hours twice a week, watch TV shows in the evening, get drunk once a week—everything seems all right. Then one day I'm awakened by a loud boom and the building is shaking. It had been raining the past couple of days with lightning and thunder, but as humid as it gets, it was a welcome relief. Anyhow, lightning hit the main power transformer and it's a blackout in the whole prison. It's not a big thing. We've had power outages before, but this one goes on and we're getting sack lunches three times a day. After about a week, the National Guard brings in generators and we stay locked down in our cells for three weeks. Not just us in Ad Seg, but the whole prison. You could look out the front windows and see the yard on the mainline. It was kind of eerie to see people walking around in military uniforms. The guys start talking.

And there's this old clause in the Inmates' Rights Title 15 Handbook that states, "If ever an invasion by foreign or domestic enemies, inmates are to be exterminated to prevent treason or a coup." At least that was one of the rumors. But then, as usual, things settled down and we're back to our normal program. For the next few months, things are quiet. Then some words were exchanged one day between one of the Nortenos and a brother named Indio from El Sereno, a gang in Northeast Los Angeles.

The story is that one day, a Norteno was going to the showers and he stopped in front of a homeboy's cell. He tried to toss a handmade bomb into the cell but it didn't light. The cops see him and bust him. These bombs were made from match heads. Back in those days, every week they would pass out supplies like soap, toilet paper, envelopes, writing paper, pens, and pencils, and also two packets of tobacco and two books of matches. Not everyone smoked but you could use the tobacco to bargain with. Hey, it wasn't Turkish blend but it was free and if you smoked you couldn't beat that deal. But as for the matches, you could use them for all kinds of stuff. You could even cook with them. Chente from Eighteenth Street was our resident chef and everyone would save something from our daily meals and Gus or Mumbles would take it to him. Then that evening, Chente would make firebombs from toilet paper.

The toilet paper Sterno is what we used to cook. Chente had scraped the paint off a section of his bunk and polished it with Ajax. He would light a couple of bombs underneath. Once it got hot, he would use butter he saved from breakfast and toss on whatever meat, beans, or rice we saved. They sold tortillas in the commissary and everyone who donated to the cause would receive one of those delicious hot burritos that evening as a late-night snack. You could smell the grill every evening and your stomach would growl. I miss those burritos as well as the comradery that went with them.

About this time, Gus and Mumbles came around collecting books of matches. So everyone gave them up. One morning during showers, we heard a big boom and the building shook. Right away, dudes were saying, "Not again," thinking it was another transformer. But it was sunny outside and the lights didn't go out. So I grab my mirror and I can see all the way to the end of the tier that the cops were wrestling with a guy from Harpys, a barrio in LA. And I could see pieces of mattress and other stuff smoldering on the tier and smoke coming out of a cell. Once the cops get the homie in cuffs, all the other cops who responded to the alarm open the cell and pull out this dude who's screaming and has all kinds of cuts and burns on him. They put him on a stretcher and take him to the hospital. The guy made it but he had some bald spots. What happened was payback for that Norteno who tried to blow up the homie. I guess our bomb lit and worked.

I picked up a couple of write-ups for winemaking, so my SHU term keeps getting extended. It's a trip, but after a while you don't even think about the mainline because you have developed a program. I know guys who have spent twenty to thirty years in the hole. It's all they know. I recently heard they're letting a bunch of dudes out because it's considered cruel and inhumane treatment. What I did see with my own eyes was a homeboy named Cornfed from the Aryan Brotherhood who spent twenty-seven years in the SHU. He dropped out of the Brand (the Aryan Brotherhood) and he was sent to Minnesota, which is beautiful country. Sure it's cold in the winter, but summer and fall are beautiful. Well, Corn-fed gets there after spending all that time in the SHU and it was kind of heartbreaking just watching him get reacclimated to the outside world. I mean the guy went to the yard and just fell to his knees in the lush green grass. He took his shoes and socks off and just stretched out. He laid out there for a couple of hours enjoying the warmth of the sun and the sounds of nature. And that was just going from the SHU to mainline. He's got a couple of life sentences to serve, but I hope one day he will get to see the real outside. It's a shame because he's got so much talent with oil paints and pastels. I've got some of his artwork and you would think they're so nice they belong in a museum.

One day we go to the yard for our twenty-five laps around the yard. That wasn't a prison rule. That was an EME rule. Everyone had to do twenty-five laps. So after our laps, my homeboy Eugene "Spider" Lopez from Logan wants to stroll around and chop it up (tell war stories). So we're walking back and forth talking. You got some homies playing cards, some on the pull-up and dip bars, and some doing just like us—enjoying the company.

Then all of a sudden the homeboy Crow from Varrio Nuevo Estrada (VNE, one of the oldest neighborhoods in Los Angeles) jumps up from the card table, holding his neck, and Marciano (yeah, the same guy I had the beef with) is walking away real fast. Spider grabs me real quick and pulls me out of Marciano's path. He says, "Watch it, homie. He's got a razor blade." All the fellas on the yard are on alert. The brothers Danny Boy from Hazard (a gang near downtown Los Angeles) and Sleepy from Wilmas (a gang located in Wilmington, California) are on the yard with us. They go to the fence to talk to Chuy, Angel Stump, and Indio, who are on the yard next to us. After discovering that no one has a shank on the yard, they tell Tomas from Placentia and Feo from Venice to take off on him. So they do. And after about five minutes of beating him down, they leave him on the ground. The brothers are still huddled by the fence and Spider is with them. Then I see Sleepy from Wilmas go talk to Gato Marquez (who would later become a brother and end up being killed down in Mexico).

Anyhow, Spider comes to me and says, "You and Gato are going to take off on him, okay. That's the punk who took it upon himself to cut you with a blade and now he did it again."

What happened was each tier back there was run like its own little village. Each had its cook, winemaker, transporters (guys who ran fishlines), and so on. Well, just like the burritos, when it came to the wine, everyone who donated to the cause got an issue. Well, it just so happened that Marciano had purchased a box of sugar from the commissary to throw into the tier's batch. He was on the third tier, the tier that Crow was tier tender on. And it just so happens that the same evening that the wine was ready and they were going to pass it out, the brother Rene "Boxer" Enriquez came to the hole. So Crow and Bobby Montenegro from Hoyo Maravilla (East Los Angeles), who was the other tier tender, gave Boxer Marciano's issue. That's because a Big Homie like Boxer at the time always took priority over rank-and-file inmates like us.

So, of course, Bobby and Crow tell Marciano that he'll be on the next issue of wine. But he doesn't want to hear that. He takes it upon himself to take revenge. So here we are.

Now, Gato also has a history. He was once my cellie in Soledad for a short time, but the guy was a pro boxer. He was rumored to have fought Roberto Duran back in the early days.

Anyhow, Gato tells me to distract Marciano but to be careful because he still has the razor blade. So I walk toward Marciano and I'm talking shit to him. "You coward. You had to do it again. Why can't you fight clean?" And so on. Gato creeps up on his blind side and hits him solid on the chin. I'm standing right there and I see Marciano's lights go out. As he's going down, me and Gato are just keeping him up with our blows. Finally he goes down and the gun tower wakes up: "Everybody down." Oh, yeah, another EME rule was that you couldn't lay down until they fired the Mini-14. There were two weapons in the towers—a Ruger Mini-14 and a shotgun. There's a lot of homies running around with birdshot from back in the day because the gunner always fired the shotgun first.

That day was our lucky day. The gunner fired a round from his Mini-14 at the wall. But me and Gato continue to kick Marciano, so they fire a round by Gato and he lays down. Then they fire one by my foot and I lay down. There's about twenty cops at the gate who responded but they don't want to come onto the yard, so they tell us to carry Marciano to the gate. But neither of us is moving. So they start yelling at Marciano, "Hey, get up. Come to the gate." This goes on for about five minutes and Marciano starts to come out of it and he looks like a baby deer trying to stand up. He just can't quite get his legs under him. After a couple of tries, he finally makes it to the gate and they put him on a stretcher and cart him off.

They call Gato and he goes to the gate and gets cuffed up. I'm called next and Spider yells, "Stay down, little homie." So I smile at him. I'm still smiling as they cuff me up and pull me off the yard. On the next yard over, I see Angel Stump, who nods his head, and I see Indio, who smiles at me. Then I see Chuy, who looks at me and puts his head down. That was his homeboy who just got sliced by the same guy who had done me. After this event, Marciano checked in (requested protective custody).

So I never did kill him myself.

Not long after all that, the SHU was closing in Old Folsom so they sent a bunch of us to San Quentin. I drove up about November of 1986. I'm put in Northblock, AC side, fourth tier. San Quentin is another place that there is no mistaking that it's a prison. High walls, catwalks everywhere. There's a lower yard and an upper yard, which is where the SHU housing units were—Badger, Northblock, Alpine, Donner, and Carson and the Adjustment Center. I got to reside in three of these fine establishments. Death Row was housed in Northblock, but that's just on the top floor. The five tiers below that were all SHU and, man, if Folsom was like a village, San Quentin was like a jungle. It's loud and you can feel the energy. There's no tier tenders here. The cops do all the work. I'm there about ten minutes when a fishline parks right in front of my cell. Like a suitor picking up a date, there's a kite tied to it. So I take it off and read it. It's from Ernie Lopez from Hoyo Maravilla. He's asking the usual—who are you, where you coming from? So I yell out, "I don't have a pen." He tugs the line twice and I pull it. There's a pen and paper attached, so I give him the scoop and he gets back with yard times, shower days, which brothers are on the tier. He wrote that Tati Torres from Wilmas was there, as well as Tablas from Florencia 13. And that's pretty much all it takes to settle in.

Over the next couple of days we go to classification and get cleared for the yard. Northblock's yard is under the pavilion on the upper yard. It's fenced in and split down the middle, so you have one side of the building on one yard, and the other side of the building on the other.

I go out and meet Ernie in person and a whole cast of characters. There's Joker from Varrio Nuevo Estrada near downtown LA, Caveman from Ontario Black Angels in Riverside County, Perico from Primera Flats. There's also Aryan Brotherhood and woods (peckerwoods who are white inmates who associate and are allies with the Mexican Mafia). Their homies on the yard were Fat Chili, Big Frank, Billy "Hoss" Frisbee from Sacramento, and Buzzard. The really senior-ranking EME brothers there were Tablas Castellanos, Tati Torres, Spider from Hoyo, Tio Pio (Ben Topo Peters), Arty Guzman from King Kobras, as well as Carlos Dias and George Ruiz. And like always, I've got a big homeboy there as well. This time it's Jessie Moreno. The last time I saw him was in Soledad. The homeboys from San Diego pull me up and tell me that they'll get at me and shoot me a couple of things until I get my property.

One evening just before Christmas in 1986, I hear music . . . it's a Christmas carol. Then all of a sudden I hear singing. I know it's not the fellas singing from their cells. Someone yells out, "It's the carolers." And all hell breaks loose. People start cussing at them, flooding the tier, lighting toilet paper rolls and throwing them at the carolers. It was crazy. I mean, I'm no saint but I felt really bad. I had not spent a Christmas at home with my family for eight years. And I'm not gonna lie. Some of those Christmas shows would choke me up.

When I asked my neighbor Tablas why they were doing that, he just said, "To cover the pain, little homie."

17

Plastic Knives

Well, after the holidays were over, I went to Unit Committee and was told that my SHU term was almost up and that I'd be sent to Max B. This was a brainstorm that the Department of Corrections came up with back in those days. This was 1987, right after the year of all those gang wars. Even though there were "peace treaties" being worked out, you still had a lot of hot spots—Tracy (Deuel Vocational Training Center, also known as the Gladiator School), Tehachapi, and San Quentin. The worst of the fighting may have been over but there was still a lot of bad blood. It wasn't like playing Army in the backyard. You were risking your life and people were losing friends.

The California Department of Corrections thought that if they take those players who were involved in the violence and are just finishing their SHU terms, they can put them all on the same yard and see if they will behave. That's where they were sending me— Max B.

"Get yours or get got"; that was the common attitude. When I go back to T Yard, I tell my homeboys, "I'm going to Max B."

So they tell me that when I get there in East Block, I should look for Macky from Florencia. He's on the third tier, Bayside, and made a fishline and he'd get at me. They told me, "Be ready. It's mandatory you get off on them before they get off on you. Macky will tell you who to hit."

When we get up to the second tier, there's a gate at the end of all the tiers. So when a cop pulls out his keys to open the gate, someone hollers "Radio," meaning cops are coming down the tier. So that warning is passed down the tier just in case you're doing something in your cell that you're not supposed to be doing.

There's like fifty cells on each tier; half are on the front bar and half are on the back bar. These are the bars that the cops slide open by handle to unlock the doors. You have the locks on your cell door, then the bar on top has a notch that holds your door closed as well. Anyhow, they take me to my cell. One cop unlocks my cell and the other slides the bar and I walk in. After I hear them leave, I wait a couple of minutes and holler out, "Macky."

Someone calls back, "Yeah, who's that?" So I tell him and what cell I'm in.

He says, "Okay. Make a line."

In a few minutes a line pulls up in front of my door. I grab it and the guy on the other end tugs it twice and I pull it. There's a kite on it, so I take it off and read it. "What's up, Nite Owl. My name is Chino for Pacoima (a neighborhood in the San Fernando Valley). I'm a couple of cells down, so when we fish, pull the line quick. We have a couple of busters between us and they're snagging lines, okay?" At least this guy has the forethought to send a pen. So I write back, "Mucho gusto. I was told to get at

Macky. Is he nearby?" After he reads it he says, "Let me go. I'll get back to you." When you send a kite on a fishline, you're "flying a kite." If Nortenos saw something that looked like a weapon, they would try to snag the line. They knew a weapon would probably be used against them.

Eastblock has their Seg Yard on the Bayside—that's the San Francisco Bay. It's got a huge wall all the way around it made of concrete blocks. There's a gun tower outside the wall and a cat-walk (gun rail) all along the front of the building about twenty-five to thirty feet high. Inside this cement fishbowl, there are six yards all separated by cyclone fences twenty feet high with razor wire along the top. Two of the yards are Max B. One yard is just for the Nortenos and the black inmates, and the other three are for Surenos and white inmates.

When I get to the yard, the cops take off my cuffs and there are two Mexicans and two blacks on my yard. One Mexican comes up to me and asks, "Are you Nite Owl?"

I'm a little cautious and get ready for anything before I answer, "I'm Nite Owl."

"Cool, homie," he says. "I'm Chino and this is another Nite Owl, from Artesia" (a Los Angeles gang neighborhood). After they ask when my property is arriving and whether I need any-thing, they explain to me that the homies upstairs are making pieces for us.

Just to get myself familiar with the enemy, we walk the whole yard and they point out some people—Manos and Babo, both of them Nuestra Familia, and a guy named Chief from the Black Guerilla Family. They tell me to be especially careful of these three guys.

That evening, the homie Chino yells out, "Nite Owl, I'm coming at you," and shoots me a line. I grab it and he says, "I'm shooting you some coffee and tobacco as well as hair grease and lotion and a couple of soups."

It's all wrapped up in a tube about an inch wide. Unlike Folsom, which just has bars, San Quentin has mesh on its bars, so fishing was a little different. There was about a half-inch gap at the bottom of the door and you could slide magazines and newspapers under that. To get stuff under the door, the procedure was to roll it up into a tube. If it was anything bigger, we used what we called the "mouse hole." This was a roughly two-inch-by-two-inch gap at the edge of the door. I untie everything and tell him "Gracias," and he pulls his line back. I sit down and start opening the packages. One tube had a few shots of coffee. Another had tobacco, rolling paper, and matches. Two others were about six inches long containing crushed-up Top Ramen soup and seasoning packets.

The last tube was about eight inches long and contained hair grease, a note, and a six-inch shank. The note said, "Welcome aboard, little homie. I'm Macky from Florencia. Here's a few things to make you comfortable as well as your piece. I hope it brings you honor. The next yard, Chino and Nite Owl are gonna get off on the blacks on your yard. You are to wait for your target. There are some more homies coming, so hang tight, okay. When you get the word, just hoop the piece and handle your business. All right, then, homie, have a good evening and let me know if you need anything else. With respect—Macky." Thoughtful.

But "hoop" the piece? I've never hooped, or kiestered, anything in my life. But now I've got to stick this six-inch plastic knife up my ass? I'm looking at it and I'm kind of laughing. So I say fuck it. I've got plastic to wrap it with. I melt it shut, grease the end, go to the toilet, bend over at the waist, and push. Motherfucker. This shit hurts. This is killing me. Fuck this. So I shoot Chino a kite and tell him, "It don't fit."

He gets back and asks, "Is this your first time?" He tells me, "Lay on your bed sideways and just relax. Push a little at a time and it will go." I try. Now I'm starting to think these dudes are fucking with me.

Well, the next day is yard, so I hide the piece in my mattress and go to the yard. Nite Owl and Chino are there as well as the two blacks. Now, each yard has a toilet, a urinal, and a shower with a small wall around it about three feet high for privacy. Chino tells me to keep point, so I'm watching the cop on the gun rail as well as the blacks. Chino goes first and squats down by the wall and poops out his piece. Next goes Nite Owl and, damn, they made it look easy.

I asked them, "Didn't that hurt?"

"No. You have to practice. Didn't you bring yours?"

I told them I hid it in my mattress. They said never to do that again. "If the cops go in your cell and find it, that's your ass." So I say okay.

Back to the matter at hand, the blacks on our yard are all the way on the far side of the yard. They see Chino and the other Nite Owl too, and since it's just the homies and me and the two of them, guess who is in the crosshairs. So they're keeping their distance. We spend the whole yard time walking laps and when it's close to yard recall, one of the blacks ducks in to use the bathroom and the other one keeps walking. Nite Owl follows one. When the other gets done and comes out of the bathroom, me and Chino get him. I'm holding the guy and Chino is sticking him. Nite Owl is on the other one. When the gunner sees all the commotion, he starts shooting. Me and Chino lay down and the black guy by us runs to the gate. But Nite Owl still has the other one and is putting in work.

The gunner fires two shots and then one more. The third round hits the wall by Nite Owl's face, missing him by a frog hair. The bullet ricochets off the wall and shrapnel catches Nite Owl and the other guy on the side of their heads and faces. Finally everyone is down and taken off the yard. The next time I'd see Nite Owl, it would be in Pelican Bay. By then, he'd become a brother in the EME. I never saw Chino again.

But now I'm up at bat. That evening I try to hoop the damned piece and it's not getting easier. It was, and still is, a part of prison life. But it's not going and I'm getting frustrated. So eventually I just say fuck it and I take the piece and cut off about two inches. It still hurt but at least it was in.

I'm on the yard and there's no one I recognize, so I'm on my own. Finally this Mexican guy comes out and says, "You Nite Owl?" I told him I was. He says, "Here," and gives me a kite. Since Chino and the other Nite Owl left, there was no one who could fish with me, so my homie says this guy is supposed to help me and that we're to hit Chief, the BGF guy from Oakland. I look over and see that Chief is playing basketball with three other dudes and he's fucking huge. He's six feet four inches, about 235 pounds, and I'm all of five feet seven inches and about 155 pounds on a rainy day. But hey. It's for the cause.

I tell the dude to keep point and I squat down and unsheathe my sword. So we start walking laps and after about thirty minutes Chief and the ballers take a water break. So I stroll over, get pumped, and make my move. I rush Chief and catch him right in the center of his chest. He throws a punch on reflex that catches me on the forehead and backs me up about five steps. I literally lost a shoe from that punch.

Chief puts his hands to his chest and lifts his shirt. I make another move but the gunner shoots and yells, "Drop the weapon." Everyone lays down on the ground. I turn and throw the knife over the wall. The cop fires another round at my foot so I lay down too. They come pull us off the yard and I get another eighteen months in the SHU. I get the official write-up later and it says the "weapon was found amongst the rocks by the bay."

I'll put you up on a secret. In the history of doing hits with those plastic knives, you probably have three or four people get killed. Sure, you can take an eye out if you're lucky. But nobody ever really got hurt that I ever seen. It was all just for principle. Even the dudes that Chino and Nite Owl hit weren't seriously hurt. But going through the motions showed that you had heart. It conditioned soldiers to be battle-ready even if you had live rounds being fired, because one day you would be called upon or find yourself in a situation to put in real work.

Oh, by the way. The date for that write-up was 2/8/87. Yeah, another birthday in the big-city jail.

18

Real Great Dudes

After that, I get moved up to the fourth tier, Bayside. I'm put in cell 401, the first cell on the tier. The first thing that strikes me when I get to my new apartment is the view. Oh, my god, I can see the whole bay, from the Oakland Bay Bridge to the San Rafael Bridge, the boats and the ferries. In fact, one of the ferries hits his horn every time he goes by and you can see him waving to the prison. For the next eight months, this is home. I've got Buzzard from El Monte below me, Macky next to him, and Bobby from Hoyo Maravilla behind me. We can talk and fish through the vent. Angel from Pacoima, Diablo from Eighteenth Street, and Psycho from Little Valley. These are all my neighbors and yard partners. Over the next few months the program goes as usual. A few hits go down, but nothing special. My grandmother writes to tell me that my mom and dad have moved back from Hawaii, but not much else.

Then one day in September I'm laying on my bed watching TV, when I hear a bunch of keys coming up the stairs. Now it's my job as the first cell to give the heads-up to the rest of the tier. So I holler, "Radio."

Anyhow, the gate flies open. In fact, from the third tier up the gates fly open.

"It's a raid!"

The cops arrive in droves. The two that stop at my door tell me to cuff up. One of them is a black officer named Jamison. He's talking shit and asking me, "Why you yell radio, snitch? What are you, the tier rat?" This guy won't stop. He just keeps going on and on and going through my stuff and tossing it around. I'm cuffed to the rail in front of my cell. He looks at me and says, "Ooops," as he drops my toothbrush into the toilet. I just laugh and shake my head. Then he gets to my pictures, pictures sent to me over the past couple of years by friends and family. It's all I have from home.

Jamison comes to a picture of my mom when she was younger that my grandma sent me. And he starts making crude remarks.

"Oooh, who's this? Man, I'd fuck her, wouldn't you?" And he shows the picture to the other cop.

The other cop just tells him, "Let's just get this done. We have a long day."

But Jamison won't stop. He keeps going on and on about my mom's picture and then he rubs it on his crotch. That's when I go off.

"That's my mom, motherfucker." I lunge at him but I'm cuffed to the rail so I don't go anywhere.

Things are getting heated so the other cop tells Jamison, "Cool it." He took the picture away from Jamison.

I'm hot. This asshole just disrespected Mom. I'm mad dogging him as they come out of my cell. Jamison looks at me and smiles. Then he says, "What? Are you mad now?"

So I kicked him. You only get one of those because now I've got about ten cops on top of me. Remember, I'm still cuffed to the rail. So they got me stretched. They put leg shackles on me and I start catching punches and kicks. Finally they disconnect me from the rail and they carry me facedown like a log, one cop on each limb. And I open every gate four flights down with my head. When we get to the bottom tier, I'm thrown into a cage and the leg shackles are taken off.

Jamison is there still talking shit and we're in each other's face. Then Lieutenant Diamond comes up to me and asks, "What's going on, Corona?" So I run it down and say the dude was disrespecting my mother's picture. Diamond asks the cops if this is true. Jamison is hopping around like an idiot, saying, "He kicked me." But the other cop just nods his head and says, "It got a little out of hand."

"Go see the nurse," Lieutenant Diamond tells Jamison.

Diamond tells me, "Look, I know sometimes some of my officers don't exactly act professional. But I can't have inmates running around kicking them. So I'm going to have to write you up. But he's not hurt so it's not going to be a serious one. Next time just control yourself and let me know if you're having issues with one of my officers."

I get seen by the nurse, then I'm shackled up and escorted to the Adjustment Center—the hole within the hole. This is where they keep the "cream of the crop," dudes who have done serious shit as well as those from Death Row who are "Administrative Problems."

I was thrown into a cold cell. These are cells in the back of the first tier. They're double-doored so it's basically a cell within a cell. The only thing in there is a cement slab with a mattress and sheet and a toilet. There's a sink, but it doesn't work. They keep you in your boxer shorts and T-shirt, which is the reason they call it a cold cell.

I can't get nothing to read over the next few days. And I found a curious-looking short curly hair in my food. After that, I was careful about what I ate. After a week of being there, I hear them put someone in the cell next to me. And the cops are real respectful to him. "If you need anything, let us know," they said. "As soon as there's an opening, we'll move you to another cell."

Whoever it was said, "Okay." Then he asks out loud, "Who's here?" I hear a couple of names called out and the new guy next door says, "Okay. Let them know I'm here."

So I'm just laying there. I didn't have many friends growing up, so I learned how to play with myself really well. After a while, I get up to take a leak and when I flush, the guy next to me says, "Hey, who's over there?" So I say, "Nite Owl de Posole." And he says, "What's up, Nite Owl? Soy Darryl from Ontario Black Angels." We start talking and he asks how long I've been back here and what did I do. And then he asks me if I have anything to read. "Nah, homie," I said. "I don't have shit. All I have is a sheet. I guess they want me to hang myself." He starts laughing and then says, "Man, that's bullshit." Then he tells me he spent two months here two years ago. Then he left for another prison and now he's back here for court.

About that time the cops come by with some stuff for him and he tells them, "Here, give the guy next door this. You guys ain't right. Give him a blanket and some clothes." So the cops come over to me and give me a book, a blanket, and a jumpsuit and they say, "From your neighbor next door." So I thank Darryl.

Over the next couple of days we get to know each other. I realize this homie is sharp. And he has some very empowering views on the betterment of our people.

After a few days they come to move Darryl. But before he leaves, he stops by my cell to look at me. "Here's some things, little homie," he says. "I'm moving upstairs. Do you want to come up to my tier?" I said, "Yeah. If I can." So trip on this. The next day I'm told to pack all my treasures and I'm moved up to the second tier chapel side about a cell over from Darryl. When I get settled in, Darryl calls out, "Tecolote ("owl" in Spanish), are you okay?" I tell him, "Now I am." Then he tells me we got some more homies on the tier and he introduces me to them. There's Mon from Jardin (a gang from Southeast LA), Chato from Arizona Maravilla from East LA, a white guy next door named John Sapp, and another white guy down the tier named Curt Kirkpatrick. Everyone says hello and I'm told to make a line and then sent a few things to hold me until my property gets there.

After a few days I get cleared for the yard and go out to meet the fellas. The Adjustment Center yards are between Northblock and the Adjustment Center. And like I said, these dudes were true gangsters. As it turns out, Darryl was a full-blown brother in the Mexican Mafia, as were Mon and Chato. The other brothers I met were Cuate from La Rana (harbor area), Jessie Bird Gonzalez from Puente in the San Gabriel Valley, Tommy Moreno from Norwalk in Southeast LA, Raul "Huero Sherm" Leon from Shelltown in San Diego, Nuchie from Indio, and Mando from Ontario. There was also Curt Low from the Aryan Brotherhood and John Sapp, who I already mentioned was my immediate neighbor. Sapp was a hit man. I came into possession of some of his transcripts and he did some really gruesome things for the Hells Angels. We became good friends because I apparently reminded him of his stepson. Like I said, these dudes are real.

Mon is running the show and the homie runs a tight ship. Under his rule, coming to the yard is mandatory. So is running twenty-five laps when you first hit the yard. After that, we have an organized workout for about an hour. Then you get thirty minutes to socialize. These are Mon's rules, not the prison's.

I meet everyone and after the workout we start talking and sharing war stories. Darryl tells me about some black guy he smoked during a peace treaty meeting. Also, Chato is a real character. He's on Death Row for killing nine people. He's a big ol' dude, so he can be really intimidating when you first meet him. But once you get to know him, he's a real great dude. He used to call me Peludo because at twenty-three years old, I had a small tuft of hair in the middle of my chest. But everyone said I looked too young to have it. So Chato would come up to me and put the back of his hand on my chest and start shaking his leg and rolling his eyes. Everyone would get a kick out of that.

Jessie Bird was on Death Row because he killed a cop during a raid. Curt Low, the AB member, was on Death Row because he cut a guy's head off with a lawn mower blade. Huero Sherm and Mando would later become EME members.

After about a week, an AB dude named Blue arrives on the yard. At that time he was the shot caller for the AB. I found out that he became legendary for hiding a small pistol up his butt when he went to court one day and pulling it out and taking the cops who were escorting him hostage. So, as you can see, I'm no longer in high school. I've just entered a university and my major is how to be a real gangster. Over the next few months I get schooled on how to make pieces from real steel or plastic with metal tips. Darryl shows me how to make a crossbow. Then he tells me about a zip gun he was given when he was in Carson block. They told him to blast this guy that they were after. So when Darryl comes out to shower, he stops in front of the guy's cell and tries to blast the dude. But the bullets are no good because they're so old. Anyhow, I'm soaking all this stuff up like a sponge. Class is in session and I'm front and center.

I don't want to glorify this lifestyle in any way, shape, or form because it's nothing to be proud of. My life has caused nothing but pain and misery for a lot of people, especially my family. Yeah, sure I've been on my own since I was thirteen, but your mother always worries about you and loves you. And my own brothers and sister don't know me because I've been away for so long. This is not to mention all the lives I will affect when I start working for the Arellanos. But at this time, these men are the only family I know and we share a true bond. These guys know I'm not getting any mail or money from home, so they're looking out for me. Shit, my neighbor John Sapp, who allegedly killed twenty-nine people, is buying me cigarettes every month. And the rest of the homies shoot commissary my way as well. Not out of fear or because they have to, but out of love for me. So this is where I find my loyalty.

One day we come to the yard and Mon calls me and Nuchie over. He asks both of us if we ever thought about "stepping up" (becoming a brother). We both say sure we have. So he says, "A suspected rat just drove up." This rat was named Willie Boy and he happened to be an EME member. Mon and the other brothers talked it over and they decided they would give me and Nuchie the opportunity to earn some "eagle feathers."

We already knew it was taboo for non-EME members to kill a member, but all the brothers on the yard were being called to court at the same time for a junta (a meeting). But they didn't want to miss the opportunity to kill Willie Boy if they were gone and he were to show up on the yard. If Willie Boy came out before the other brothers left, Nuchie and I would still get our chance to kill him. Nuchie and I both agreed to do it. Mon then tells us to be ready and not to say anything to anybody. So for the next couple of days we wait to see if Willie comes upstairs. Soon after, I get a kite from Darryl with a big eight-inch shank and he tells me, "Start practicing." Here we go again. These dudes are determined to wreck somebody's butthole. I don't want to miss the chance to "step up," so I'm trying my damnedest.

Anyhow, I get to the yard and Nuchie is there. He asks, "Are you good?" I say yeah and he says, "Me too." We're both armed. So now we're waiting to see if this guy comes out. By now, everyone is on the yard except Willie Boy. Mon asks the cop if Willie Boy got cleared for the yard.

The cop says, "Yeah. But he won't be coming to this yard."

To us, this means that Willie Boy checked in. He went into protective custody as part of his agreement with the authorities to debrief and spill his guts about everything he knows about the EME. We realized he was a genuine rat and we had every legit reason to kill him.

One more story about a serious dude in the Adjustment Center: There was this well-known cult leader who ran a hippie commune back in the 1960s, convicted of conspiracy to commit murder, nine life sentences, Charles Manson. Anyhow, he was there with us and he had a cell next door to the brother Cuate from La Rana. This hippie white boy gave Cuate a bunch of trinkets over the time they were neighbors—scorpions, spiders, and centipedes all made out of string. Real prison art stuff. He also gave Cuate an autographed picture of himself. One day he gave Cuate a page from a letter.

Cuate read it and asked, "What do you want me to do with this?"

Charlie says to just tear a small piece off the letter and eat it. So Cuate does it and it turns out to be LSD. So Cuate tears it into a bunch of small pieces and brings it to the yard and passes out the papers. Even Mon takes one and Mon never does anything in the way of drugs. But he said back in the 1960s, that was the only drug he liked.

Well, we're all on the yard frying our asses off and the homies start playing basketball. It gets wild during the game because everyone is high and elbows are flying and there's even a couple of busted lips.

So when the cops come for yard recall, the cops start tripping. They ask the homies, "Who got hit?" But everyone is sizzling on acid, so we all start laughing and pointing at the cops, who keep going, "Come on, we just want to get them off the yard so they can get some help."

That makes us laugh even harder. The cops get on the radio and call the lieutenant. The lieutenant comes out and starts acting all hardass. "You better tell me who got hit or you're all getting write-ups." We just couldn't stop laughing. We were already in the Adjustment Center. What were they going to do to us? Send us across the bay to Alcatraz? The lieutenant calls the captain and when he comes out, he takes one look at us and says, "Nobody got hit. These assholes are high. Leave them out there until they sober up."

That night we all got to see something we hadn't seen in years—the stars over the San Francisco Bay.

PART THREE

PROFESSION

19

A Big Enterprise

By the early part of 1992, I was back in prison. This time it was Donovan State Prison in Central California. They arrested me while I was riding my Harley. I was carrying heroin and a meth pipe. By this time, I was a well-known and reliable soldier in the hierarchy. The same day I hit the yard, I got a kite from Sal, the Big Homie that was running that prison at the time. Basically, Sal tells me that I'm now holding the keys to the yard for him. That means that when it comes to matters concerning the EME or their activities, I speak for Sal, and Sal of course is speaking for the Mexican Mafia. I was essentially the chief executive officer of the EME franchise in Donovan. I had become one of the dudes that I had admired and respected for years.

Some time after my arrival, Johnny Romero, a good friend from Shelltown, told me that he was leaving. He'd been transferred to New Folsom, and since I was now "driving the car," he wanted to get some things squared away before he left. Johnny and I went back a long way, so we had a lot to talk about. He asks me to take a walk with him and he starts talking to me in a way that was more serious than he'd ever spoken to me before. We start walking the track and he told me that for years, he'd been taking care of a youngster, guiding and protecting him, as a favor to another Big Homie from "down south." He said that this Big Homie from down south is the real deal. He said that if I agreed to take this youngster, Bugsy, under my wing and keep him from getting hurt or getting into trouble, the Big Homie would take care of me.

I was given that chance of having a lot of prison daddies who guided me and kept me from trouble, so I felt it was my obligation to do the same for the next generation.

As it turned out, Bugsy was a solid young kid. He was smart. He kept himself in good shape and he showed a real willingness to learn. He also happened to have the heart of a lion. He was serving a triple life sentence for homicide. He got dragged into a triple homicide and the guy who dragged him into it turned around and became a confidential informant for the prosecution. So basically, Bugsy would be spending the rest of his natural life in prison. That's a tough thing to face for anybody, but for a nineteen-year-old? Bugsy never showed any bitterness.

Johnny introduced me to Bugsy and I can see right away that he's shy. I remember having been the same way when I was that age and introduced to guys who I'd only heard about on the streets as men who were bigger than life. So it was sort of amusing to see him being shy. Johnny leaves and I tell Bugsy to walk with me around the track. I have some weed and we smoke it as we walk. By the time we circulated the track the first time, I had put him at ease and I could see some of this kid's qualities. Of course I knew he was from Logan Heights, one of the ally gangs to my varrio, and I knew a lot of the people he knew.

But in fact, looking out for him wasn't that big a job. He'd already been schooled by Johnny and his predecessors and it didn't hurt that Bugsy had a good head on his shoulders and had a sense of humor. Soon after we met, Bugsy was transferred to Calipatria State Prison deep in the desert of Southern California. The area is brutally hot, dusty, and miserable in the summer and it doesn't get much better in the winter.

When he told me he was being transferred, I paid off one of the clerks in the office to get some paperwork started to have me transferred there as well. There are a lot of ways to work the system in prison if you know how and can grease the right people. Soon after Bugsy leaves, I'm on the bus to Calipatria. When I got there, I paid off some more people so that Bugsy and I would be celled up together.

By this time, I was getting close to being paroled. But Bugsy and I decided that we needed a program. First things first and that was smuggling dope into the prison. So we set up regular visits with people on the outside and we started moving dope. I also decided that I needed some tattoo work done. I never had a chance to actually sit down and figure out what kind of ink I wanted on me. But I found this little homie in Calipatria, Baby Ray from Keystone, who did some great work that I'd seen on people I spent time with in other prisons and figured he was a good guy to do the ink. So Bugsy and I were just doing easy time and trying to fill up days with any activity we could think of. But I knew I was getting "short on the house," meaning that my parole was coming up and that I'd be leaving.

Then one day Bugsy told me that David Barron was his brother.

Bugsy was David "Popeye" Barron's little brother. In my world, being asked to take care of Barron's brother was like being asked to take care of Bill Clinton's kid. Instantly the job of looking after him had a whole new sense of serious responsibility attached. As well as high visibility with Barron and people at his level in the hierarchy.

Barron had asked Bugsy to ask me if I wanted to go to work for him in Tijuana. At the time, I knew there was stuff going on in Tijuana (we called it TJ) involving the Mexican Mafia and the cartels, but I didn't have any details on what was really going on. I asked Bugsy what I'd be doing for David in Tijuana.

Bugsy said, "Moving big dope." David Barron was working for the Arellano Félix Cartel and he was recruiting people to work for him. There was a lot of money to be made.

At that time, the only things I knew about the cartels was what I'd seen in *Scarface, Carlito's Way,* and *Tequila Sunrise.* I was picturing huge mansions, guys in suits driving Ferraris, and fine women scattered around swimming pools. "Where do I sign up?" I asked him, sort of kidding.

While this notion of working for a cartel was completely alien to me, there seemed to be some possibilities there. By this time, I was twenty-nine years old. I had a wife I'd married between stints in prison who I wasn't very close with and two kids that I was crazy about. I thought about what I'd be doing once I was paroled, but there was nothing on the horizon that seemed worthwhile. I could hit the streets again and sling dope. Party until I passed out? Then go sling more dope. Get a job somewhere on a loading dock driving a forklift again? The things that got me out of bed in the morning as a younger man—the dope, the women, and the partying—no longer seemed as appealing. I'd be acting like a thirty-year-old teenager.

So the more I thought about the possibility of joining a big enterprise like a cartel, the more it seemed like a natural evolution. This may be the last opportunity to actually do something bigger with my life than any alternative I could think of. This next phase could be the big payoff and I could make enough to provide for my kids, at least for a long time while they go through school. And—this was crazy thinking on my part—I could finally do something that would make my father proud of me. I figured once I made enough money working for the Mexicans, I could just walk away. Get out of all of it forever and start fresh.

Needless to say, it was pure fantasy. Wishful, uninformed thinking. What finally steered me toward working for David Barron was the news I soon got from some of my homeboys who were coming through Calipatria. My wife, Tutu, was running around "wide open" all over town. She wasn't even making an attempt to hide her activities. I wasn't even important enough to her to keep it from me.

The day of my release, I was picked up at Calipatria by Bugsy's wife, Veronica, and one of her girlfriends. They drove me to Logan Heights, where I was told that someone would contact me soon. Around five thirty that afternoon, I was told that the person I was waiting for had just crossed the border from Tijuana and would be there soon.

I was nervous and a little frightened by this whole deal. But I gathered up the clothes I thought I'd need, swallowed hard, and waited. Eventually, a clean-cut guy about my height shows up. He's got one of those film noir 1950s pencil mustaches and he's all business. There was nothing about him that would make you think "cartel" when you saw him. He introduces himself as Marcos but he says that I should call him Pato, like everyone else does. I found out later he was married to David Barron's sister. He asked me if I was ready and I said I was. Then he asked me if I had any ID on me. I said I just got out of prison, but my California driver's license was at my mother's house.

He seemed a little put off, so he made a phone call. When he finished he said, "Let's get your ID. But we need to move fast because they're waiting for us."

We shoot over to my mother's house and by the time we get there, it's 7:30 P.M. My mom knew I was coming home and she cooked my favorite food—chili Colorado and Spanish rice. I felt awful. She went to all this trouble and here I was running in and out after eighteen months in prison and not even having the time or good manners to eat the food she cooked. I felt like the most ungrateful bastard on earth.

I told her we had to go and asked her where my license was. She told me it was in her bedroom. So we went in there and she looks at me and says that she has a really bad feeling. There was no hiding anything from her. I felt what she was feeling. There was something not quite right about any of this. She hugged me and then she gave me a blessing. I promised that I'd call her.

When we got back to the kitchen, Pato said, "Go ahead and eat. They can wait a little longer." So Pato and I sat down and wolfed down all that good food until we couldn't eat any more. After we ate, Pato thanks my mother in the nicest way possible and tells her, "Don't worry, senora. He'll be okay. I promise you."

She thanks him and then she blesses him as well. It's a Catholic Mexican ritual where the person giving the blessing makes the sign of the cross on your forehead to bless your thoughts, then over your heart to bless your emotions, and they perform the sign of the cross on your forehead, chest, and both shoulders to symbolize the Father, the Son, and the Holy Spirit. It always made me feel better after she did that. It was a brief, fleeting moment of peace. Or grace. Or maybe a reminder of my mother's love.

We got to the border in no time at all, but it took a long time to get through customs and the usual checks. By this time, whatever fear I had was replaced by simple excitement and curiosity. I got the feeling this was going to be an adventure that only happens once in a lifetime and I didn't want to miss anything or forget even the smallest detail of this night.

Pato and I were getting along so well and speaking so freely that before he realized it, we were at "the office."

"Oh, shit," he said. "I forgot to tell you to *agachate de avestruz*." I asked what that meant. He said, "You were supposed to put your head down between your knees for the last few miles so you wouldn't be able to tell anyone where the house is or how to get there." I told him not to worry. I couldn't remember any of this ride, let alone the street names or where we were. "In case they ask, just tell them you did that, okay?"

He made a call on his cell phone and within a minute a garage door slid open and revealed a large three-car garage and we drive right in. There was a white van and a black Suburban already parked there. As the garage door closes behind us, some guys come into the garage from the back. I recognize a couple of them from jail—Big Smokie and Booboo. The rest are all strangers.

They start making introductions. I meet Puma, a youngster I'll be spending a lot of time with in the next few months, Roach, another guy I'll get to know well, and Big Popeye. Big Popeye should not be confused with Popeye Barron, the boss of this crew and Bugsy's brother. Out of the three, Big Popeye is the one guy in that group you could guess was an actual gangster. You could tell from a combination of the way he carried himself and this hollowed-out, jaded look in his eyes. They were eyes that said they'd seen a lot and could no longer be concerned about the tiny, inconsequential details of life. You'd need to have something big and important for those eyes to take you with even a grain of interest. There was Cottoro, who I would later see in action in Mexico City, and Gorilla, who would eventually get arrested for the murder of Archbishop Ocampo in Guadalajara.

And then there was a huge crew, all from Logan Heights in San Diego, who made up the bulk of our crew in that office—Tarzan, Cougar, Zigzag, Little Smokie, yet another guy named Nite Owl, and Cracks. After the introductions, they asked me about Bugsy and how he was doing. He was their homeboy and they all had a fondness for him. He was like everybody's little brother. As we were talking, Big Popeye's police radio crackles to life. I found out later this was an actual Tijuana police radio. They could hear everything the Tijuana cops said. The radio message said that Big D was on his way. I knew that meant David Barron. Big Popeye said, "Let's get this place cleaned up."

This particular "office" is actually a five-bedroom house with a second floor, a big three-car garage, a backyard with maid's quarters that was turned into a gym, and a basement that I got to see later. When they got the word that David was coming, the whole crew ran around cleaning the place up. Barron was a stickler for hygiene and cleanliness and he was always riding this crew because they lived like pigs. I asked Big Popeye if there was anything I could do, but he said to just kick it. These guys made the mess and they should have known better and not have waited until the last minute to clean the place up.

Big Popeye's radio crackles again and this time it's David asking to have the garage door opened.

Pato, Big Popeye, and I walked out to the garage to greet David. He stepped out of a silver Town Car looking every inch the drug gangster that you see in the movies. He was well dressed, perfectly cut hair, in great physical shape, and had the aura of a guy who was used to being in charge. He was no taller than I am, but he seemed bigger just from the way he carried himself. He smiled and shook my hand and asked me how it felt to be out. I told him it felt great. Then I told him that Bugsy gave me a letter to give him. David took the letter and walked off into a corner to read it. The other guys are talking to me while David is reading and I kept an eye on him to see if he had any reactions. I didn't know what the letter said. For all I knew, the letter could have said, "Take this dude out." Not that I had any reason to think that, but I was in a new world . . . I saw David chuckle a few times, and a few times I could see that he actually got emotional.

When he's done reading, he walks over to me and says, "Thank you, homie, for taking care of my little brother." And then he gives me a big hug. He asked me if I had any money and I told him I had the $200 gate money that they give you when you leave a California prison. I asked him if he wanted it. He laughed and pulled out a knot of American dollars and peeled off $2,500 and handed it to me. "Is that enough?" he asked. "Hell, yeah," I said. "How about pussy? You get any yet?" I told him no. "Not yet." He told Puma, Zigzag, Roach, and Cougar to be ready when he got back. Then he said to Big Popeye regarding me, "Set him up and explain the rules to him." Then David looked at me and asked, "You do know why you're down here, right? What we're doing?" I told him, "To move big dope."

The whole crew was suddenly quiet and I thought I'd said something wrong. It wasn't actually wrong.

"Yeah, we're doing that too. But we're also taking care of business for the Arellano brothers. Putting in a lot of work. Do you have problems getting dirty?" That was slang. He was asking me if I had any issues with killing people.

If I'd said I had a problem with that, I would never have left that house. I had stepped into the lion's den and there was no gracious way of stepping out. Even though I'd only been there an hour, it was already way too long and I already knew way too much. If I didn't sign on right there, I was a liability. And they don't like liabilities floating around loose in the world.

I said, "It's all good," smiling as convincingly as I could while my heart was pounding in my chest and throbbing in my ears.

"Good," he says. "Glad to hear it." The tension in the room dropped by about one hundred percent. They started talking again. "Go with Big Popeye and he'll show you some tools and how to take care of them. I'll be back later."

20

Bullet Hoses

After David left, Big Popeye took me into a room and opened a closet door. There were about twenty rifles in there—AK-47s, AR-15s, and M16s. He asked me if I knew how to operate an AK-47 and I told him that I did. He took one AK out of the rack and checked the condition of a 100-round drum magazine. It was fully loaded. He racked the slide, checked the chamber to make sure it was empty, and he handed it to me. He reached farther into the closet and came up with a semiautomatic pistol chambered for .38 Super.

This is sort of an oddball chambering for that weapon. That weapon is usually chambered for a .45 ACP or sometimes a 9 mm, but I found out later that the cartels and the cops both loved the .38 Super chambering in that gun. One of the reasons is that military-caliber ammunition in Mexico is completely banned. Since the .38 Super is not military ammunition, it's a legal round under Mexican law. Not that they needed to worry about having illegal guns, but that .38 Super chambering is something of a tradition down there and they all grew up shooting it, so it retained its popularity.

He checked the magazine on the .38 Super and then racked the slide to make sure he had an empty chamber and handed me the gun. He rummaged around the closet some more and asked me, "Do you want any hand grenades?" I was a little shocked but tried not to show it. He must have noticed.

"We have a lot of enemies. The Mexican cops. American cops and rival cartels. So you never know when they're going to hit and you have to be ready to hit them back hard."

So I told him I'd take a couple of grenades and he hands me two of them. Later on, he said, he'd show me how to fieldstrip them and clean my weapons. He also said that they had weapons training once a week and that I always needed to keep my weapons clean and ready to use. "A clean weapon can save your life."

He ran the rules down for me. The crew worked for five days straight and then we had two days off. While we were working, we were expected to be at the house twenty-four hours a day waiting for "calls." We couldn't leave without permission and we always had to have our mochilla (our bag with the weapons and grenades) ready to go anytime day or night.

When we were on duty at the house, there was no drinking or doing drugs. When we got our days off, we would use them to take care of whatever personal business we had but we weren't allowed to go off committing crimes or selling drugs. If we wanted to sell drugs, we had to ask David for permission and he needed to know the who, what, where, why, and how we were selling those drugs. The pay was $500 per week and there were bonuses if the brothers thought that we deserved them. Under no circumstances were we allowed to bring anyone to the office.

Big Popeye showed me the rest of the house and said that all the beds were taken right now but not everyone sleeps in the same bed all the time. But, he said, no matter where you sleep, "you keep your guns with you all the time. You never know when we could get hit."

This was basically my indoctrination to "office" life.

The crew was running around getting ready to go out—showering, shaving, putting on their fine clothes, and spraying the place up with cologne. Puma came up to me and gave me a bottle of Polo Sport. I sprayed some on me and he said, "Wait 'til you see these bitches. They're fine. And freaks."

David Barron finally shows up and asks me if I was all set up and squared away. I told him I was. He said we're going out for a little ass tonight but I'd be on duty when we got back and that I'd have a few days off later in the week. He asked me about my clothes and I told him they were at my wife's house but I had no idea who'd be there right now. He laughed and said, "Yeah, I know what you mean." He said he'd give me more money for clothes and I could wait for my days off to buy them. He told everyone to leave their weapons behind and to get into the Suburban. Once we're all loaded up, he yells out, "Agacharse!" So we all duck down with our heads between our knees and he goes roaring out of the garage into the street.

After driving for about five minutes, David said, "Okay. You can look up now." When I did I saw that we were driving on Avenida Sanchez Taboada and heading toward downtown Tijuana. I recognized the area because my homeboys and I would go down there occasionally and hit the clubs on Revolution Avenue. So the area wasn't at all foreign to me.

We pulled into a parking lot and the crew got out all excited and jabbering away. We followed David into a club called Mexico Lindo and as soon as we got in there, I could see there was nothing but an ocean of girls all wearing lingerie and prancing around. It was clear that this wasn't David's first visit or the first time this crew had been there. The crew was welcomed like visiting royalty. They took us to a large booth and we all turned to David for direction. He says, "Okay, cabrones. Two drinks each. Maximum." The crew seemed happy with that. It was obvious that David was enforcing the no drinking or drugging rule. There was something about it that appealed to me. It was the kind of move professionals make. When they asked me for my drink order, I took a pass. David asked me, "Are you sure?" "Yeah," I told him. "I'm sure." When he ordered a Coke, I told the waitress that I'd have a Coke as well.

The place was crammed with beautiful women from all over the world. There were Mexican girls, for sure, but there were black and white girls from the US and Europe, girls from Central and South America, and some from places that I couldn't pin down. No matter where they came from, though, they were stunning. A cute short-haired girl came and sat on my lap. Her most striking feature was a pair of almost unnatural-looking emerald-green eyes. They almost looked like they had a light shining from behind. The combination of those green eyes and thick black hair was amazingly exotic and beautiful. Her name was Desiree, or so she said, and she came from Colombia. She put her hands on my chest and felt the muscles and asked me if I worked out. I told her I did. Every day. One by one, the boys are peeling off with girls and heading upstairs. Although he wasn't rushing us, I could tell that David didn't want us hanging out there all night. He came over and asked if I was okay. I told him everything was just fine.

I asked Desiree if she wanted to go upstairs to a room. She said she had a cousin who had just arrived from Colombia and she didn't want to leave her alone her first night there, so would it be all right if her cousin came with us. That was probably a lie but I didn't care. The more the merrier.

I looked at David and he shrugged and said, "Go ahead if you can handle it." Desiree goes off to get her cousin and a minute later the three of us are upstairs in one of the rooms. It was a huge room with two enormous beds and a hot tub in the corner. Desiree starts filling the hot tub right away and when it was good to go, the three of us got naked and got in. The two of them were amazed to see my tattoos. This was 1993 and tattoos weren't as popular as they are now. Not even with gangsters. In fact, David discouraged people from getting tattoos and he paid to have a few of my more visible ones removed. He was especially concerned about the tear tattoo near my eye. He didn't want any easily visible physical descriptors that could help identify me in case someone saw me doing something that could get me and the crew in trouble. David ran a tight ship.

After messing around in the hot tub, the three of us got into bed and less than a half hour later, there was a knock on the door. I put on my shorts and see that it's David holding a grocery bag. Fun time was over. He tells the girls he's going to pay them in one-dollar bills. The girls looked puzzled but money was money. He asked them how much he owed them and Desiree said $300 apiece. David counted out $600 in singles, paid them, and we left.

Back at the office I found my weapons right where I left them by the couch. There was a blanket and pillow on the couch as well and I figured that would be my bed for the night. Big Smokie was still up; obviously he was working the night shift, ready to answer the phone or the radios if something popped up. I lay down. I had my pistol under the pillow and made sure I had the AK and the grenades within arm's reach. This had been a long, long day. I'd woken up that morning in Calipatria State Prison as a released convict and now I was going to sleep in Tijuana as a hired gunman for one of the most notorious cartels in Mexico. Nobody I knew could claim the kind of day I'd just had. I fell asleep thinking, "You're not in Kansas anymore."

Over the next few days, I started to familiarize myself with the routines at the office. Cottoro, Gorilla, and Big Popeye didn't live at the office the way the rest of the crew did. They arrived in the morning and worked a day shift. The rest of the crew basically did nothing but lay around all day monitoring the radio and lounging around. There was always a lot of radio traffic, but it was all Tijuana police talk that had nothing to do with us. We'd only get interested if something happened that was of interest or concern to David or to the Arellano brothers. I found out that there were three offices. Ours, which was David's office, and then two other ones for Ramon Arellano Félix and Benjamin Arellano Félix, his older brother. Ramon did the day-to-day work of keeping the drugs moving and the pipeline into the US filled. Benjamin was the money guy and the man who was sent out to pour oil on the waters in case there was any trouble with the cops or the local politicians. He was the smooth-talking public face of the Arellano Félix Cartel. The face that was acceptable to some degree to the Mexican public. He didn't look or act like a killer and he always had the right touch of conciliation when he was called upon to make some public announcement.

Other offices dealt mostly with the business of the drug business. We knew practically nothing about them because we were the shooters and enforcers. David and the health and safety of the brothers was our concern.

Puma from Logan Heights in San Diego was one of the first guys on the crew that I got to be friendly with. Although he was only eighteen or nineteen at the time, he was a lot more mature than his age. He grew up in the same kind of circumstances I did and we had the same sort of criminal history—running around his varrio slinging dope and getting himself involved with the local neighborhood gangsters. But he had a very funny side to him. For instance, I worked out almost every day I could, and most mornings at the office, I was in the gym early. One morning I ran into him there. I was there to lift weights. He was there to get high. He asked me if I wanted to smoke weed and I was a little surprised and said no, it was against the rules. He said the rules didn't really apply to weed. Ramon just wanted us to stay away from cocaine, heroin, and PCP, the really hard stuff. That may have been true but I still wasn't about to get high on the job. Puma was skinny. There wasn't much meat on him at all, so I offered to show him how to lift weights. He tried some light weights and gave up. Then he lay down on the bench, held his joint over his chest with fingertips of both hands, and started bench-pressing the joint—making all the noises of a guy trying to bench-press a couple of hundred pounds. "Arrgh. Yeah, this is really giving me a burn." Like I said, he was funny.

When we had days off, Puma and I would try to take them at the same time. Early on in my stay, David came by and gave me and Puma a bunch of money and told us to use our day off to buy some clothes. He gave us each something like $1,000. We got a ride from Big Popeye to the border and we crossed into San Diego. We took the trolley into Logan Heights so he could show me around his neighborhood. Roach let us borrow his truck and we hit all the clothing stores. Since we weren't allowed to dress like gangsters, we went to places like Banana Republic, Old Navy, Fila, Miller's Outpost, and Nike. We bought a bunch of clothes and then went over to Horton Plaza, where we met some girls from Imperial Beach. We took them to the movies and later to a hotel in Chula Vista just off the 5 Freeway.

That's pretty much how we spent our days off. We actually didn't need much in the way of personal items because we had everything taken care of for us. Even when we scored some big bonus money, we never spent much of it. We either put it away or reinvested it by buying some dope and reselling under David's strict supervision and with his okay. Considering what Puma and I would turn into later on, the money wasn't much of a reward for what it cost us in the destruction of our souls and the waste of years of our lives.

When we got back, David wanted to check out the clothes we bought to make sure they met his approval. He was a real micro-manager that way. David was always a sharp dresser and made sure that none of us looked like gangsters or wore stuff that made us too noticeable. David had closets full of high-end Italian shoes and expensive suits even though most of the time when he was in the office he wore jeans and a sweatshirt. Occasionally he'd ask us if we wanted any of his "old" clothes. To him, if something had been in his closet too long and even if he'd never worn them, they were old clothes.

David Barron was always willing to help us learn something that made it safer for us to do our business and not get killed.

The next day, I got a real education from David and a look into the depths of corruption in Tijuana and probably the rest of

Mexico. Big Popeye told us to get our weapons ready and load up in the van. We all got excited thinking this might be a mission but they didn't tell us where we were going. I heard David talking on the radio and he mentioned something about Posole—my own neighborhood. I thought it might have something to do with me or something happening back there.

Big Popeye put me in the Suburban with Big Smokie and we rode off. By this time, they weren't bothering us to get our heads down when we left. We knew where we were and they had to trust us at some point. The neighborhood we lived in was called El Hipodromo and it was located behind the Agua Caliente Race-track. We drove around the track property and turned onto San-chez Taboada Boulevard. We eventually pulled up to a building and parked. I noticed that the front of the building had a lot of double-parked cars all sort of jumbled together. But what caught my attention was the huge Mexican flag hanging off the building and the words POLICIA JUDICIAL FEDERAL. Holy shit. We were at the Federal Police station.

As soon as we park, two federal cops in uniform come up to the Suburban. One of them is carrying an Uzi submachine gun. The other is carrying a Heckler & Koch MP5 submachine gun. Technically, both weapons are machine pistols since they're chambered for pistol ammunition, but most people just call them machine guns. A real machine gun fires a rifle-caliber bullet.

I was so nervous that I never caught their names. Pancho? Nacho? Who knows. All I'm thinking is just don't bust me or kill me. They did neither. They got in the Suburban and Big Popeye drove. Big Smokie is on the police radio talking away. We hit the Via Rapida and catch the highway going to Rosarito. I never thought I'd ever find myself sitting in a car with automatic weapons on my lap and some cops sitting in the back, also armed to the teeth. And all of us not shooting at each other because we were on the same side.

After driving for twenty minutes, we stopped at a gate by the side of the highway. One of the cops got out and unlocked it. We drove through. I saw a sign that says RANCHO .357. We drove up the road for a couple miles and then I saw a bunch of what looked like buildings but with the sides missing. It's just framed two-by-fours but with windows and doors framed out. Beyond the buildings were silhouette targets and the hulks of bullet-riddled cars. We were at some kind of shooting range. A range that the cops were using. What the hell? Smokie is on the radio and tells David that the gate is open and he should come on up.

We dismounted and a few minutes later, one of the cops pulled out his pistol and shot at one of the silhouette targets. The other cop did the same and they both then went forward to check their targets. The cops asked me if we brought any more targets and Smokie says that "CH" was bringing them. This was the first time I'd heard David Barron referred to as CH. Apparently, after a disco shoot-out, Ramon Arellano Félix started calling David Barron "Charles Bronson." Partly because of the way he looked but mostly because of the way he got the two brothers out of the jaws of an assassination attempt by shooting and killing everything that the assassins could throw at them. CH eventually became David's radio call sign and the designation for our "office."

The cops tell Smokie to step up and shoot at a target with his pistol. He does and when he's done, it's my turn. I fire fairly rapidly but carefully and when we go forward, I can see that my grouping was a little wide but that seven out of the ten rounds I fired would have been fatal, or near fatal, center mass chest shots. Not too bad. It was a lot better than Smokie had done and he was impressed. He asked me if I'd fired guns a lot in the past. "A little bit," I told him.

Actually, I grew up around guns. My father and I would often go to the range and shoot shotguns at clay pigeons. He also taught me to shoot .22-caliber pistols and rifles. One time, for my ninth birthday, my dad took me to the base for a war game event they had. He arranged it so that I got to fire an M60 tripod-mounted machine gun. This was a real machine gun that they refer to as a "crew-served" weapon since it has a gunner who does the firing and an assistant who carries the ammo and the tripod and loads the weapon. I didn't want to brag or anything, though. For some reason, I didn't want to expose my hand too much with these cops around.

After we got done shooting the pistols a few more times, Smokie told me to go get my AK. "You ever shoot one of these before?" he asked me. I hadn't and told him so. He walks me through the operating system quickly, showing me how to insert the magazine, rack the slide to load the weapon, and then switch the lever on the receiver that was marked SEMI and AUTO. In SEMI mode, the weapon fires with each pull of the trigger. In AUTO mode, the weapon keeps firing as long as you keep your finger on the trigger—what they call full auto.

I put it on SEMI just to get a feel for the weapon and determine how bad the recoil was. There was definitely recoil but it was very controllable. I put the AK to my shoulder and fired a string of single rounds into a bush. Firing at a bush isn't really marksman-ship of the first order, but it does represent what I might come up against in the real world. And if you can keep your rounds hitting into an area that small, you're basically overwhelming your opponent with firepower.

I got a couple of congratulatory noises from the cops and Smokie. "Try it on full auto," Smokie says. "Do it Bronson-style from the hip." This is not the most accurate way of firing an AK or any weapon, really, but it looks cool. So I flipped the lever to AUTO, braced the stock against me, and unleashed a long string of fire into the same hapless bush. They all hit where I'd want them to hit if this was a gunfight and some guy was taking cover behind the bush. No wild stray shots bouncing around all over the country. It was a rush.

It's amazing how fast you can go through a 100-round magazine when you fire on full auto. Even though I was wearing earplugs, my ears were ringing and I had a huge smile plastered on my face. I ran out of ammo and watched the other guys shoot. I fell in love with the one cop's MP5. Since it fires a smaller, 9 mm pistol-caliber bullet, there's a lot less recoil than with the AK-47 so it's easier to control and you can put a lot of lead on a small target. It's a light weapon, shorter than an AK and a lot handier to use if you have to fire from a car or a confined space like a small room. The other thing about the MP5 is that it has three modes of fire. One is the SEMI mode that fires one round at a time. There's another mode that fires three-round bursts. And then, of course, it has the full-auto mode that will basically empty a thirty magazine in about three seconds if you keep the trigger pressed. Of all the guns we had, that MP5 was my favorite.

A little while later, David and the rest of the crew showed up. David shakes hands with the cops and asks me if I had a chance to shoot yet. I told him I did. Then he asked one of the cops how

I did. "*Este carbon tira bravo*," he said. "This fucker shoots good." Then David looks at me and says, "Let's see what you got." We walk over to the van to get some more ammo. There was maybe 20,000 rounds of AK ammo in two wooden crates. There were also thousands of rounds of 9 mm and .38 Super ammunition. David also brought out these blocky-looking machine pistols— MAC-10s that spew out something like 1,200 rounds a minute. They're not really accurate but they're basically bullet hoses that you can use to spray down a whole room full of people. Except for the .38 Super pistols, none of the guns we used that day were legal in Mexico or the US. They weren't the kinds of guns you could buy at a gun show or, frankly, anyplace in the US.

After we all got reloaded, David said, "I want to see how you guys would approach that car and how you take out the occupants when you get there." He had a couple of the crew guys line up and gave them the signal to attack. They basically rushed the car like a mob and spraying bullets all over the place.

When it was my turn, I approached it a little differently. I put myself in the place of the guys in the car and I thought to myself, what would be the hardest way for them to shoot me if I was approaching the car. So I angled my approach to the car using the C-pillar of the car as their blind spot. Everybody knows that the C-pillar of a car is a big blind spot when you're driving, so it would be the same if someone was standing there shooting at you.

With the AK to my shoulder I crouch low to make myself harder to see and approach from that angle and I use two- and three-round bursts to pin down the occupants. Once I get close enough, I swing around to the front to take out the driver and unload on the rest of the occupants in the car. I had a hundred rounds to play with, so I really let the car have it.

When I was done I looked over at the cops and David and they were all smiling. David asked me, "Where did you learn to shoot like that?" I told him, "I watched a lot of TV when I was in jail." They laughed some more but that was the truth. Then David said, "You keep this up and you'll be putting in work real soon. Remember. No nuts. No glory."

21

The Fat Guy

To us, the mansion was just "The Office." But it was a mansion with a huge atrium, a pool, waterfall, koi pond, and a staff. We had women that cleaned, cooked, and did our laundry and we had local old men who maintained the grounds and did maintenance.

The office was located in one of Tijuana's best neighborhoods. It would be the equivalent of Beverly Hills in Los Angeles, or Sutton Place in New York. Our neighbors were the cream of Tijuana society. They were judges, politicians, millionaire businessmen, and old-money families that made their fortunes a hundred years ago in gold, oil, cattle, and crops.

Of course, everyone in the neighborhood knew exactly what was going on behind the walls of the office. They couldn't help but see the twenty-four-hour heavily armed security force that constantly patrolled the grounds. And how could they possibly not see the caravans of ten to fifteen SUVs, packed with armed men, coming and going in the middle of the night or in broad daylight? But the neighbors kept their mouths shut because we didn't bother them or have any dealings with them. Our business was dope and murder and our enemies were other people whose business was dope and murder.

Occasionally, the two worlds did collide and we had to handle these "legitimate" people who either got in our way or decided to play with fire. Oddly, some of the young people in these wealthy families were fascinated by the life of a narco-terrorist and did business with us. Some did well. Others ended their lives melting in a barrel of acid.

Growing up as a street kid in San Diego, living the life of a millionaire was something I never thought I'd experience. At the time that I raised my hand to join the AFO as a sicario, I didn't care if the price for the life of a king was killing people. The people that Ramon Arellano Félix targeted were no better or worse than we were. They were just adversaries, our opposite numbers in the drug business. Everybody on both sides knew that competition in the drug trade basically comes down to how many people on the other side can we kill before they give up. And that was the goal. Kill as many of them as we can, as fast as we can, until the attrition just wears them down.

Of course, they were trying to do the same to us.

A month after I'd left Calipatria State Prison in California and crossed the border to work for Ramon, David "Popeye" Barron gave me my first assignment.

Like I said, David Barron was a Mexican Mafia brother, but years ago he traveled to Mexico and offered himself up for service to the Arellano Félix brothers, the AFO. Barron had personally killed something close to one hundred people for the AFO. He used everything from pistols, shotguns, rifles, machetes, knives, sledgehammers, chain saws, to plain old meat cleavers. He liked to think of himself as a specialist, a methodical killer with a deep knowledge of the human body. Later, on some of our missions, he'd show me how and where to plunge the knife into a bound man who was screaming for his life.

David pulled me aside one morning and told me that Ramon had ordered two assassinations. I never knew their names. And I didn't need to. All I was told was that these two guys lived in LA and they'd been part of the assassination team that tried to kill Ramon at Christine's discotheque in Puerto Vallarta the year before.

That was the incident that got Ramon Arellano Félix calling David Barron Charles Bronson. Chapo Guzman had sent forty assassins into Christine's to kill Ramon and his brother Benjamin. Hundreds and hundreds of rounds had been fired from both sides during the gunfight between Ramon's people and Guzman's killers. Eight of Ramon's bodyguards were killed, ten of Guzman's assassins were killed, and something like a dozen innocent civilians were killed in Christine's that night.

It was a bloody massacre that should have made headlines all over the world. Or at the very least in the United States, the biggest consumer of the drugs we moved. The fact that it didn't just indicates to me that American society is deluded in thinking that personal drug use is a victimless crime. Every ounce of pot or bindle of cocaine or eight ball of heroin that changes hands on the streets or in an executive suite or an Oscar after-party has blood on it. A lot of it is innocent blood, like the young "civilians" who were killed at Christine's that night.

Ramon needed to show Guzman that even though the assassination had failed, Ramon wasn't about to let any of Chapo's guys live to brag about the tale. And it didn't matter that they were no longer in Mexico. Chapo needed to be sent a message that even his people living in the US would not be safe from the long arm of Ramon's retribution. These two shooters had to die. And I was the one just tasked with killing them.

This was the thing I'd sweated about since I was recruited the month before. This was going to be my first hit. And it was critical to Ramon Arellano Félix that it get done and done right. No fuckups. No arrows pointing back to him. No footprints that could implicate the cartel. It had to be clean and fast. And I was going to be in charge.

One of the people on the target list, a fat, slow-moving shooter, was now living large in LA, dealing drugs for Chapo Guzman and probably feeling safe from any retaliation from the Arellano brothers. After all, he was in the US. And everybody knows that the cartels don't commit murders in the US. It was to our advantage that people kept believing that. The reality is, more killings in the US are committed on orders that originate in Mexico than the cops and media let on. No one wants to talk about how little control they have over who comes in.

Chapo and the Arellanos had been at war for a decade, since 1989, and nobody has any clear idea of the body count on both sides. Thousands.

David gave me $15,000 in "desfanar" money—getaway cash in case something went wrong. If I needed to buy a car, bribe a hotel clerk to give me a room without checking in, or buy a gun on the street, I'd have enough for me and my crew to make it back to Tijuana.

Besides actually killing one or more of my boss's enemies, what I was worrying about was going back to the US. I was a parole violator. I never checked in with my PO after I left Calipatria State Prison. I could get violated just for that. Could I make it across the border into San Diego without a nosy border agent running me through the NCIC? Would some gang cop in LA spot me at a gas station and decide to see what was up?

The truth is, I'd grown up on the streets and had developed ways of how to behave around cops. And I was good at profiling people and analyzing situations that could get too hot for me.

There was no way we could bring our weapons across the border. So David gave me the names of two Border Brothers (Mexican nationals, also known as paisas) who lived in LA. These paisas also knew our targets and they'd be our local facilitators. These US-based locals were part of Ramon Arellano's network of intelligence, communication, and enforcement. They'd set us up with the guns and show us who this fat dealer was and where he lived.

The cartels would not be able to ship a billion dollars of dope into the US every year without a huge network on US soil. It could be anybody. A middle-aged mother handling money and phone calls for the AFO in Palmdale. A construction worker standing outside a Home Depot in LA. A couple of teenagers slinging dope in Compton and keeping an eye out for AFO competitors. A civilian employee of the LAPD. Someone on staff in a city council member's office. A Border Patrol agent. A corrections officer in Pelican Bay State Prison. They can be anywhere and anyone.

David asked me to handpick two guys to go with me. There was no question. I picked the only two of my San Diego homeboys who I could halfway trust to shoot straight and follow orders. They were both only seventeen at the time.

I picked Roach and Puma. Roach was an awesome driver who didn't lose his shit in a gunfight or a police pursuit. Puma was a solid soldier with a lot of heart. They were proven quantities.

When you're working for the Dark Side, you've got nobody to rely on except the guys standing next to you. Going deep into enemy territory, which, face it, is what we were doing, is nothing like gangbanging or hitting up an enemigo from the neighborhood across the boulevard.

I wasn't a gangbanger anymore. I wasn't even just a Mexican Mafia camarada. I was now the sharp tip of the spear of an international criminal organization. And at that level of operation, you're expected to perform like a professional. Excuses only make you dead.

Guzman and the Arellanos were all billionaires. They did what they had to do to keep the other guy from eating into their business.

So at 3:30 P.M. the next day, Puma, Roach, and I waited in line at the San Diego border crossing. Puma was driving a red Toyota pickup truck. Roach and I were in a brand-new white Jetta. Both vehicles had California plates that, if the cops ever ran them, would come back to legally registered owners in California. That's what a billion-dollar organization can buy you—an enormous support system of safe houses, safe registrations, routes of entry and exit, intelligence networks, and all the guns and people required to keep the organization running smooth.

We had people inside the Mexican government that fed us information on American cops working in Mexico. We had people inside the Mexican phone companies that tapped the phones of anybody we wanted. Including the US DEA agents that were working in Mexico. There was nothing we could not know or could not buy.

It turned out I had no reason to sweat crossing into San Diego. The Border Patrol guys saw the plates and barely gave us a second look when we flashed our California-issued driver's licenses. Actually, I didn't even show a driver's license because I didn't have one. I flashed a California DMV-issued identity card.

The border was so loosely enforced that the cartels could move anything they want through it. I had a warrant because I never showed up to my parole meetings. I was in the US law enforcement computer system as a parole jumper. A few keystrokes on a computer would have shown that.

By 6:00 P.M. that afternoon we were in Los Angeles. We checked into a Ramada Inn and called the two Border Brothers at the phone number that David had given me.

An hour later, Chino and Chuy, the two Mexican nationals living illegally in the US, showed up at the room. They were both in their twenties. They brought us our weapons and gave us the briefing on where our targets lived and how they operated.

They brought us a fully automatic Uzi submachine gun equipped with a huge silencer. They also gave us an M1 carbine, a .357 revolver, and a couple of 9 mm semiautomatic pistols.

The carbine is a semiauto weapon that the US military used in World War II. It's a good, reliable weapon that was designed for hard use in combat situations. The Uzi was developed by the Israelis for close-quarter combat. It has a short little barrel that's perfect for using from inside a car or in a room. The problem with the one they gave us was that it had a massive, eighteen-inch silencer on it. That made the handy gun less handy. I didn't want a long barrel getting in the way in case we had to use it from a car or I had to carry it under a shirt.

The way we worked was to use a light-caliber weapon for the

initial engagement and then back that up with the heavier calibers. Basically, the Uzi sprays a lot of lead real fast but it's not that accurate. The procedure is to hose off the opposition and get at least enough holes in them to get them down. Then we finish them off with head shots at close range with the heavy calibers like the .357 Magnum and the .30-caliber bullet of the carbine. Believe it or not, it's hard to kill somebody with a single shot in a gunfight. The only absolute, instant kill shot is in the head. And you need to be close and the target has to be still to get that shot.

It was a point of honor to use the least amount of ammo to kill a guy. The ideal hit was a single shot to the head at close range. When someone came back from a mission and had to use a lot of bullets to get the job done, we'd haze them for wasting ammo. Sometimes, like the guy who killed the police commander in Mexico City, a sicario would apologize for using more than a few rounds to kill his target.

I told Chino to see what he could do about losing the silencer. But I realized the next day he had no idea what I was talking about.

I gave Puma and Roach one hundred dollars to go get some food, and I started thinking how to run this mission based on the information the two Border Brothers had given us.

A few hours later, Roach and Puma came back with a couple of girls they met on the street and they basically partied and screwed until three in the morning, when the girls left.

They were young. And although they didn't say it, they were probably thinking that this could be their last night on earth so why the hell not get loaded and laid. I was thirty at the time. I had already reconciled myself to the fact that I wasn't going to live much longer. Getting drunk and laid wouldn't make me feel any better than I was. Besides, getting loaded is a hazard. It makes you stupid and tired the next day and if I was going to survive, I needed to stay sharp and on my game.

Maybe the best I could hope for was a cartel funeral with a big headstone and a statue of Santa Muerte planted in the dirt over my body. I didn't care. I had nothing holding me to the world of the living. I'd cut myself off from my parents and my siblings. I didn't have a relationship with my wife or children. I was a fugitive from the California justice system. I didn't have a single thing to look forward to or live for. I was already dead.

The next day the two Border Brothers came back and they took us to a canyon in the hills outside of Pomona, California. The guys in the crew that trained me were former Mexican Army or Mexican Federal Police members. They told me that when you prepare for a mission, you have to function-fire your weapons to make sure they work. Then clean them, load them, and make sure nobody else handles the weapon except the guy that's going to use it. That's what I drilled into Puma and Roach.

Then Chuy threw me a curve. He wasn't supposed to be part of the hit team. But he said he wanted in. I don't know why but I figured he probably needed to earn some stripes with Ramon or his gang or the Mexican Mafia. Or all of them. I could see he was like me in a lot of ways. He wanted to prove himself. Even though it all worked out well in the end, I should not have let him be part of the hit team. It was unprofessional.

I assigned Puma the M1 carbine. Chuy got the .357 revolver and Roach got one of the 9 mm semiautos. I was supposed to have the Uzi, but Chino the Border Brother had taken the Uzi to a guy who supposedly knew about guns. This idiot thought the silencer was a flash suppressor that wasn't made right. So he drilled about one hundred holes in the silencer, thinking that was the way flash suppressors work. He basically destroyed the usefulness of the gun.

When we got back to the Ramada, I called David about the Uzi and that I needed another weapon. A few hours later, a fully automatic TEC .22-caliber showed up. It had two forty-round magazines loaded with hollow-point bullets that had been dipped in mercury. The idea was that if the bullets didn't kill the target right away, the mercury would eventually poison him. These rounds were reserved for the fat guy, who we knew for sure was one of the shooters at Christine's discotheque. He was the primary, must-kill target. If we got anybody else connected to him, that was a bonus.

Once we had our weapon situation figured out, we started the surveillance part of the mission.

The street where we'd do our hit was in East LA, not too far from the post office in the LAPD's Hollenbeck Division. That part of LA is about as deep in Sureno gangs and Border Brothers as any part of the city. It's been a spawning ground for street gangs and Mexican Mafia shot callers since before World War II. Legendary EME brothers like Joe "Pegleg" Morgan, Mundo Mendoza, and Alfie Sosa all came from those streets.

We parked where the dealers wouldn't see us watching them. Roach and Puma were in the Toyota. Chuy and I were in the Jetta. We had Tijuana police radios and we were using those to talk to each other. It turned out there were three of Chapo's people working that street. They had rented houses and apartments on both sides of the street. And the way they worked was that they'd hang around in the front yard, looking to the casual observer as just a couple of residents relaxing. But we could see that every few minutes, a car would pull up to the house and wait. One of the dealers would approach the car and serve the drugs.

Then the car would pull off and the guy would go back to sitting in his yard. It was a drive-up franchise for dope—a Burger King for coke, meth, and pot. And this was just one of hundreds, if not thousands, of Chapo Guzman's retail dope outlets all over California and the rest of the country.

"That's him. That's the cabron," Chuy said when the fat dealer first showed himself. I told my guys to memorize his face. He was the guy we needed to kill.

22

Getting It Done Right

He was working with two other guys, both Mexican nationals working for Chapo Guzman. I decided right there to hit all of them. I wanted to go back to the office with a high body count. We watched them dealing most of the day. They were busy.

Once we had the guys' faces, their houses, and how they worked completely memorized, I started looking for ways to get in and out of the street fast. I sent our two Border Brothers away and drove all around the neighborhood with my shooters. We analyzed entry and escape routes. We went through a lot of "what if" scenarios. What if they spot us early and run? What if they have shooters in the houses? Dope houses are a prime target for home invasions from rival gangs, so a smart dealer will always have a security team in place right behind the entrance, with large-caliber weapons. So there was that to think about.

And then there was the issue of what would happen if the cops showed up. The Hollenbeck Police Station is only a few blocks away and cops are driving in and out of the station all day. They could get to us in half a minute once the bullets start flying.

We decided on where to meet up in case something went wrong and we had to scatter. The military calls this a "rally point." We had two rally points in case everything went completely sideways at the first rally point and we needed that secondary fallback position.

Then we started getting deeper into the mechanics of the kill.

You need to do all this groundwork ahead of time if you're in any way serious about committing an assassination and getting away with it. Little gangbangers and hotheads get caught because the only thing they're thinking about is pulling the trigger. An assassin who's worthy of the title knows that pulling the trigger is only about ten percent of the job. The real work is the setup, planning for the "Oh, shit" moment when the plan falls apart, getting in, and getting away with it.

Once we had our scenarios down, I took the crew to a swap meet for our clothes.

We were operating in what the press likes to call a "gang-infested" neighborhood. To us, it's just the neighborhood. None of us grew up in neighborhoods that were not "gang-infested." We know how gangs operate.

What the average guy on the street doesn't know is that when you enter a gang neighborhood, you're being watched. We profile the hell out of everybody that walks through our varrio.

What does your hair say about you? What about those tattoos? We can tell the difference between a tattoo made in prison with sewing needles and shoe polish and the professional ones. We can look at a tattoo and make an accurate guess as to what neighborhood you're from, your status in the gang, if you're a camarada, a shot caller, or a soldado.

I picked out clothes for me and my crew that would send the

local gangsters the message that we were "casual," not gang affiliated.

I picked out a jacket with a hoodie in a different color for each of the team—weird colors like brown, yellow, black, and green. To a gangster, those colors mean nothing. Casuals. The only color that counts to a Sureno is blue. Blue is the color of the Mexican Mafia–affiliated gangs in all of California. Don't get caught in Norteno territory wearing a blue jersey or a blue LA Dodgers ball cap. It could get you killed.

Then sweatpants, shorts to wear under the sweatpants, and T-shirts to wear under the hoodies. This was for the benefit of the cops. The idea was that, right after we did the hit, we strip off the jackets and sweatpants and dump them. After the shooting, the radio call would go out looking for three Hispanics in hoodies and sweatpants. By the time the units got that information, we'd be in T-shirts and shorts, looking like every other Hispanic on the street.

Then I got everyone different-colored bandanas and gloves. The plan was to dump the guns. They were expendable tools. But we couldn't dump them with our prints all over them and we didn't want GSR—gunshot residue—on our hands in case we got stopped and they got curious enough to give us a GSR test. So we got gloves that were thin enough to work a slide, press the mag release button, and anything else we needed to do to keep a gun working in the middle of a firefight but thick enough not to leave GSR on our skin.

We were committed to not getting stopped by the cops. We didn't want to kill them. We thought, they're just working guys like us. But they belonged to a government that wasn't our government. And if it came to it, it was their tough luck that they can't shoot first. We could.

I briefed my guys that after we did the hit and got back in the car, we would reload with topped-up magazines and lock and load for battle with the cops if we had to. I told Roach, the driver, not to drive away fast from the scene. Drive like every other guy on the road so we wouldn't attract attention.

If we did get a cop on our tail, we wanted to be ready to light them up. If a cop car just got behind us, we'd be cool. But if the lights came on, that was our signal to bail out of our car, fire everything we had at the windshield of the cop car, and take off on foot.

We had one more day of surveillance and planning ahead of us. We showed up early in the morning and set up our monitoring of the three dealers.

We had everything we needed in terms of weapons and gear. We had the plan. We were spooled up and ready. All we needed was the opportunity to get these three guys out in the street at the same time.

And then. There it was.

We hadn't planned on doing it that day or at that moment, but it looked like the patron saint of sicarios, Jesus Malverde, had heard the assassin's prayer and gave us the perfect opportunity.

All three of our targets were out in the street serving cars that had pulled up. It was right around 9:00 A.M. on a Monday morning and business was great.

I didn't have to say much to the crew other than "We're doing it now."

Roach drove the car and parked it to within a foot of where we agreed to park it. It was in front of a closed machine shop.

We tied off the bandanas, pulled up our hoodies, grabbed our guns, and started walking the half block to where the three were serving.

I don't know what it's like being in an organized war in an army. But when I stepped out of the car with a full-auto weapon in hand, dressed up in my battle gear and focused on my enemy, I felt an enormous calm. Even though we were moving fast, everything seemed to slow down and I got a sort of tunnel vision. At the same time, I became aware of everything around me in sharp detail.

They were busy selling and we got to about ten feet of them before one of them yells out, "Agua! Agua!" That's the distress call. What he saw were three guys in hoodies and bandanas walking toward them with their weapons raised and fingers on the trigger.

The first guy closest to me wasn't the fat dealer. He looked me in the eye and froze for less than a second. It's all it took.

I already had the muzzle of the TEC .22 centered on his chest. I pulled the trigger and four mercury-tipped bullets hit him center mass. I found out later that he was dead before he hit the ground.

The second dealer took off on foot and Chuy followed him down a side street.

Puma, as he was ordered to do, immediately straddled the guy I had just shot and was about to put one in his brain to make sure he was dead. I yelled at him not to bother. I could tell the guy was already dead. I yelled at Puma to go help Chuy find the runner.

All this took a handful of seconds. But it felt like forever.

Next was the fat dealer who was on the passenger side of his customer's car. The car was between me and the fat guy. I yelled at the driver to get the hell out of there. But the guy froze up. He wouldn't move.

I fired two rounds into his car and he finally pulled away. Slowly. So slowly that by the time he was clear, the fat dealer was about twenty feet away and running toward his front door.

I took my time, aimed, squeezed the trigger, and eight rounds blasted out the barrel like a garden hose. The fat dealer rolled onto the ground. It looked like his legs just got chopped out from under him. But I could see he was still moving and crawling to his front door. I took a quick look to see if anyone was hiding behind the door with a weapon, but didn't see anything.

I walked up to him and I could see that I'd only hit him in the ass and the legs. The fat dealer rolled onto his back and said, "Non me mata. Por favor. Non me mata." (Don't kill me. Please. Don't kill me.)

It was way too late in the game for mercy. This guy was a si-cario. Just like me. He was one of the forty people who walked into Christine's discotheque and sprayed lead all over the place, not caring how many innocent people he killed. If the situation were reversed, he wouldn't hesitate to kill me. I didn't hesitate either. It's an ugly business. But it is a business.

I said to him, "Si, puto. Por Ramon."

I leaned over him and emptied the rest of the forty-round mag-azine into his body.

When bullets hit a body, what the body feels first is something like an electrical shock. The nervous system is basically over-loaded by the impact of each bullet and the body reacts with muscular spasms. This guy was twitching like somebody had plugged a generator to his feet. That somebody was me.

I looked up and down the street and it was completely empty. This was a Monday morning around the time that people were on their way to work or school and there wasn't a single person in sight. We'd just committed what we believed to be a triple ho-micide on a street in one of the biggest cities in the country, and for a long moment, I was the only living thing visible on the land-scape.

Where were my guys?

I started off for the car and Roach was already behind the wheel and he and Puma were stripping off their bandanas and hoodies. But where was Chuy? I told Roach to wait and give me a few seconds.

I jumped out of the car with my weapon still in hand just in case I needed it. I ran up the street and there was Chuy, bent over at the waist, his gun still in his hand and both his hands on his knees. He was gasping for air. He'd chased the guy for a long time and finally hit him.

Chuy saw me. He smiled. He said something like he thought we left him behind. Then he told me he hit his man.

Time to go.

We ran back to the car, jumped in, and took off the bandanas.

I told Roach to go slow. Don't make it look like we're escaping the scene. And the good soldier that he was, he drove down the street right past the bodies as cool and slow as Joe Citizen.

Our first turn out of there was Whittier Boulevard. It was three blocks away. If we could make it to Whittier, we'd blend in with the traffic and we'd be gone.

But then we had to stop for a traffic light. And, as things like this happen, a Hollenbeck black-and-white cruiser stopped be-hind us.

"Be cool," I told the guys in the car. I also told them to check their weapons and make sure they were loaded with fresh mags.

It was a female cop driving without a partner. My stomach

tightened because she might be a mother or a wife or both and the thought of killing a woman, even if she was a cop, made me sick. But not sick enough to give her a pass.

I reminded my guys again. "If she puts her light on, we bail out. We light her up with everything we got and meet up at the first rally point."

We sat frozen waiting for the red light to change. And then. Her light goes on. We went on full alert. We had our hands on the door handles, ready to swing out and kill her.

Then she cranked her wheel hard. She made a high-speed U-turn behind us, and disappeared going in the opposite direction. She must have just gotten the shots-fired call. She'd come about three seconds from being executed.

We looked at each other. This was some crazy shit.

We pulled over at the place we had arranged to dump our weapons and clothes and finished stripping. We threw the weapons and the clothes into a plastic bag and handed the bag to one of the Border Brothers who was waiting for us.

As he took the bag to dump it, we started hearing sirens coming our way. A lot of them. We pulled out into traffic and drove down Whittier Boulevard to get to the freeway. A couple of cop cars actually drove past us to respond to the scene of our crime. It was beautiful.

We were back across the border and at the office that same afternoon.

The next day, David Barron came in with a suitcase and told us that the killings had started a shit storm in LA. He opened the suitcase and gave us each $25,000 in cash. He didn't ask for the $15,000 he'd given me as getaway money.

The body count turned out to be only two out of three. The

first guy I shot died on the spot. The fat dealer took two days to die from the bullets and the mercury. The third guy that Puma shot eventually survived.

I was a hero to David Barron and Ramon Arellano. I led a team on a successful assassination and not only got away with it, but it kept the LAPD and the entire California justice system in the dark about those homicides for over a decade. Those murders remained unsolved until I eventually became a prosecution witness and told them how and why they happened.

Getting it done right that time does not make me proud now, but it did then.

23

Respect

I came back from that mission in Boyle Heights, East LA, with the hit under my belt. In that world, there can be respect and that was what I was craving. The morality was completely turned on its head. Right was wrong and wrong was rewarded.

But it wasn't just the fact that I could assault and kill people on demand that raised my status with David Barron. It was also the fact that I could follow orders even in the small things. David was a fancy dresser and he liked things around the office to be clean and straightened up. Most of the other guys in the crew lived like frat boys. They left their clothes laying around and they never cleaned up the place unless they knew that David was on his way. I was the opposite. I guess it came from being raised by a Marine but I always had my shit squared away. My bed was made, my clothes were clean, and I kept my guns and equipment in good shape. David noticed and gave me props for it.

Don't get me wrong. I wasn't the only guy like that. There was another guy, named Chi Chi. He was a sharp dresser, like David, and he worked out a lot. He owned a couple of gyms in Tijuana

CONFESSIONS OF A CARTEL HIT MAN

that I sometimes used to work out in. So Chi Chi looked good and he owned a Porsche and a Mercedes. Naturally, he had a lot of girls always hanging around him. He was also a little older than most of the guys in the office and I guess that was part of the reason for his discipline as well.

The other thing is that I like to cook my own food. Whenever I cooked, everybody would start asking me to make some for them. So before you know it, I was the unofficial cook of the office, and David had respect for that too.

About a month after we came back from the mission in Boyle Heights in LA, David assigned me to do another mission in California. He made me the lead guy on it and told me to pick my own crew for it.

The target was a guy named Guero Palmas of the Sinaloa Cartel and therefore an enemy. He was Chapo Guzman's right-hand man. He was just an enemy. Palmas lived in a small town called Maywood. When I say small town, it wasn't something out in the woods or anything. Maywood is its own town in the greater LA area that has its own city government. At the time, Maywood also had its own sixty-man police department. Maywood and a neighboring town named Cudahy are only two square miles big. Sixty cops for that small a town is a lot, but they needed that many.

Maywood and Cudahy didn't have the kinds of budgets to hire top people. And that included the police force. The Maywood police force was in large part made up of cops who were fired from their previous cop job for everything from corruption, prisoner abuse, sexual crimes, and bribery. It was known as the town where all the bad cops landed. The town itself had a high proportion of fully mobbed-up gangsters. One of the most popular nightclubs in Cudahy, for instance, had pictures on the wall of Al

Pacino in *Scarface*, and pictures of Chapo Guzman, Pablo Escobar, Al Capone, and a bunch of other notorious criminals. They also played a lot of narcocorridos over the PA system. It was that kind of place.

I decided to take my reliable crew with me for this one—Chuy, Puma, Roach, and Trigger. We got across the border into California with no problems. We hooked up with our local guys who gave us guns, ammo, hand grenades, and showed us where Palmas lived.

We checked into the Maywood Inn and started doing our recon. Palmas lived across the street from a big swap meet that isn't there anymore. He had one of the apartments in a small, four-unit building. Once we started doing the recon, we realized that this guy almost never came out of his house. People would come and go to see him to do their business, but he never stepped out of his pad.

Palmas had two Thunderbirds, a blue one and a maroon one. So we sat in a park across from the apartments and waited day and night for him to show his face. It was long and boring, and naturally, when you sit in cars all day using binoculars and talking on radios, you draw the attention of the local gang. In this area it was Los Compadres. At first they thought we were cops. After a week of hanging around and getting to know these guys, we finally dropped David "Popeye" Barron's name and they stopped being suspicious. In fact, we bought some dope from them to pass the time at night when we weren't working.

One night we caught a break. We watched Palmas and his crew come out of the complex and pile into the two Thunderbirds. It was him and seven other people with him. We were already in the custom van Ramon had given us in TJ so we followed him until he pulled into the parking lot of a club called La Aquilla in South Central LA.

We were all ready to go. We had our rifles, pistols, and a couple of hand grenades and we were just about to make the move on him, when a couple of LAPD police cars pulled into the parking lot. We waited but the cops didn't leave. So we scrubbed the mission and I decided to call David.

I told him the trouble we were having with Palmas not coming out of his house, so I told him I had a plan. We knew his apartment was on the second floor, so I wanted to have my guys with AK-47s set up downstairs and I'd throw a hand grenade into his apartment. Once the grenade went off, he'd either be dead or he'd run out of there. If he ran down the stairs, we'd get him with the AKs. David asked me if there were any kids living in the complex. I told him there were kids' toys like Big Wheels in the yard so there probably were kids in the building. David didn't like the sound of that. He didn't want to stir up a shit storm by accidentally killing kids. He wanted us to do it as stealthily as possible. You can imagine what would have happened. The publicity it would have brought down would have been dramatic. This was 1993. A hand grenade and full-automatic weapons? Not stealthy.

So while we went back to the surveillance, David called me and told me to come down to San Diego. "I need you to meet some people." So me and Puma went down there because David wanted me to have an extra body with me. When we got down there, I got a call from David and he told me, "Somebody's going to call you and I want you to do something for him." I told him that was cool and I waited for the call.

So we get a call and they tell us to meet up in Horton Plaza. When Puma and I get down there, they scoop us up in a van and it was Kity Paez and Chi Chi. And Kity told us, "Look, man, we're going to go down here and find this guy. And when we find him, we want you to go ahead and put in some work."

Kity is a really cool dude. He looked like a big kid. Normally, I would have been suspicious. But this was something that David put me onto and I was positive that David wouldn't throw me to the wolves. If he was backing this guy's play, it had to be part of David's business. As it turned out, Paez struck me as a good dude that I could trust. He was open-minded. He would listen to us when we had a suggestion. He wasn't the kind of guy that just issued commands and expected you to follow them blindly or without some feedback from you.

Years later, after I was arrested, I found out that Paez had asked David for me personally. They all knew about the Boyle Heights mission and they liked the way I handled myself and ran my crew. So when Paez wanted to have somebody taken care of, I was the guy he wanted. I never really found out why this guy in San Diego had gotten on the wrong side of Paez or David Barron. Most of the time, I never got those kinds of details. Sometimes, though, out of respect, David would give me details like that after the job was over.

Paez, Chi Chi, Puma, and me were sitting in a white minivan and Paez started shooting questions at me. Paez was in the front passenger seat and turned around in the minivan and asks, "Look. Let me ask you something. If we were to pull up next to a car right now, and I tell you that's the guy and you had an AK-47, what would you do?"

I told him, "I'd stick the gun right out the window and spray the guy while we were driving." Then he said, "Show me how you'd do it." So I walked him through how I'd do it and he said, "Good. Good. If we do this, we want it done right." So I said, "Cool."

So he takes us down to the Gaslamp Quarter in San Diego. This area is full of nightclubs, restaurants, and shops. It's the sort of place that tourists flock to like the Third Street Promenade is in LA or Greenwich Village in New York. The guy we were looking for owned a nightclub in the area. We pull up to the place and Chi Chi gets out and goes in there. After about twenty minutes, he comes out and tells us that he talked to a couple of people in there and that the guy wasn't there. The target had to take care of some kind of business in Mexico and that's where he was. So Kity says he knew where this guy lived in Chula Vista and we drove there next.

We looked at the cars in the driveway and the car he normally drove, a black Mercedes, wasn't there. So we missed our chance. Kity called David and told him that we couldn't find the guy. David got on the phone and told me to chill out overnight in San Diego and go out the next day looking for him.

Then he said, "If things don't work out, don't worry about it. Go back to LA and take care of the thing I sent you on." We spent a couple more days looking for the guy but he never showed up, so I went back to LA and took up surveillance on Huero Palmas.

They ended up killing this guy sometime later. When they got him, they used the same white Jetta that I had used in the Boyle Heights mission. After they got him, they took that Jetta behind a supermarket and set fire to it. They poured gasoline all over the interior, and Tarzan, one of the guys on my crew, threw a match in there not realizing that the fumes are more flammable than the liquid. When the match hit the fumes, the whole car flashed out in a huge fireball, and Tarzan ended up getting some second-degree burns and had his hair and eyebrows completely singed off.

I found out later that Tarzan and Zigzag had killed him in his Mercedes and they found something like $170,000 in a briefcase in the backseat that they took off with.

After I get back to LA, I got a call from Marta, who was my girlfriend at the time. She called to tell me that she wanted to go out with her best girlfriend to a nightclub in Tijuana. She asked me if that was okay if she did that. I said, "Yeah, go ahead and have a good time. I'm up here in LA and I'll see you when I get back."

Then around 2:00 A.M. she calls me back. I was dead asleep at the time. I could tell she'd been drinking but she wasn't drunk. She asked me, "Baby what are you doing up there?"

I told her I was asleep but I was in LA taking care of business. She kept insisting, "But what are you doing?" I told her, "Look, I told you never to ask me about my business." She was living off me at the time. I was renting her apartment for her, I was taking care of her, and she had at least $25,000 that she was holding on to for me. I had told her that she could take out what she needed, but I wanted to know what she was taking out. She knew that I was in the drug business because I was bringing home dope and I had her brother selling it for me. So she was aware of all that. But she thought it was strictly drugs.

Then she told me that when they were in the nightclub, one of the Logan boys, a guy named Cracks, was hitting on her. She told him to leave her alone because she was already living with me.

Cracks said to her, "Fuck Nite Owl. It's all Logan boys. He's the only one from Posole."

Some of the other guys from my crew were there as well and

they're telling Cracks to shut his mouth. They told him that I was one of their crew and I was all right with everybody down there. But Cracks was one of those bad drunks that gets belligerent and he continues to try to hit on her. He finally decides to go up to her and says, "I bet you don't even know what your old man's doing." She told Cracks that I was up there slinging dope. He says to her, "You don't know. He kills people for money." She told him it was bullshit. He kept telling her that I killed people for money.

She asked me, "Baby, is it true?"

"Don't listen to him. He's not going to hit on you anymore."

I was pissed at this. And it's not just because he was hitting on my girlfriend. He was shooting his mouth off in a crowded bar about my business and the cartel's business. This was something that could put us all in jeopardy. And not just from the cops but from the Sinaloa Cartel as well. The next morning, I jump in the car and drive down to Tijuana. As soon as I get there, I see David, and David is surprised to see me. He's also pissed off that I left my assignment in LA unfinished and came back without his approval or even alerting him. I explained to him the situation with Cracks and Marta. He said he'd let it go for the moment, but Amado Carrillo was coming to town for a face-to-face meeting with Ramon. David told me to go suit up and get my stuff. They needed me for the escort mission. So I got my bulletproof vest and my guns and loaded up in David's truck.

Amado Carrillo Fuentes was the head of the Juarez Cartel, which had sided with the Sinaloa Cartel against the AFO, and he was known as el Señor de los Cielos, the Lord of the Skies. Among his other assets, he owned a large fleet of airplanes that he used in his drug business. He was supposed to be the richest criminal in history with something like $25 billion in assets. Carrillo got into the drug trade through his uncle Ernesto Fonseca Carrillo, who was known as the legendary Don Neto, who was the head of the Guadalajara Cartel. We'd been warring with Carrillo for a decade and even though there was supposed to be a temporary truce during the time of the meeting, neither of them trusted each other to keep the peace. The war was basically over who would control the plazas, the ports of entry for drugs into the US. The cartel that controls the plaza controls the drug trade. You either have to pay a tribute to the owner of the plaza to get the drugs across or you have to declare war to control the plaza yourself. This meeting was supposed to iron out some problems and see if Ramon and Carrillo could come to some arrangement.

Carrillo brought twenty security guys with him, all armed to the teeth. Our mission was to go pick up Carrillo at the Tijuana airport and escort him and his team to Benjamin Arellano's fortress just one block from the bullring in Tijuana. Benjamin's house had a wall twenty-five feet high with guard towers. It was a fortress.

This convoy duty was a demonstration to the world of how much power Ramon had over the entire Tijuana government and judicial system. We had about twenty SUVs at the airport, all of them filled with our security people. After we picked up Carrillo and his people, we headed to Benjamin's house in a big convoy. The local Tijuana cops worked traffic control for us. They blocked intersections and ran interference the entire way from the airport all the way to our destination. It's the same kind of traffic control and security that any president would get. We blasted the whole way with nothing to stop us. Except for an old man.

Somehow, this old guy in a pickup truck gets himself in the middle of the convoy. As luck would have it, he was stuck just in front of our SUV. David was riding in the front passenger seat and Puma and I were in the back seat. The old guy is poking along slowing everybody down. David tells the driver to ram the old guy to get his attention. After we bump him, the old guy gets pissed and slows down even more.

David was on the radio with Benjamin, and Benjamin was telling him to be cool and not do anything that could draw some heat. David tells us to open the doors and show the old guy our guns. The old guy apparently wasn't impressed and just kept driving slow. So David bumps him off the road and pulls over. He radios the convoy to keep driving. David gets out of the SUV, pulls open the old guy's door, and throws what must have been $2,000 at the old guy. He gets back in the SUV and we take off again. This was crazy shit, especially when you realize that he was doing this in front of the local cops.

When we got to Benjamin's place, the giant steel gates slide open and we all drive in. There must have been another seventy-five of our security people inside the walls, all armed with full-automatic weapons.

Ramon and Carrillo had their meeting and we escorted them back to the airport. On the way back, Ramon asked us if we were afraid of heights. We said we weren't. He had a plan to get us all into a couple of helicopters and get to Carrillo's landing strip before his plane touched down and kill him on his own turf.

He asked if I was ready to go out to Sinaloa in the choppers and kill Amado for him.

I said, "Yeah. Sure I'll go."

By that time, I was down for anything. I was already anticipating my life ending down there. My thinking was if I'm going to go out, I'm going to go out. I never refused to take an assignment. This kept me on good terms. It may have been the only thing that kept me alive. I was very sure that with all the politics the way they are with the cartel, the first time I refused anything, I would have been taken out. I was expendable. Regardless of how good you are, you're always expendable.

For some reason, Ramon couldn't pull off this stunt and they canceled the helicopter assault.

As it turned out, the helicopter intercept and any other plot to kill him was all for nothing. Carrillo eventually died from complications from having plastic surgery performed on his face. He died on the operating table. The two surgeons that operated on him were tortured and then put in fifty-five-gallon barrels and then they poured concrete into the barrels. It turns out that Ramon had his own people in the hospital and somehow got the doctors to kill him or caused the equipment to fail. A year later, the Mexican cops along with US law enforcement seized $10 billion from Carrillo's various bank accounts.

After David realized the helicopter intercept wasn't happening, David said, "Listen, I need you to go back to LA. I promise you. I give you my word right here right now, that when you get back, I'll have Cracks tied up for you and you can kill him any way you want to." You got to remember that Cracks is his homeboy from Logan. So I figured, all right, the guy gave me his word and I accepted it. So I went back to LA.

We went back to our surveillance the next day and spent another couple of weeks just watching. Palmas never showed his face.

When I came back to Tijuana, I found out that they already took care of Cracks. They caught him in an alley and shot him seven times. But Cracks survived. He's all messed up but he's alive to this day.

I was angry at David for breaking his word to me about Cracks. Soon after I found out about Cracks, I walked away from David and the Arellano brothers. I got in my car and came back to San Diego. In my mind, I was through with them.

Not long after I landed back in San Diego, I was picked up by the local cops for a parole violation. After leaving Calipatria State Prison, I never reported to my parole officer and they'd had a warrant for my arrest ever since. At first they put me in Donovan but after pulling a few strings, I eventually worked my way back to Calipatria. Bugsy and I were cellies again, just as we were before I went to work for David and Ramon. I'd be in Calipatria for at least a year.

I heard through Bugsy that David was angry with me for leaving the way I did. Bugsy was on my side and told David that the whole episode with Cracks wasn't done right and David should have waited until I got back to let me take care of my own business.

While I was in Calipatria waiting for my one-year sentence to end, Ramon, David, and the crew sparked off a battle that made headlines around the world and almost crippled the AFO.

The event I'm talking about happened on May 24, 1993, at the Guadalajara airport. David's crew, made up mainly from Logan Heights boys, assassinated Cardinal Juan Jesus Posadas Ocampo. Hundreds of rounds were fired and the cardinal was hit with fourteen gunshots. Six other people died in the shoot-out. The fallout from the Ocampo assassination drove Ramon and the whole organization underground.

There are a lot of theories on what actually happened that day. The first reports were that Ocampo was just caught in the cross fire between David's crew and Chapo Guzman's crew, who were protecting Chapo Guzman. The other theory is that Chapo was at the airport and driving away in the same kind of car that Ocampo happened to be driving in—a white Mercury Grand Marquis. And they thought it was Guzman in the Grand Marquis. The last theory is that this was an assassination plot that started in the Mexican government to silence the cardinal. The rumor was that the cardinal was going to name names of corrupt Mexican politicians who were working with the cartels. And it was those politicians that ordered Ramon to kill the cardinal.

What's not in doubt is that most of the shooters that day were David's crew and most of them were Logan Heights homies.

Like I said, the aftermath almost put a complete stop to Ramon and the cartel. Everybody went underground and they were told not to do anything. They had heat on them everywhere. Interpol. The Vatican. The United States. All the Catholic nations in South and Central America. They're mad at Ramon. So for the whole time that I was in Calipatria, nothing was going on in Tijuana, and David had bigger things to think about than me walking out on him.

24

Wasn't for Her

After I got out, I was running around the neighborhood like usual. But this was the time I met my second wife. She's the mother of my daughter. And I got to say that she is the love of my life. To this day she's the only woman I ever really opened up to. I've never been able to open myself up to anybody else the way I opened up to her. I married her and we had a child. She was everything I ever wanted.

And the life I lived just wasn't for her.

When we first got together, we ended up living at my cousin Roy Boy's house. Roy Boy Rivas was an EME member. At the time, he was in county waiting for his trial on a murder beef. (He lost that case and he's serving life.) He was married to Myrna.

He had asked me, "I need you to do me some favors."

I asked what kind of favor and he said, "I need you to take a dude out."

I said okay. I'd do it.

He asked me to meet up with my ex-wife, Tutu. "I'm going to have you meet up with Tutu because she knows where this guy lives." He was going to have Bobby Perez come down from San Diego to help. He asked me to meet up with her in Tijuana and if I had any guns.

"Yeah, I got some guns." At the time, I had a full-auto Uzi, a .45, a 9 mm, and a few guns I accumulated while I was in TJ.

"When Bobby gets there, you meet up with Tutu and she's going to take you where the dude's at and you take care of him."

So Bobby and I meet up with Tutu and I told her that I had to go to Oceanside because that's where my guns were at. So I get my guns and as we're coming back, the cops pull us over. I grew up on the East Side and I know how the East Side is. They see more than one homeboy in a car or even one homeboy late at night and they're going to pull you over. It's just their thing. They see me and Bobby in the car and they get on our tail.

Bobby asks me, "What do you want to do?" I told him we can either bail out and make a run for it or we can spray the cops with the Uzi and take off. "What do you want to do? It's up to you." You got to keep in mind that Bobby had just got out after doing seventeen years in the state penitentiary. And I can see now, after doing all that time, him not wanting to go back.

Bobby says, "Maybe they're just going to give us a ticket." I know better. We got guns in the car, we both have records. There's no way they're going to just give us a ticket.

Bobby is in total denial. He said, "Nah, nah, dog. Just pull over. They'll just give us a ticket." I asked him if he was sure he wanted to do that and not run for it. He was convinced we were going to walk on this one. So we pull over and the cops ask for license and registration. I had neither so I gave them a fake name. The cop goes back and runs it and then he comes back to our car and asks Bobby his name. The dude gives him his real name—Robert Perez. As soon as they run his name, they come back with the Fourth waiver. That's the California law that says when you're on parole, you waive your Fourth Amendment right and they have the right to search you, your property, or any place you happen to be without a warrant. That includes any car you ride in.

The cop says, "You're going to have to step out. We're going to search this car." It's over with. The only thing I had going for me was that I gave them a fake name. My name came back clean. But they search the car. They find the Uzi. They find the .45. They throw us on the ground. They cuff us up. And they take us to the county jail. By this time, I was already on the ladder. My reputation had grown while I was in Mexico and after I came back and went back to prison. So when we land in county, I was considered a Big Homie. A senior shot caller.

After they put me in a cell, I got hold of some staples and started cutting up my fingertips so the prints would get screwed up. When they called me out to have my prints taken on the scanner, the cop asked me, "Why are your fingers so tore up?" I told him I was an electrician and that's what happens when you're working with wires all day. Your fingers get chopped up.

The amazing thing is that they set bail at $7,000. Here I was with my history, getting caught with a full-auto Uzi and a .45, and they let me post $700, the ten percent for the bail, and they let me out.

By the time I got out of that one, Bat Marquez had gotten out of prison and he was with David in Tijuana. Bat was a made EME brother and he was also David's compadre. Bat talks to David and asks him about me. "What do you want to do about the homie?" David tells him, "Look. Have him stay in San Diego and wait for word until we can have him cross over." They phone

Myrna, Roy's wife, with that message and she's the one that re-layed it to me.

My wife and I end up going to Roach's house in Chula Vista and they put us up in a garage apartment. After a while, David asked me to come down. So I crossed over and stayed with my wife's mother in Tijuana. Her mom had six small kids in the house and they were barely making ends meet. While we're staying there, one night the local cops bang on the door and want to search the house. They all look at me because earlier in the day, David and Pato had come by looking for me to see that I was all right and dropped off some money for me and some for them. They knew who I was involved with. They're all thinking it's the Arellano thing. But it wasn't. It turned out that somebody had reported a man with a gun earlier and they were doing a door-to-door search. I'd never seen that side of it, of how seriously they took something like that.

The cops leave and everything was cool again.

The next day, David called me and asked if I was ready to start working again. I said I was. He told me to pack up my stuff because I'd go back to living in the house. Pato picked me up, I kissed my wife good-bye and told her everything would be all right. She was worried and I could see it in her face. Like I said, she was the love of my life. She was beautiful, ten years younger than me. It's hard for me to open up like that.

So I leave with Pato and we go to Rosarito to the Tres Torres Oceana, a high-end complex right on the beach. I meet up with David again and he gives me a big hug and says that he's glad to have me back again. Then he says, "I have somebody for you to meet." And out of the back of the condo comes Bat Marquez. I met Bat a couple of times, but I never really had any interaction with the guy. I know about him and he knows about me and he comes up and says, "What happened the night you got arrested with Robert Perez?" After some dancing around, I finally found out what he was talking about.

The night we got arrested for the Uzi and the .45, I had a Costco credit card on me that a little homeboy gave me. He'd done a burglary or something and he was showing me what he got. I saw the card and I asked him to give it to me. At the time, I was doing crystal meth and I was using the card to cut up the meth. When the cop asked me about the card, I told him exactly why I had it. I told the cop it was to cut up crystal meth. The cop told me that they found meth residue on the card. That was the extent of my conversation with the cop about the card, or anything else.

After I bailed out and left, Perez sent his arrest record, and mine, out to the street. You have to do that so the carnals know what you said or did during any arrest to make sure you weren't talking. And if you did talk or didn't carry yourself the right way, they used the paperwork as proof that you needed correcting or some more serious kind of retribution. Bat took that small credit card conversation I had with the cop as proof that I was talking about the drug business to law enforcement. Which is total bullshit. He was trying to make an issue of it when there was no issue. He was an idiot. He was trying to make himself look good or look big or like he had all this secret information about people.

But David was sharp. He told Bat, "Hey, cut it out. The homie is good. He already showed me his colors." David already knew where my heart was at. David shut him down and told him that my conversation with the cop amounted to nothing. There was a little tension in the air after that, but I let it go.

Right after that, David asked me to do him a favor. He knew I was good with firearms and all that military stuff. He says he wants me to get rid of something for him. He goes to the refrigerator and pulls down a big basket of artificial flowers from it. He sets it on the table and takes the flower arrangement off it and there's like six hand grenades underneath. He says, "Dog, these hand grenades have been buried for a couple of years. I don't know how good they are but, man, I got to get rid of them. My family is getting ready to come over for Christmas and I don't want them around. You want to go get rid of them?" I told him, "Yeah, I'll get rid of them for you."

So we jump in a big truck and drive south into the hills above the beach. Then we take a dirt road that goes right to the cliffs above the ocean. And we just start letting them loose, pulling the pins and throwing them. After we blew them all up, we jumped back in the truck and drove back. After we got back to the condo, Bat asks, "Hey, dude, you want to smoke a joint with me?" The dude doesn't fascinate or impress me but I said, "Okay, I'll smoke a joint with you." So we go out on the balcony and start smoking. I guess he's just trying to be sociable. But the truth is I never had much respect for Bat and neither did any of the other people on the crew. Bat was living in the shadow of the respect people had for David.

After I came back we started getting organized again after laying low for over a year after the Ocampo assassination. The story was that Benjamin Arellano had personally tried to visit the president of Mexico at the time and ultimately a deal was made involving ten million US dollars and future promises to take the heat off us. The other part of the deal was to offer a sacrificial lamb for the benefit of the press and to show the world that the

Mexican government was serious about shutting down the cartels. Ramon threw a guy named Spooky and another soldier to the Mexican cops and they basically admitted to shooting the cardinal. Spooky wasn't completely right in the head so it wasn't hard for the cops to get a complete confession from him. Eventually, the cops beat him to death in prison. The other guy was to serve nine months in a Mexican prison for possession of firearms, but I hear he is still in prison.

After all this went down, we started getting new police uniforms, radios, and documents. And we started training again with the federales and the Mexican military. We needed to get back on our feet because the other cartels were going to take every opportunity to take over our business.

Instead of moving right back into the office, though, we were staying in the condo in Rosarito. Each floor of these buildings had two condos on it. I was living there with Pato and Bat in one condo. Across the hall was a guy named Gino Brunetti, his wife, and his cousin, a guy named Blanco. He was a Colombian. He was the middle man for the transactions with the Colombians. He'd go down to Cali, Colombia, to set up the deals, getting the shipments made from Cali to Tijuana, and then from Tijuana we'd send it to the United States. These were big dudes.

Gino Brunetti eventually got arrested in Cancun, Mexico, and was extradited to the US. He eventually received two life sentences to be served concurrently, plus 120 months to be served concurrently and a $25,000 fine.

Gino kind of takes a liking to the way I carry myself. By this time I was basically David's bodyguard, and Gino liked the way I protected David. Everywhere we go, I'm strapped and I'm maintaining the position of a bodyguard. I always check first when we walk into a place. I go in first, make sure everything is safe before David goes in, and keep people away from him. Pato's a coward, he's not going to step up. And Bat is too cool for school. He's on that whole "I'm in the EME. I'm that guy, I'm a carnal" attitude. Bat thinks he's the shit.

David also asks me if I know anybody from California who wants to come down and be part of the crew. I knew that Big John had just gotten out of jail. Big John and I go way back to when we were youngsters. He's six feet five inches, he's got a lot of heart, he's a gangster, he's a thug, and I know he'd be perfect for the job. So I asked him if he wanted to come down to make some money. And he says, "Hell, yeah." I told him he'd have to live down there and he couldn't be running back and forth from Mexico to the US. He said that was good with him.

By the end of the year, just before Christmas, I had my wife set up in her own apartment and I'm seeing her on a daily basis. Everything was going well between me and my wife and she's living off the spoils. My wife grew up so poor that I had thirty or forty thousand in the house and she wouldn't touch it, even to go grocery shopping, without asking me if it was okay to spend some money on food. On my end, I was spoiling her rotten. I'm buying her dresses, I'm buying her jewelry, I'm buying her everything she ever dreamed of. And I was helping her mom too by giving them money. Because of what I was contributing, her and her whole family were living a great life.

As it turns out, Big John's girlfriend is a friend of my wife. So when he comes south, they go to my house. I drive down to pick him up and bring him to the condo in Rosarito.

One day, Brunetti borrows me from David for security. I told him that I wanted to take Big John along as part of the security detail. Brunetti was cool with that.

Big John and I were as professional as we could be when Gino and his wife went out to dinner the first time. Anybody that tried to approach the table got stopped. When his wife went to the bathroom, we escorted her there and stood outside the door. And Gino liked that flashy, pomp kind of thing. Gino totally got off on it. The next day, he gave me $5,000 just for that one night. And he gave Big John the same thing. He thanked us for the job we did and then he said that if I ever wanted to buy some coke, I should come to him and he'd give me a good price. He said, "I got you. I like your style."

When Christmas comes, all of David's family arrives. I meet his mom and dad. I'm sitting up with his sisters, who are beautiful. We're staying up late at night playing Scrabble and they're treating me like part of the family and I'm feeling like part of the family. Of course, they all know what David's business is and one day his father turns to me and says, "I'm going to ask you one thing. Please, please protect my son. Take care of him. Don't let anything happen to him." So I give him my word. I said, "I promise you, señor, I give you my word that as long as I'm with David, nothing will ever happen to him." His dad then said, "David told me that you're one of his strongest soldiers he's got." Then he shook my hand and we went on a store run.

There's a place called the Rock & Roll Taco in Rosarito. And they were looking to have a famous band come in. It's a big club in the Hilton Hotel. They knew the guy that owned that club. So David makes arrangements to get a table near the stage and he wants a long table set up. They also made arrangements to have the whole table cordoned off. And he was going to have his own security going. So when we go there that night, it's Gino Brunetti and his wife, Barron and his wife. Then it was me, Big John, Blanco, and Pato. Bat had gone to San Diego to be with his family.

It was a real trip. I was told to go to the bar and tell them we only wanted one waiter serving, the same waiter serving us all night. I was given certain codes like if I touched my nose, this was from Gino. They also gave me a bag of coke to hang on to. Gino told me, "If I touch my nose, bring me the coke because I want to do a line." David, on the other hand, is opposed to all drugs. He doesn't like that shit. But Gino, he uses dope. And his wife does dope. So whenever he touched his nose, I'd go over to the table, give him the bag, and they'd do some lines.

David's code to me was "If I touch my shoulder twice, that means there's somebody here that we don't like being around. And it's time for us to leave." But the night went smoothly. We do a couple of escorts for the women when they want to go to the bathroom. And the girls are getting pissy. David's old lady and Gino's old lady are both getting drunk. And they start talking to each other about me right in front of me. Gino's old lady says, "We should set him up with a girl." And the other one says to me, "You need to have a girlfriend. We can set you up with a good girl."

I told them that I was cool and that I already had a girlfriend. But they keep insisting that I needed a girl. I told them I appreciated their concern. Whenever they went to the bathroom, Big John and I would open a path through the crowd for them. And the people in the club were tripping out. This was the holidays and there were a lot of Americans down there. One guy even yells out, "Damn, girl, who are you?"

The next day, once again, here comes Gino and he pays me and Pato and Big John five grand for maintaining security for them.

25

Bad Karma

After the New Year, things started popping again. Since we went underground, Chapo and Amado Carrillo were moving dope through our plaza and we had to stop that. One of the first missions after we came out from hiding was a woman in Imperial Beach.

A story hit the San Diego papers that the cops had found a van with one thousand pounds of cocaine parked at the curb in front of this woman's house. Although the cops were sure she was using her house as a drop pad for the dope, they couldn't prove it. Although she was living in Imperial Beach, this woman owned a couple of beauty parlors in Tijuana and she'd drive back and forth across the border every day to run her business. If she was smart, she would have just run her business and be quiet about it. But she wasn't smart.

She liked to do a lot of partying and one of the guys she liked to party with was a real mama's boy named Bon Bon. This Bon Bon guy was one of those well-off Tijuana civilians who was fascinated with the cartels and had been hanging around the same places we did. This woman couldn't keep her mouth shut and one night she bragged to Bon Bon that she was working for Amado Carrillo, the guy that eventually died from complications while he was getting his face-lift.

From Bon Bon, word reached Ramon that she was working for Carrillo. Ramon decided that she had to go. My crew was assigned to take care of her where she lived. We got Bon Bon to agree to take us to her house, where we'd do some surveillance and put together a plan to get rid of her. Since Bon Bon was a complete idiot, we tried on three separate nights to find her place but Bon Bon kept getting lost. Finally, Ramon told us to bring Bon Bon to him. After they had a conversation, Bon Bon finally remembered exactly where she lived.

Drak, Pato, Panther, Bon Bon, and me were driving in Panther's brand-new black Cadillac. We normally wouldn't use one of our own cars, but Panther was getting another new one so he didn't care if we had to burn this one afterward. Once we found the house and memorized how to get there and get out, we drove Bon Bon back to Tijuana to drop him off. We didn't want that guy anywhere near us.

After we dropped him off at around three in the afternoon, we came back to San Diego and went to collect our guns. There was a junkyard in Chicano Park in Logan Heights called Sunshine Auto Body that we used as a drop place for dope and guns. There were empty junked buses and cars full of dope, guns, and anything else we might need while doing missions in California. One of the buses was like a complete arsenal. We could have picked a lot of heavy firepower like machine guns and shotguns, but we only had a single target that night and by that time we were sure the target didn't have anything like security for herself. So instead of big guns, we got three .38-caliber revolvers—two were blued and the other one was chrome plated.

We got to Imperial Beach around 7:00 P.M., but since it was January, it was already dark out. We had a plan worked out. I dressed up the cleanest of them. I was wearing Guess jeans, a nice jacket, J. Crew button-down shirt, a nerdy pair of glasses, and a hat. I was going to knock on the door while the rest of the crew would hide by the side of the garage. As soon as the door opened, we'd bum-rush the door and take care of business. We also talked about going through the house real quick because we were sure there was probably dope, money, jewelry, or some other valuable stuff in there.

I walked up to the door and knocked. I heard a young female voice from the inside asking who it was. We knew the woman had a daughter so it was the daughter that answered the door. I told her, "My mom asked me to come by to talk to your mother."

The girl asked, "Who's your mother?" I told her, "Gloria." Then she asked which salon did my mother work at.

Since I already knew what stores she owned, I said, "The one in Plaza de Oro."

A legit answer. She opened the door with the chain still attached to get a look at me. What she saw was a clean-cut nerdy guy, so she took the chain off.

As soon as she did that, I pulled out my gun and the rest of the crew rushed into the house. By this time the mom was with the daughter by the door and they both tried to take off screaming. We let the daughter go and three of us sort of tackled the mom. Pato shoots her in the head and Drak and I shoot as well. We were pretty certain she wouldn't survive the five rounds she'd just taken.

We weren't all that rattled or anything, but we completely

skipped looking for anything else to take in the house. We later found out from the newspaper story that the cops found $500,000 in cash hidden in a closet.

We got in the Cadillac and took off. But as we're driving, Pato starts yelling that he's been shot. He looks at me and says, "Dog, you shot me. There's a fucking hole in my hand."

I knew there was a cluster when all three of us tackled the woman, but I know for a fact that I didn't shoot Pato. He was bleeding and started to lose it and I kept telling him to chill and not trip out. It wasn't going to kill him and it's the kind of thing you got to expect in this line of work. I told him, "Even David got a bullet in his leg from a homie. Shit happens. Just chill."

We decided to skip dropping the guns off at the body shop and shot straight across the border to Tijuana. I called my wife and told her to meet us in TJ. I was going to hand the guns off to her and she'd give them to me later on. We drove to the condo in Rosarito and told David about the mission and that Pato took a bullet in the hand.

David didn't seem all that pissed. He was experienced enough to know that stuff like this can happen. He took Pato to the hospital and told us to chill out at the condo until he came back.

After Pato got fixed up, David and I went through the whole scenario move by move, and even David admitted that it looked like Drak had shot Pato in the hand. But convincing Pato that I didn't shoot him was impossible. Just to keep things calm, I volunteered to pay $7,000 for the hospital costs, but Pato never got over it. He even wrote Bugsy in prison that I shot him in the hand and that he'd never be able to fully close his hand again.

Not too long after that, David shows up at the Tijuana office one day and tells me and Pato to get ready to roll. The first thing

I asked him was how should I dress. Depending on the mission, we could go as uniformed cops, full-battle tactical, or casual. David says to just wear casual clothes so I put on jeans, a button-down shirt, and a cowboy hat. I asked about weapons and David said to just bring a handgun. "We just need to check something out." He told us to hang tight and someone would pick us all up.

A little while later David's sister Marta shows up and asks me, "What kind of knives do we have?" We went to the kitchen and picked out a few big chef's knives that I rolled up in a towel and stuck in my pants. We get in one of David's cars and we roll up the Via Rapida to Ensenada. The place David was looking for was a huge walled compound that must have been almost a block long.

When we get there, David and I go over the wall and see at least eight cars, a nice collection of vintage and new Porsches and SUVs. As soon as we land on the other side, a couple of little dogs come yapping at us. Apparently, the little dogs didn't disturb anybody in the main house. David said, "We're going in. Tie up everybody in the house. There's a family living in the back house, so go in there and march them all in here."

As we get to the secondary house, a guy comes out and we jump him. We take him, his wife, and two little girls around five years old back to the big house. David marches them all into the kitchen and tells me to tie them up. He then makes a call to Pato, who is outside with the car, and tells him to come in. The gate opens and Pato drives in and meets us in the house.

Usually when we go in casually dressed and with just hand-guns, it isn't a big deal. But I could tell that Pato knew something and he was more nervous than I ever seen him. I asked him, "What's up, dog?" Pato whispers to me and says, "David's got something big going on, bro." The people we had in the kitchen were the family of the brother that we were there to take care of.

David pulls me and Pato aside and tells us, "This guy's brother burned Benjamin. He owed Benjamin millions of dollars, but when we went underground after the cardinal, the guy kept the money." Then he said, "This guy treats his own brother like shit. He's an asshole. He pays him minimum wage and forces him to live in a shack on the property."

We went through the house and found the guy, his wife, a teenage boy, two young girls around ten and seven years old, and an infant. David told me to watch the family downstairs while he and Pato went upstairs to search. After about an hour, Pato comes down the stairs with a pillowcase full of stuff and a large suitcase that looks heavy.

David takes the homeowner upstairs and we hear a lot of noise. The guy is pleading for his life, begging not to be killed. After a while there's no more pleading. Then the woman is taken upstairs and I heard the sounds of a struggle. David killed the two of them with a knife.

While this was going on, the homeowner's brother asks me why we killed his brother. I told him, "I don't know. I don't know. Just be quiet." Then he said that if we're going to kill him he wants his whole family killed at the same time. He doesn't want to live without them and they don't want to live without him. All the while his wife is holding a crucifix in her hand and I could see she was in agony. Then her baby started crying and she looked at me and said the baby was hungry. Her hands were tied, so I untied her. But I told her that if David came back down, she should pretend that her hands were still tied. I told her to go ahead and feed it. She put the baby to her breast and began feeding him.

I was sickened by the thought that David would want to kill these people too. But he didn't have anything against this family. They were victims of the homeowner, even though they were his family too, so I didn't think David would kill them. It wasn't unusual in cartel hits that they wiped out entire families, including little babies. I had a gun and I started thinking that if David made a move against these people if I had the heart to shoot him.

As David and Pato came downstairs again, there was a knock on the door. David went to the door and it turned out to be the guy that took care of the horses. There was a stable with horses on the property and this guy had no idea of what was going on in the house. David pulled him in and pistol-whipped him with a Desert Eagle. It's a really big handgun and the guy was getting his head smashed in. He wasn't killed but he was sure bloody and we all got hit with his blood spatter.

Then Marta called and that was David's cue to get us out of there. We got in the cars and went back to the office. Once we got there, I tore off my clothes and gave them to Marta, who took all our clothes and went somewhere to burn them. I went into the shower and rubbed my skin raw trying to get the blood and the stench of that place off of me.

I went downstairs and saw that Pato and David were going through all the stuff they took from the house. David calls out to me and says, "Hey, fool. This is for you." He tossed me a Rolex watch that was worth around $8,000. Pato had already grabbed another Rolex with diamonds around the dial that was worth $25,000.

Then David tells me, "Hey, there's more." He dumped a drawer full of jewelry on the table and said, "Take whatever you want. Give it to your old lady." The truth is I was afraid not to take. I was already real quiet and not talking and if I started showing any kind of remorse or feeling, I know it would have started David wondering if I still had the heart for this business. He had already seen me freak out over some women he called the cambio girls in a job we did before the one in Imperial Beach, and he didn't like it.

David called Benjamin and told him what we hauled out of the house. Then he told Benjamin, "We painted the house wall to wall." Benjamin asked David who was with him and he said Pato and me. Benjamin told David to split the money with us but he wanted all the paperwork because he needed to study it and see exactly how much the guy had stolen from Ramon. "This is what happens when you turn your back on Ramon," Benjamin said.

David told me to go in the kitchen and help myself to the money. There were three stacks of money in there about three feet high and three feet wide, one stack each for me, Pato, and David. Our share was something around $35,000. But mixed in with the American currency, there was some Mexican pesos that Pato didn't want to be bothered with. He just gave all his pesos to me. That came out to about $20,000 in value.

Later on, I gave my mother-in-law the pesos to hold for me.

Sometime after that, we were in the office as usual just hanging out and waiting for orders. David suddenly shows up without warning and tells us all to get ready and put on our Federal Police uniforms. We needed to take care of something right away and he needed everybody that was in the office at that time. We get dressed and strapped and we all pile into a van. It was me, David, Pato, Drak, Panther, Rafa Camacho, and Lino Quintana.

As we approach the target house, we see a car just starting to pull out. David yells out, "Stop him! Don't let him leave." The van blocks the car and we get out, grab the guy, and rush him back into his house.

Once we get in there, David and one of the other guys take the man, tie him up, and David says, "Put him in the bathtub." I knew this was going to be ugly. There was an old woman and young girl around seven in the house as well. They told me to tie up the girl and her grandmother, take them to one of the other bathrooms, and watch them.

David and the rest of them are searching through the house, looking for anything valuable or anything that might be important paperwork. I was supposed to tie up the girl and the old lady but the little girl looked at me and asked, "You aren't going to kill me, are you?" I said to her, "No, mija. I'm not going to kill you. And nobody else will." I told her to pretend to be tied up and just hold on to the rope. "When we leave, you can let go of the rope and call for help."

David told everybody that "We got to make this look like a dirty job. Throw weed all over the house and make this place look like a dope house." They took handfuls of dope and threw them all over the place to make it look like this was a home-invasion drug robbery. David kept going through everything in the house looking for something in particular, but he never told us what it was or if he ever found it.

At one point I left the two I was watching and went into the bathroom where they were holding the man. He was in the tub with a sheet over him. I asked Lino how they were going to kill the guy. Before I even finished the sentence, I heard this disgusting, cracking, squishy noise from behind me. David had just smashed the guy in the head with a five-pound sledgehammer. Then David hit him a few more times with the hammer. David lifted up the sheet and made a disgusted-looking face. He called me over to look at the ugly mess he'd just made of a human being.

I don't know if they ever found what they were looking for and I didn't care. But right then I made up my mind that if any of them made a move against the little girl or her grandmother, I would kill them. Even if it was David. I didn't know it at the time, but that was my last mission for Ramon. I was through. I was going home. I just had to find the right time and place to get out.

Fortunately, I didn't have to shoot anybody on the crew that night. Once they killed the guy, we all got back in the van and went back to the office. The little girl and her grandmother were left unhurt.

That night I woke up in a cold sweat. I was having a nightmare. The cold sweats and the nightmares continued to happen for years after that last homicide. I wanted to commit suicide and I now know that the only reason I didn't was because of my wife and soon-to-be-born child. I couldn't imagine my child growing up without me in Tijuana. I had to stay alive for no other reason than to keep my child safe.

As I said, before we did the mission in Imperial Beach, David had put us on a surveillance mission of two women he called the cambio girls. They were sisters and both of them were beautiful and rich. They supposedly made their money from running a cambio, a money exchange office in San Diego. One of them even dated Ramon for a short time. After Ramon and the girl broke up, he started suspecting that she was talking to the cops. From what I heard, the sisters had a brother who worked for Ramon for a while but he did something that Ramon didn't like. So Ramon had him killed. The girls were pretty sure that Ramon had killed their brother, and they took it hard.

I'd be with Pato or Drak or one of the other guys on the crew and we'd follow them for days. Most of the time they just went from their house to the exchange office and back. But one day we followed them all the way to Chula Vista in California. They drove to the sheriff's office and we parked in the sheriff's parking lot. They were there for a long time and when they left, we followed them back to their house.

It was obvious they were talking to the cops and Ramon decided to get rid of them. At first he said he wanted them tortured and then chopped up to send everyone a message that you don't snitch on Ramon. But after a couple of times of trying to find them and then not being able to get the business handle for a bunch of problems that weren't our fault, he said to forget the torture and the rest of it and just shoot them.

The job fell to me because by now I was the only one that Ramon and David could trust to get the job done without a mistake and do it as stealthily as possible.

Drak and I followed them for days in a couple of throwaway cars. These were used cars that we bought cheap but under false names. We bought them instead of stealing them because we didn't want to be out driving around and take a chance on having a cop run the plates in case he didn't like the way we looked. Whenever we drove those cars, we always wore some kind of gloves and we had the interiors steam-cleaned in case we left any kind of blood or forensic evidence behind. David and Ramon were smart about that and they always gave me money to legitimately buy a car we would use for a job. Guys like Bat were so stupid that they'd keep the money for the car for themselves and then go steal one to go on a mission. It screwed him up a few times, but David would always let it slide because he was his compadre.

Drak and I finally pinned the two women down in an alley behind one of their offices in San Diego. As they were pulling out, Drak blocked the alley with his car. I was wearing a big Afro wig, a long coat, and sunglasses even though it was ten thirty at night.

I had a Colt 1911 semiauto pistol loaded with hollow-points. I approached the car, leaned in, and shot the both of them. I hit one in the head and the other in the neck. In those last few seconds I realized the one I shot in the neck was pregnant. And then I heard the screaming from the backseat. It was a little girl around seven years old. She was naturally terrified. That's when my life changed. I froze looking at her and felt devastated. I had killed her mom. I didn't know which of the women was her mom, but I knew for sure they were both gone.

Drak and I got out of there and went straight back to Tijuana. We went to David's place and told him it was done. David said we should wait for the news that night to confirm the kills. I wasn't in control of myself anymore. I'd lost my shit and started getting paranoid, scared, and remorseful all at the same time. The thing was that my wife was pregnant and we were expecting our first child. I didn't know if I could face her after what I'd just done.

I started walking around the apartment like a zombie, just saying, "It's bad karma. It's bad karma," over and over again. I couldn't watch the news because I didn't think I could handle it, so I kept asking David, "Are they dead, bro? Are they dead? Did the baby die too?" David was getting pissed off at me. "Forget it. Just let it go." But I couldn't let it go. Bad karma, I said to myself over and over again.

Finally, when the news came on, David told me that the job was finished. Both women died and the baby couldn't be saved. The news didn't say anything about the little girl in the backseat.

Every time I'd go home and see my wife pregnant and happy with our child, I started tripping in the worst possible way. I honestly considered suicide for the first time in my life. I started using heroin again just to blot out the memory and find a few hours of peace where I wasn't tortured by the things I had seen in the car that night.

I started thinking about leaving Ramon and going back home, but I was worried about my wife and child. I knew that if I quit on the spot, I'd never leave Mexico alive and neither would they.

26

Neglected Business

Now that the AFO had come out from underground, there was a lot of catching up to do. The business had been neglected. That meant a lot more missions than before the cardinal was killed. We had two of them back-to-back.

We had a mission in Mexico City and the target was another commandante who was working for Chapo. I wasn't the primary. Ramon pulled together a local crew and a few of us from the Tijuana office were there as backup in case this commandante had a security escort too.

Big John was one of the guys I picked to go down there with us. We spent a whole week in the Mexico City office waiting for the call. We were there long enough that Ramon decided to give me and Big John two days off, and he told Tiburon, his right-hand man, to take us to a mall for a shopping trip.

The three of us went to Colonia Sarange and I bought some clothes and a few CDs. We weren't there very long, when Tiburon gets a call that they need us back at the office right away. By the time we got back, they were loading a motorcycle into a truck and everybody was getting strapped. Big John and I got our guns and bulletproof vests and made sure we had enough ammo and grenades.

Ramon was going on this mission with us. When Big John and I got there, he yelled out to us to ride in his minivan with him. Big John and I rode in the back and Ramon was up front. He's on the radio and getting intel from whoever he has out there keeping an eye out for the commandante. I hear Ramon ask, "Is he there? Is he there?" He got his answer. The commandante was still there.

That morning, the commandante was at a gymnasio, a gym, working out. And whoever Ramon was talking to had eyes on him in the gym. The designated shooter was a guy named Gordo, who was riding on the back of a motorcycle. We waited there for about twenty minutes with Gordo riding around and around the block, waiting for the commandante to come out.

We finally got the word. We hear on the radio, "There he is. That's him." He was an older guy with a bald head and he's walking across the street to his car with his keys in his hand. Gordo pulls up next to him with his .38 Super semiauto already in his hand. It was supposed to be a one- or two-shot kill, but the commandante got slippery and Gordo didn't get off a clean shot to the head. We couldn't tell if Gordo had trouble with the gun and allowed the commandante to move around or the reverse of that. In any case, it took five rounds to drop the commandante. Gordo got back on the motorcycle and we all headed back to the office. Once we're back, Gordo apologized to Ramon for using so many rounds to kill the target. Gordo said to him, "My finger got stuck in the trigger. I'm sorry." Ramon said, "No problem. As long as it got done."

After the killing of the commandante, Ramon and David took

a plane to Guadalajara. Big John, Tiburon, and I were told to take a day off and then meet up with a Mexican Army general. The plan was for the three of us to drive with the general to Guadalajara and take all the guns we had and meet up with David and Ramon. The general was a little guy and not really impressive as a military man. But he had the uniform and he could pull enough rank that no cops or Army personnel would stop us on the road.

On the drive up, the general says that he's up for a promotion and when that happens he'll be in charge of the entire district. He told Tiburon that he could guarantee safe passage for Ramon's business throughout the whole district. He told Tiburon straight out that it would cost Ramon between $1.5 and $2 million a year for the privilege.

When we got to Michoacan, Tiburon dropped me and Big John off because he had to take care of some business. We set a time and place to meet later. So John and I just hung out and did the tourist thing along with a lot of Americans who went to live there for their retirement.

John and I were eating in the patio of one of the restaurants on the main drag. Along with the tourists and the local residents, there were some beggars on the street. One of them was a ten-year-old boy who was begging for money. He was barefoot and the clothes he was wearing were ragged and dirty. When he came up to us, the waiter tried to chase the kid away. I told the waiter to leave him alone and told the kid to sit with us. At first he didn't want to. He asked for money and cigarettes. I asked him when was the last time he ate anything and the kid just looked down.

I ordered burgers and fries for him but I noticed that he was constantly looking up the street to a median divider where some people and a wrecked old wino were hanging on the benches. As we were eating, he eventually told me that the old wino was his father. The father didn't work and the kid never went to school. His job was to panhandle and beg for money and cigarettes so his father could get drunk and smoke.

After he finished eating, he asked me if I could give him some money. I made the kid take us to a market where I bought shoes, socks, pants, and a shirt. At least he'd have something to wear. Before we left, I gave him twenty dollars even though I knew where that money was going. Whatever I gave him would end up as liquor going down his father's throat.

Tiburon came back and we got in the car and drove to Jalisco. It's the best place to buy tequila, so I bought three bottles of top-brand tequila for my father. We drove on to Guadalajara, where we met up with Ramon and David and spent three weeks doing some surveillance and putting in some cartel work.

A Guadalajara police commandante was working for Chapo and was working to get Ramon and the whole cartel out of Tijuana. David explained to me that this was going to be a real hard mission. The commandante was always surrounded with a Grupo Tactito—which is just what it sounds like. An elite unit of bodyguards. After David finished his briefing, it sounded like a suicide mission. At this point, I didn't care. I was using a lot of heroin and still feeling terrible about the cambio women.

We had crews all over Mexico, and the guys in Guadalajara assigned to watch the commandante were a retired Mexican cop and a Mexican Army officer. Because of who they were, they were able to keep track of the commandante. Ramon knew this was dangerous, so he had a big Denali pickup truck reinforced with armor plating. The plan was for me and the ex-cop to ride in the armored pickup bed and be ready to hose down the commandante when we got our chance. I had an AK-47 with a 100-round magazine and a spare 100-rounder in case that first one wasn't enough.

We got the call at 6:00 A.M. one morning and we loaded up the truck. For insurance and scouting, there were two guys on motorcycles riding along with us. When we got to where he was supposed to be, we got on his tail. I couldn't see anything because I was laying in the truck with the ex-cop, so I didn't know if the commandante was alone or if he had a whole squad of security men around him who would outnumber us and probably shoot the shit out of us and the truck. The ex-cop was smiling like a fiend. He had a gun and grenades and dressed like a fool—shorts, sandals, and a simple T-shirt. I was decked out in black and tactical boots.

We drive around for a while and then over the radio we hear one of our guys yell out, "There he is! There he is! Pull up, pull up!" The commandante was stopped at an intersection, so I got myself ready and as soon as our truck stopped, I was ready to pop up over the bed and spray the guy, not knowing how many security guys were ready to spray back.

The one thing I knew I had going in my favor is that the Mexican cops aren't allowed to carry weapons with a round in the chamber. The only advantage was that after I started shooting, they'd have to chamber a round to shoot back and in that one or two seconds of advantage, I could hit enough of them that the return fire wouldn't kill me. They called it "Los van a ganar al gatillo" (Beat him to the trigger).

As the truck came to a stop, the radio blared out again. "It's not him! Abort! Abort! It's not him!"

We leave the area in a big hurry and go back to the local office in Guadalajara. By that time I was sick with nerves. As soon as I was alone in one of the rooms, I went down on my knees and started praying to God and thanked him for making this thing go the way it went. I was sick of killing and I knew I wanted out. While I was praying, one of the guys on the crew walked in on me.

At the end of the three weeks, we pack up and fly back to Tijuana. We split up and went our own ways. One of the bottles of tequila I had started leaking in the luggage. One of the security guards at the airport sees the leak and pulls me out and starts harassing me about what was in my luggage and they want to search all the bags.

Fortunately, Tiburon hadn't gotten out of the airport yet and he makes a quick call to Ramon. A short time later, Ramon shows up at the airport with eight guys and starts flashing official police badges to the security people and forces them to let me go. Ramon told the airport security people that he was on an "operativo privado"—a classified operation way beyond their pay grade. And just like that, we were sprung and I was on my way home.

27

"Are You Against Us?"

My child was only weeks away from being born. The expected due date was July 4. I wanted to stay around the house to be with my wife when the baby came, but Ramon had decided it was time to go on a full-scale war with Amado Carrillo. This war would either see us all killed or the whole Carrillo cartel killed. It was all or nothing.

Ramon and David rounded up thirty of us and took our cell phones away. We were going into the boonies and we'd be training for two straight weeks with no contact with the outside world. The place where we trained was a 550-acre ranch outside of Ensenada that belonged to a friend of Ramon's. It was as close to hard-core military training as any of us would ever see outside of a real military organization. We had to bring just about everything we needed to stay fed, watered, and equipped for the next two weeks.

We lived out of tents and we trained every day from sunup to sunset. We ran obstacle courses, learned how to do dynamic entries through doors and windows, how to lay down suppressing fire and flank an enemy position, perform vehicle ambushes, how to estimate distances for sniper fire, and every other military maneuver you could think of. The only luxury we had was a generator for lights at night and a camp cook. Everything else from doing laundry to stitching up cuts we had to do ourselves.

As it turned out, David, Gordo, and me were the only ones who could hit a target reliably at three hundred yards. Ramon had brought in a military-trained sniper to teach all of us how to do it, but the three of us were the only ones who could do it on command. By the time the two weeks were done, we must have fired hundreds of thousands of rounds and the place was practically knee-deep in spent shell casings.

On the day we left the training area, we headed down the road and stopped in Puerto Nuevo. It's the best place around for seafood and Ramon decided to give us a break and buy dinner for everyone. He sent Tiburon and Gordo into a restaurant and told the owner that we had thirty people coming in and we'd all be armed. He told us all to bring our rifles, handguns, grenades, radios, and tactical gear with us into the restaurant. The owner pushed a bunch of tables together so we could all sit down and face each other. Ramon said we could eat all we wanted but we were restricted to one beer each. After the one beer, it was strictly soda. When the food came, it just kept coming. After two weeks eating camp food, we ate like animals.

While we were eating, three musicians walk into the restaurant carrying a drum, a guitar, and a horn. Ramon gave them permission to play but only if they played a narcocorrido that was written about him years earlier by a group called Los Tucanes de Tijuana. Some of the song lyrics that they sang were:

They say that the law is looking for me.
But I'm roaming with two men in the trunk.
And I'm armed to the teeth in the streets of Tijuana.
And they never find me.

Nobody ever told the owner or the musicians which of us was Ramon or if Ramon was even in the restaurant that day, but thirty heavily armed men having dinner in a public restaurant like that must have given everybody a clue who we were.

Ramon knew my wife was expecting any day and he said that if it was a boy, he'd give me a million dollars if I named him Ramon and he could be the godfather. Ramon never had boys, so he really wanted somebody to carry on his name. I thanked Ramon for the honor but I told him that David already had the claim on being my child's godfather.

By the time we got to Ensenada and into cell phone range, my phone started buzzing. I got a lot of messages. All of them from people looking for me to tell me that I was a father of a little girl. She was born on July 8. I was thrilled. I told David that I had a daughter and David congratulated me. But he told me not to go home that night. We all needed to stay in the office because he was expecting a call and needed people to respond when he got it. David said he'd give me a month off to spend with my family after whatever he was expecting had happened.

He told me to collect all the guns and get them cleaned and ready to go if we needed them. So I went back to the office and spent the next four hours cleaning all the guns, topping up the magazines, and making sure that all the weapons were in good shape. We'd been gone for two weeks and I needed to get some money to my mother-in-law for her rent and expenses. I knew I wasn't supposed to leave the office, but this was only going to take a little while. I asked Big John to come with me.

Instead of going right to my mother-in-law's house, John said, "Let's go out and celebrate your daughter." We went to a club called the Acropolis, where everybody knew us because it was owned by Ramon. They knew about my daughter's birth, and the bartender, a guy named Huero, starts sending over champagne and coke. I know it was stupid and unprofessional but once we started drinking and drugging, we ended up staying out all night.

John and me get back to the office the next morning and run into Hernan. He's David's cousin and he told us that David was there ten minutes ago and got mad at us when he found out we weren't there and had stayed out all night. Hernan said, "David had a bunch of money for you and he wanted to go see the baby. He told me to tell you to get all your stuff and get the hell out."

I told Hernan, "If David has a problem, have him come see me. If you're gonna come at me, make sure your guns are blazing because mine are gonna be blazing too." I never talked like that before about David but I was mad. I started pulling all my stuff out of the office and drove home. Just as I'm pulling up to the house, here comes my wife, her mother, and the baby. This is the first time I have ever seen my daughter. My wife put my daughter in my arms and things are going through my heart and my head that I never felt before.

My wife noticed that my car was all full of the stuff I had at the office and asked me, "Is everything okay?" I told her David was mad at me but it wasn't a big problem.

I spent the rest of the day and night with my new family and spent a lot of time thinking about getting out of TJ and leaving the AFO. I knew that I might have to pay a price, but I had enough confidence in my ability to stay alive.

The next morning around 7:00 A.M., there's a ring at the gate and sure enough, it's David. He came alone. Just in case, I had my pistol in my back pocket. I wasn't sure how David would react to me leaving the office without permission.

"I told you to stay at the office," David said to me. I told him right back, "This is my first kid. I needed to see her and my wife. I know I broke your order and didn't consult you first, but I didn't do anything stupid." That wasn't exactly the truth.

Then David pulled out a leather bag that looked like a shaving kit, hands it to me, and says, "Here. I had some things planned for you. This is my gift to you for your daughter." There was $20,000 in the bag.

I don't know if Ramon would have gone as easy on me as David did, but David and me still had respect for each other.

"I apologize," I told David.

He said, "It's not that big a deal you going off like that."

"Do you want to see the baby?"

David came into the house, took the baby in his arms, and right away started tearing up. "She's beautiful," he said. "When you get ready to baptize her, let me take care of everything." While he's still holding her he said, "Take a couple of weeks off. We're going down south to take care of a few things. When we come back, I'll check with you and see if you're ready to go back to work."

That was the last time I saw David. After he left, my wife and I spent a lot of time talking about what to do next. We both knew that I couldn't just leave. I knew that I'd never rat them out, but they didn't know that and wouldn't believe me if I told them.

I finally told my wife, "I don't want to be here anymore. I don't want to raise her in this world."

She asked me, "What about my mom? We can't leave her here."

"We'll take her with us."

We loaded up whatever we could and drove to my mother's house in Oceanside. Once we got settled in, I knew it was a matter of time before I'd start hearing from David or Ramon.

In the next couple of weeks, I went around the neighborhood and let people know that I was back for good and I was ready to go back into the dope business. By this time, I was a superhero in the neighborhood. Everybody knew where I'd been and what I'd done and they all wanted to go into business with me. I had a lot of dope connections in Mexico and I could get anything I wanted.

During that period of a few weeks, a homie named Phantom got shot and killed over some stupid gangbanging. People came to me like they came to Marlon Brando in the *Godfather* movie and asked me to help with the funeral. I gave them $7,000 for a proper burial ceremony. I still had a lot of money then and it didn't seem that much at the time. But to the homies, it was really generous.

A couple of weeks later, Big John shows up at my door. I wasn't surprised to see him. I knew this was coming. "David is asking about you," he said. "He heard you moved and he wants to know if you turned on us, giving up or what." I told him, "I don't want to raise my kid over there. I'm done." Then Big John says, "Ramon doesn't think you'll turn on us. He says he wants to give you a job on this side of the border." I told Big John that I was cool up here and making deals so I didn't need a job. Big John went back to TJ and told David about our conversation.

A couple of days later I get a visit from a homie named Chato. Chato tells me that Ramon wants to talk to me on the phone. Ramon wanted me to go to Chato's house and he'd call there at a specified time and he wanted me to be there to take the call. I told Chato, "Just have him call me." Chato said, "Nah, dog. This is the way Ramon wants to do it."

I knew from experience that this could be an ambush, so I go on alert. I knew Chato from when we were youngsters. And my mother knew his mother since they went to high school together. We were close enough that when we were growing up, I used to call Chato's mother my auntie. So I wasn't too concerned about Chato. But I didn't know what was waiting for me on the street on the way to Chato's house.

On the night that the call was supposed to happen, I took a gun with me. We waited around for the phone to ring and I could tell that Chato was real nervous. He was acting funny and I suspected he knew more than what he was telling me.

Finally the phone rings and it's Big John on the line. The first thing he said was, "I lost your number is why I called you at Chato's house."

Then he hands the phone to David.

"What's going on?" he asked.

I said, "Nothing. It's all good. Have I ever turned on you?"

"No, you didn't."

I said to him, "I don't want to raise my daughter over there. We're not eye to eye anymore."

"Are you against us?"

I said, "No, I'm not. I'll still do my obligations to the carnals.

We're just trying to do some things over here. I'm leaving you guys alone for a while and working with Roy Boy, Black Dan, and Wimpie."

What I meant by obligations is that I was kicking money upstairs to the Big Homies whenever I made a deal. I wasn't a carnal yet and I was expected to show respect and let them know that I knew who still had the horsepower in prison and on the street.

David didn't press the issue.

He said, "Give the brothers my regards. But Ramon still wants to see you and talk to you. Ramon wants to ask you himself."

I told David, "Have Ramon call me. Tell him that if he needs something done, I'll take care of it for him."

We hung up and left it at that for a while.

But I could see that Chato was still acting strange. I told Chato, "I don't like the way you're coming at me. This business is my business and there's no need to get you involved. If they call you next time asking about me, you tell them to call me direct. I got nothing to do with your phone."

A few days later, the cell phone that I brought back from Tijuana rang. It was Ramon.

"Hey, carbon. Que esta pasando? I'm sitting here with my compadre Tiburon and we were talking about you." I told him to say hi to Tiburon.

Then he asked me, "I know you're working with the cousins up there. But are you with us or against us? Because you know how it is."

I told him what I told David. "I don't want to raise my daughter down there. You know I've always been loyal to you. I didn't turn against you."

Then he dangled a carrot in front of me. "Maybe we can set something up for you to work on that side."

I told him, "That would be cool."

"Come down and see me. I just bought a new yacht."

I left it vague and said I'd do that once I got settled in. If I took a ride on that yacht, I'd never see the shore again.

28

Out of My Life

After the last conversation I would ever have with Ramon, I started dealing dope in a very big way. With my history, my reputation, my drug connections on both sides of the border, and with the backing of the brothers, I had crews organized all over San Diego.

I told everybody that was working with me that gangbanging was forbidden. From now on, it was going to be all business. If one neighborhood had a beef with another one, they had to come to me to straighten out. No more shootings, drive-bys, or dealers stealing drugs from each other. I set up territories and put people I could trust not to be stupid in charge. What I wanted to do was put away as much money as I could and then move the family someplace where nobody could find us.

Then one night, I was walking home to get a 9 mm pistol that I had stashed. A cop car was rolling in the opposite direction real slow. I think we probably saw each other at the same time, so they saw me duck into the bushes. They turned on their spotlight and they caught me in the beam. I decided not to run. I gave up without trouble because I wasn't carrying the gun and I thought I could slide out of whatever they wanted the same way I slid out from the night they caught me with the Uzi and the pistol.

What I didn't know was that my face was on posters as one of San Diego's Ten Most Wanted for the murder of the woman in Imperial Beach. The other thing I didn't know was that a cop named Steve Duncan was part of a special task force investigating the AFO. And I was on his radar. He's the one that put me in those posters.

As a parolee, the cops had a right to search my house and they found the 9 mm. They arrested me and I got three years for the Uzi and pistol possession. That usually meant about eighteen months.

As hard as it is to believe, at that point in my criminal career, I didn't have any violent felonies charged against me. All my previous charges were for drug possession and nonviolent burglaries and robberies. That's the reason I only got three years. The case in Imperial Beach was just supposition based on information that Duncan got from an informer. They had nothing solid against me at the time.

So about a month after leaving Tijuana, I was back in state prison. This time it was Corcoran. After I was processed, the assistant warden brings me into his office and has a file in front of him. He looks at the file and asks me, "Is this true?" I had no idea what he was talking about.

"It says here you were a hit man for the Arellano Félix Cartel and that you received paramilitary training from Mexican Army officers."

I told him, "I have no idea what you're talking about. You

must have me mixed up with somebody else. If that's in my file, I want a copy of that."

"But is it true?"

I told him it wasn't.

Three days later I got a copy of the file and it spelled out my time with the AFO. The file mentioned Steve Duncan as the cop who put the report together. This was the first time I'd heard of him. I figured out real fast that the task force had snitches all over the AFO and they had a lot information on me. They didn't have everything, but it looked like they had enough that sometime real soon, the feds would come to the prison and scoop me up.

After Corcoran, I was transferred to Tehachapi. Right after Thanksgiving 1997, my wife came to visit and told me, "Your tio is gone." I knew she meant David.

"Are you sure?" I asked.

"It's all over the news and papers."

"When did it happen?"

"On Thanksgiving Day in Tijuana. They said it was friendly fire but nobody knows for sure."

I told her to send me every clipping and piece of news she could get. I needed to know what happened.

What happened was that David, Bat, Raton, and some other guys from the crew tried to kill Jesus Blancornelas. He was the editor for a newspaper in Tijuana called *Zeta*. Blancornelas ran a lot of stories about the AFO and even ran pictures of Ramon and Benjamin. So Ramon sent the crew to kill him right on the street as the guy was being driven to the airport. The cops counted 180 bullet holes in his car and they killed his driver. The editor was shot four times but managed to survive.

But during the shooting, David was hit in the eye by a ricochet off the car body and died instantly. There was a picture of David slumped against a wall with his rifle on the ground where he dropped it. Just like the cardinal killing, shooting the editor made headlines all over the world.

On one of her next visits, my wife told me that they had killed Big John because he was using too much and getting paranoid. They also killed Raton because they blamed him for shooting David. They convinced themselves that Raton had been paid off by one of the other cartels to kill David. The truth is that it was one of Bat's bullets that killed David.

Right after that, most of the Logan Heights crew left Ramon and went back to San Diego. The reason was that Bat was next in line to get David's job and nobody who knew Bat wanted to work for him. That's when the whole organization started to fall apart. All the soldiers left.

The whole time I was in prison on the gun charges, the feds were putting their AFO case together. I knew they were doing that because Duncan tried to contact me to meet with him. But I refused. I told the COs that they had the wrong guy and I wasn't involved with the AFO. They were looking at anybody with a connection to the AFO to see if they could get them to flip to build their case.

At the time I was released, they still didn't have anything on me that they could use to prosecute. So I went back to San Diego and picked up where I left off moving dope. The one major event that happened in prison before I was released was that Darryl raised his hand for me and got a few other brothers to do the same. In their eyes, I was now a made man and a full-fledged brother. The day that I'd been looking forward to when I could call myself a carnal was also the day that I became completely disillusioned with the EME. The same moment Darryl told me I was a carnal, he asked me to kill somebody for him. The target was another brother that he had a personal beef with. It was crazy. I expected to be in an organization that was united and the brothers treated each other like family, but here was this fool asking me to kill another member. That wasn't what I signed on for.

After I was on the street again, I completely lost interest in running my little dope empire and making sure that all the little egos in the EME were being satisfied with the money I was putting into their prison accounts. I started to let things slide. It was right at this time that my wife left. She couldn't handle the stress anymore. She wanted out of my life and I couldn't blame her.

One day, Freddie Gonzalez told me that he was having trouble with somebody on the street. He told me to go find somebody and to use my name and have him killed. I told him straight out, "I'm tired of all this, dog. I'm old and tired of going to jail and putting in work for somebody else. You don't know what I've seen and been through." This floored Freddie. He couldn't believe it was me talking like that.

"I'm just being honest," I said. "I don't want to put somebody through the shit I been through." Freddie shot a kite to Huero Sherm in prison about my change of heart and word got around fast that I was through. Sherm sent a letter to my new girlfriend that she should stay away from me. By that time, she was pregnant with my second child. And she didn't want to raise the child by herself. We talked about the future and the both us tried to figure a way out of the mess.

My lawyer kept talking to me about meeting Steve Duncan and the US Attorney in San Diego, Laura Duffy. They weren't offering a deal sight unseen, but they did want to talk to see if I was interested in cooperating. We had lots of meetings and it was during one of those meetings that one of the biggest weights of my criminal life was lifted from my shoulders.

I was talking to them about all the missions I'd done and how badly I felt after some of them. I mentioned the two cambio girls and how that episode still gave me nightmares. The room got real quiet and Laura Duffy looked at the other cops in the room and said, "He doesn't know?"

They explained to me that neither of the cambio women had died. The bullet I fired at the first one's neck just went under the skin, traveled to the other side, and came out. The other one survived three bullets to her head. It knocked her teeth out and gave her brain damage but she survived. They were both alive.

After I heard that, I wrote them a seven-page letter telling them what had happened and why and told them that I would happily spend the rest of my life in jail to make up for shooting them. I gave Duncan the letter to pass on to them. Sometime later, I got a letter back telling me that one of them forgave me and they didn't blame me for what happened to them or to their brother. She saw me as much of a victim as they were.

I spent the next eighteen months in the Federal Building in San Diego telling Duncan and the task force everything I knew about the AFO. After I testified truthfully about everything I knew about, the federal judge sentenced me to 292 months in the federal prison system. My entire family was provided with funds to move out of the state.

During the time that I served in federal prison, the task force took the AFO apart one piece at a time. In 2002, Ramon was killed by a cop in Mazatlan. Ramon was there to kill one of his rivals. While driving, he violated some kind of minor traffic law.

Not knowing that it was Ramon in the car, the cop pulled him over. Because of the kind of guy he was, Ramon pulled out a gun and shot the cop. The cop fired back as he was falling to the ground and killed Ramon in his car.

A couple of weeks after that, Benjamin was arrested and sent to jail for his part in the AFO business. In 2006, the youngest brother, Javier, was detained off the coast of Cabo San Lucas by the US Coast Guard. Because he was in international waters, he was taken directly to the US and prosecuted. The Arellano brother Eduardo was arrested by the Mexican Army in 2008. In 2014, the eldest brother, Francisco, was murdered at his own party in Cabo San Lucas by the Sinaloa Cartel. All five of the Arellano brothers involved in the drug business are either in jail in the United States or dead in Mexico.

After I finished my years in prison, I began to rebuild my life, trying however I can to make up in some small way for the violence I inflicted on people and the family that I should have been taking care of. This book is part of that atonement.

About the Author

Martin Corona, after serving as an enforcer in the Tijuana drug cartel, turned state's evidence against the organization and made possible the federal prosecution that brought an end to it. He lives with his family. He speaks to law enforcement organizations on the subject of his crimes and to at-risk youth on the importance of avoiding his mistakes.

Tony Rafael was the author of *The Mexican Mafia* and a researcher and reporter on complex issues of gang crime in Southern California and Mexico. He passed away in the final stages of the production of this book.